The Hero

LORD RAGLAN

The Hero

A STUDY IN
TRADITION, MYTH, AND DRAMA

GREENWOOD PRESS, PUBLISHERS
WESTPORT, CONNECTICUT

Library of Congress Cataloging in Publication Data

Raglan, FitzRoy Richard Somerset, Baron, 1885-
    The hero.

    Reprint of the ed. published by Vintage Books,
New York.
    Bibliography: p.
    Includes index.
    1. Heroes. 2. Mythology. 3. Folk-lore.
4. Drama. I. Title.
BL325.H46R3 1975b   291.2'13   75-23424
ISBN 0-8371-8138-0

TO

JANETTA AND FITZROY

WHO ENJOY FAIRY-TALES

WITHOUT BELIEVING THEM TO BE TRUE

This edition originally published in 1956 by Vintage Books,
New York

Reprinted by permission of Sir Isaac Pitman & Sons Limited

Reprinted in 1975 by Greenwood Press
A division of Congressional Information Service, Inc.
88 Post Road West, Westport, Connecticut 06881

Library of Congress Catalog Card Number 75-23424
ISBN 0-8371-8138-0

Printed in the United States of America

10 9 8 7 6 5 4 3

PREFACE

It is often said that "there is no smoke without fire." What those who use this expression mean by it is that their wish to believe any story or part of a story makes it historically true. They never apply it to a story which they know to be historically untrue, however much "smoke" it may have emitted.

Those who are convinced that Bunyan was an earnest and truthful man, who meant every word that he wrote, do not conclude that Christian and Faithful were historical characters. Those who are delighted with the realism of Dickens's descriptions do not conclude that the *Pickwick Papers* are the embellished adventures of a real Mr. Pickwick. Those who remember how many clever people were convinced by the story told by the Tichborne claimant do not conclude that that story was founded on fact.

It should be clear that the veracity and earnestness of a narrator and the vividness and verisimilitude of a narrative are no criteria of historicity; that many clever men have believed stories which are now known to be quite untrue; and that the truth of a story is to be judged by evidence alone. As regards modern stories, all this would no doubt be generally agreed, but towards ancient stories a totally different attitude is commonly adopted. It is at least possible that Homer, though he meant all that he said, may have intended it to be understood in a religious and not in a historical sense. It is at least possible that the saga-writers, like Dickens, may have collected sayings and incidents from a variety of sources and attached them to persons who never existed. It is at least possible that the story of Hengist and Horsa, like the story of the Tichborne claimant, may have been invented to support a false claim. But whereas modern stories, such as those I have mentioned, are assumed to be fictitious unless there is good reason to believe them historical, old stories are commonly assumed to be historical unless they can be proved to be fictitious. Interest in historical fact, which is notoriously rare among moderns, is gratuitously assumed to have been universal among the ancients. In the following pages I shall try to show that the "smoke" which arises from these oft-told tales is the outcome of mythical and not of historical fires.

The main thesis of the book was put forward in the Presidential Address that I gave to Section H of the British Association in 1933. Part of Chapter II appeared under the title of "Fiction in Pedigree" in the *National Review* for December 1933. The greater part of Chapters XV and XVI were given as a paper to the Folklore Society, and printed in *Folk-Lore* for October 1934. A series of articles, embodying much of the material relating to Robin Hood, Sigurd, King Arthur, Cuchulainn, Helen, and Falstaff, appeared under the title of "Quasi-Historical Personages" in the *Illustrated London News* in the spring of 1936.

Many friends, too many to mention individually, have helped me with suggestions, criticisms, references, and the loan of books; I cannot, however, omit a reference to Mr. R. Bowen, B.A., Librarian to the Monmouthshire County Council, whose wide knowledge of English literature has been of great service to me.

That the book has many defects I am only too well aware. They are due in part to the fact that it has been written in the depths of the country; in part to my limited knowledge of foreign languages; and in part to the variety of treatment which the subjects dealt with (including the names) have met with at the hands of those who have written upon them. Further research is needed on many points, but I am satisfied that the thesis, in its broad outlines, is established beyond all reasonable doubt.

RAGLAN

June 1936

PREFACE TO THE
VINTAGE BOOKS EDITION

WHEN this book first appeared, it received some good
notices in the American press, and I am proud to think
that it will make its reappearance in such good company
as that afforded by the Vintage Books. For three years I
sat down to my typewriter about 10 p.m. and spent an
hour and a half in copying out passages from the books
I had been reading and in sorting out my notes till they
gradually took shape as chapters. I feel that my pleasant
labours have been well rewarded.

As most of the book is concerned with the more distant
past, there is little that directly concerns the American
continent, but the literature of the Old World at least till
the seventeenth century is part of the cultural heritage of
the New, and it seems that much of it is now being studied
more intensively in the United States than in the countries
of its origin.

The idea that the story of Leif the Lucky is a fable based
on Irish mythology may come as a shock to some readers,
but hardly to those who know how many alleged vestiges
of the Norsemen in America have been shown to be spurious. On the other hand, the possibility of Asiatic influences
on the old civilizations of Middle America is coming to be
more generally realized, so that the idea that the Mexican
Quetzalcoatl follows the hero-god pattern of the Old World
should cause less surprise than formerly it might have.

When the book first appeared, criticism was mostly di-
rected to my contention that tradition is never historical,
and examples were given purporting to prove the contrary.
I should like to give one. A visitor to Tewkesbury Abbey
was given what was practically a first-hand account of the

battle, and on making enquiry was told that the office of verger, and the account, had passed from father to son ever since the time of the battle (1471). I too made enquiry, and was told that the authorities there knew nothing of any such family, and that their records did not show two vergers of the same surname.

October, 1955

RAGLAN

CONTENTS

✳

PART ONE

Tradition

*

CHAPTER I

THE BASIS OF HISTORY

Only the smallest fraction of the human race has ever acquired the habit of taking an objective view of the past. For most people, even most educated people, the past is merely a prologue to the present, not merely without interest in so far as it is independent of the present, but simply inconceivable except in terms of the present. The events of our own past life are remembered, not as they seemed to us at the time, but merely as incidents leading up to our present situation. We cannot persuade ourselves —in fact, we make no attempt to do so—that undertakings which ended in failure or fiasco were entered upon with just as much forethought and optimism as those which have profoundly affected our lives. We suppose our beliefs and mental processes to have been ever the same as they now are, and regard the story of our lives not as a cross-country walk upon which we are still engaged, but as a path, cut deliberately by fate and ourselves, to the positions which we now occupy.

In our consideration of the story of others, our minds work in the same way. We judge every event by its consequences, and assume that those consequences must have seemed just as inevitable to those who took part in it as they do to ourselves. We find it difficult to believe that when the ship went down, those who were to be drowned felt just the same as those who were to be saved. We say that coming events cast their shadows before them, but what we really mean is that later events cast their shadows back over earlier ones. This lack of mental perspective, from which we all suffer, displays itself in the saying: "Call no man happy until he is dead," which implies that a few hours or days of pain or misfortune can outweigh long

years of happiness and success. All this is characteristic of
our study of history. We regard the events of the reigns of
Louis XV and Louis XVI as leading up inevitably to the
French Revolution, though Voltaire and Gibbon saw no
sign of an impending catastrophe. We regard Stonewall
Jackson as having fought in a losing cause, though at the
time of his death the Confederates were getting the best
of it. In a word, even those of us who take a genuine
interest in the facts of history tend, either by our mental
limitations or by the defects of our education, to see them
in a false perspective.

Before discussing history any further, I ought to follow
what should be a universal practice by defining the term.
History, then, is the recital in chronological sequence of
events that are known to have occurred. Without precise
chronology there can be no history, since the essence of
history is the relation of events in their correct sequence.
We might know something of the Battle of Marengo and
something of the Battle of Waterloo, but we could not
attempt to compose a history of Napoleon unless we knew
which came first.

Why do people study and transmit historical facts? It
cannot be with the sole object of studying and transmitting
historical facts. Educated people study history for a
variety of reasons—because they hope to find in it an
explanation of the present and an indication of the future;
because their curiosity is aroused by survivals from the
past; because the classics were long regarded as the source
of all knowledge, and a knowledge of the classics involves
some knowledge of history; because the Bible and other
religious works contain historical references; because they
get a living by it; because for these and possibly for other
reasons some knowledge of history has come to be regarded as part of the mental equipment of an educated
person. Our interest in history, however, is inseparable
from books. It is very remarkable that our dependence
upon books is so little realized, even by teachers and
writers, who live by books. An illiterate person, if he were
interested in history, could learn it only from the lips of
a historian, or from a person who could read a history

book to him, and if he forgot a fact he could regain it only by having recourse to his teacher. The amount of historical knowledge that he could acquire would be limited by the fact that he would have no means of tabulating or classifying it, and could therefore have no idea of chronology outside the very limited range of his own experience. All history depends, as I have said, upon chronology, and no real idea of chronology can be obtained except by seeing facts tabulated in chronological sequence.

This was brought home to me when I was showing my five-year-old son round the amphitheatre at Caerleon, and telling him something of the Romans in Britain. He looked rather puzzled, and asked: "Were you there then, Daddy?" When we read of the Irish blacksmith who said that his smithy was much older than the local dolmen; it was there in his grandfather's time, and he died a very old man—or of the English rustic who said that the parish church (thirteenth century) was very old indeed; it was there before he came to the parish, and that was over forty years ago—we are apt to suppose the speakers exceptionally stupid or ignorant, but their attitude towards the past is similar to that of the Australian black who began a story with: "Long, long ago, when my mother was a baby, the sun shone all day and all night," [1] and is the inevitable result of illiteracy.

It would be almost impossible to make an illiterate person realize that the date A.D. 1600 had any meaning at all. Calendar sticks are used by tribes of both Africa and America to keep a record of events within living memory, but there is no means by which such a record could be preserved longer. Bundles of sticks convey nothing except to those who tie them together, and if you were to tell your illiterate that a stick represented a year, and then count out 335 sticks, he would be little the wiser. And if you were to tell him that Queen Elizabeth and Shakespeare both lived then, he would find it difficult to believe you, since if Shakespeare were really connected with some ancient monarch, which since a play of his was performed

[1] *Folk-Lore,* xlv, p. 233.

quite recently seems highly improbable, it should be King
Lear, whom he tells us all about, rather than Queen
Elizabeth, whom he hardly mentions.

The fact that chronology depends upon reading and
writing seems quite unknown to historians. Thus, according to Professor Chambers,[2] "it is probable that, even in
heathen times, despite the absence of written records, the
succession of monarchs and the length of their reigns
may have been committed to memory with considerable
exactness." Yet he suggests no motive for committing
such facts to memory, nor any possible machinery for
transmitting them, and he asks us to believe that the
Anglo-Saxons of the Settlement had conceptions of chronology which were quite foreign to their descendants
even a thousand years later. The editor of the *Paston
Letters* tells us[3] that "the mode in which the letters are
dated by their writers shows clearly that our ancestors
were accustomed to measure the lapse of time by very
different standards from those now in use. Whether men
in general were acquainted with the current year of the
Christian era may be doubted; that was an ecclesiastical
computation rather than one for use in common life. They
seldom dated their letters by the year at all, and when
they did it was not by the year of our Lord, but by the
year of the king's reign. Chronicles and annals of the
period which give the year of our Lord are almost always
full of inaccuracies in the figures; and altogether it is
evident that an exact computation of years was a thing for
which there was considered to be little practical use."
That the exactness of chronology which Professor Chambers postulates for the illiterate Saxons of the fifth century
was quite foreign to the literate English of the fifteenth
indicates that his postulate is nothing more than an ill-
considered guess.

That English illiterates have in fact no sense of chronology at all has been noted by several writers. "The folk

---

[2] R. W. Chambers: *England before the Norman Conquest,*
p. 69.
[3] *Paston Letters,* ed. J. Gairdner, vol. i, p. ccclxv.

have no sense of history," says Mr. Fox Strangways;[4] "there would be nothing improbable to them in St. George meeting Napoleon in the same ballad." Sir E. K. Chambers tells us that in the Mylor (Cornwall) folk-play the battles of Agincourt and Quebec, and the capture of Porto Bello by Vernon in 1739, have all been mixed up together.[5]

"There is another characteristic of the folk-play," says Mr. Tiddy,[6] "which has an interesting connection with popular taste. The absence of any historic sense . . . cannot be passed over. For us it is quite impossible to realize the state of mind to which a century, let alone five hundred years, means nothing at all; and yet that is the normal condition even of the majority of those who have been subjected to the modern elementary education. Thanks to this state of mind our village ancestors a century ago could pit St. George against Bonaparte without the least sense of incongruity; and even without the evidence of Chaucer we should have good reason to believe that our ancestors of the Middle Ages were liable to the same kind of absurdity. To the folk, it might almost be said, 'a thousand years are but as yesterday.' "

These plays are acted and ballads recited by members of what is at any rate a semi-literate community. The ideas of St. George and of Agincourt, if not derived originally from books, have certainly been reinforced by book-learning. In a semi-literate community all the members, including the illiterate, not merely benefit from the existence of books, but learn to understand something of the meaning and purpose of books and written records generally. In totally illiterate communities, however, such as still exist in central Africa or northern Australia, the whole structure of society is based upon a system from which reading and writing are completely absent, so that the purpose of writing is not merely unknown, but totally inconceivable. And since the purpose of writing is incon-

[4] A. H. F. Strangways: *Cecil Sharp*, p. 51.
[5] E. K. Chambers: *The English Folk-play*, p. 83.
[6] R. J. E. Tiddy: *The Mummers' Play*, p. 93.

ceivable, the idea of any form of knowledge which might
be preserved by writing is also inconceivable. Forms of
knowledge which depend, even in part, upon written record, can have for the savage no existence at all. Since
history depends upon written chronology, and the savage
has no written chronology, the savage can have no history. And since interest in the past is induced solely by
books, the savage can take no interest in the past; the
events of the past are, in fact, completely lost. We shall
realize this fact better if we consider how soon the past
is lost among ourselves whenever it is not recalled to us
by books. How many women of today know, for example,
what is meant by a sprunking, a palatine, or a farthingale?
Yet it is not a great many years since these words were
as familiar as the word *jumper* is now.

Even the most familiar facts are soon forgotten. In
the Neolithic Age polished stone axes were made by the
thousand, but soon after they were superseded by the
introduction of metal all knowledge of them was lost, and
a few centuries later it had come to be believed that anyone who happened to find one had come upon a thunder-
bolt.[7]

When, therefore, we attribute to the savage an interest
in the past comparable to our interest in the history of
England, we are attributing to him a taste which he could
not possibly possess, and which if he did possess he
could not possibly gratify. The savage, again, has far less
than we have to remind him of the past. There may be
ancient ruins, but since he has no means, even if he had
the wish, to learn their history, he contents himself with
attributing to them a supernatural origin, by which he
means little more than that they must have been made by
people whose customs were unnatural, since they were
different from his own. He thinks about them to this extent, if they thrust themselves upon his notice, but if they
have no use they have no real interest. The attitude of
most Europeans to relics of the past is very much the
same.

In illiterate communities all transmitted knowledge

[7] A. B. Cook: *Zeus*, vol. ii, p. 510.

is traditional, and tradition is strictly utilitarian. There are so many things that must be remembered—all the means of procuring, storing, and preparing food; the ways of building houses and canoes, and of making weapons, tools, clothes, and ornaments; all the magical rites, songs, dances, sacrifices, and purifications, as well as the relationships, upon which depend marriage, inheritance, and social obligations. All this would mean a good deal to a literate person, who could make a note of the facts, file it for reference, and then banish the matter from his mind, but in an illiterate community nothing that is of any value can be banished from the mind, since once lost, it can never be recalled. It is not that the savage is mentally incapable of transmitting the events of the remote past, but that there is no inducement to transmit them, no machinery by which they can be transmitted, and a great deal of other matter which has to be transmitted and remembered. He may remember that there was a great drought in his grandfather's time, because his village still has a claim to lands which were then vacated; he may remember that there was a war with the next village in his father's time, because it led to a blood-feud which has not yet been settled. But when all the participants have died, and all the feuds have been settled, then the war is forgotten. There is no inducement to remember it, and no machinery by means of which its memory could be preserved.

"When a man grows old and feeble," says Colonel MacNabb,[8] writing of the Chins of Burma, "and is unable to exact his dues by force . . . and when at the feast his voice is no longer the loudest and his hand no longer the strongest, then his son gradually begins to take his place. Instead of the son deferring to the father, the father defers to the son, and finally he is turned out of his house and made to end his days in a small hut. Before death claims him he is forgotten and set aside . . . and a man who in his prime may have been a power in the land, the hero of a hundred raids, and the owner of much property, is, in his old age, a nonentity." The Chins, it

[8] D. MacNabb: *Report on the Chins,* p. 16.

seems, completely lose interest, not merely in the remoter
past, but in the events of thirty years ago, and in my belief
this is the case with illiterates in general, except in so far
as their own personal exploits are concerned.

Speaking of the Jukun of Nigeria, Dr. Meek[9] comments
on "the singular absence of any interest or pride in the
past, or of any knowledge of events prior to the beginning
of the last century. . . . There is no clear tradition among
the Jukun relating to the "destruction of their principal
city," and even its site is uncertain, though the Fulani
conquest is believed to have happened only about one
hundred and twenty years ago.[1] Things are much the
same in Europe. We are told that within fifty years of
Napoleon's death the French peasantry had completely
forgotten the facts of his career, and that ten years earlier
it was difficult to find anything surviving of the songs
about him which had once such a widespread popularity.[2]

Most illiterate communities have, of course, traditional
stories, and these stories may seem to be memories of historical events. They tell of the journeys and victories of
heroes, and with some rationalization and rearrangement
these journeys and victories can be made to represent
historical migrations and conquests. These stories, however, are really myths. What a myth is we shall consider
later; here I may note that, according to van Gennep
(the writer whom I have just cited),[3] the leading heroes
of French tradition are not Charlemagne and his successors on the throne, but Roland, Gargantua, and the
Little Red Man.

If illiterate people really took an interest in the events
of the past, we should expect to find that when people
began to write, they would soon begin to make records
of past events. So far is this from being the case, however,
that it is doubtful whether the ancient inhabitants of
Egypt and Mesopotamia had any history at all in our
sense of the term. Such records of fact as were kept

[9] C. K. Meek: *A Sudanese Kingdom*, p. 21.
[1] Ibid., p. 43.
[2] A. van Gennep: *La Formation des légendes*, p. 193.
[3] Ibid., pp. 185–6.

seem to have been merely the by-product of a system of
drawing up elaborate calendars for the purposes of ritual.
"Religious and magical factors," says Dr. S. A. Cook,[4]
"have also been prominent in the rise of history-writing,
and Mesopotamian astrological tablets record, for the
warning of all concerned, portents, signs, catastrophes."
Kings may have recorded their victories as a charm to
secure further success; at any rate they seem never to
have recorded the victories of their predecessors.

In the Egypt of Herodotus' time there seems to have
been no corpus of recognized history at all. The discrep-
ant tales that the priests told him were almost entirely
mythical, and the only fact upon which they were agreed
was that the Egyptians had invented the calendar.[5] Most
of Herodotus is myth, but I believe that he has a good
claim to the title of father of history, since I can find no
evidence that before his time the idea of history had ever
occurred to anyone. The history of Herodotus was defec-
tive because his materials were inadequate.

Let us now consider what the materials of history are.

In the first class we will place accounts written at the
time by persons who were present at the events they describe—letters, dispatches, reports, diaries, memoranda.

In the second class are accounts by eyewitnesses, but
not written down until some time after the event—auto-
biographies, reminiscences, pleadings, inscriptions.

In the third class I would place the archæological evidence. This, though it can seldom give us actual dates,
yet often produces clear chronological sequences, and indicates unmistakably the presence or absence of certain
groups at certain places.

In the fourth class are accounts written by people who
obtained their information from actors or spectators
shortly after the event—annals, chronicles, minutes of
evidence, press reports, news-letters, and other forms of
contemporary correspondence. These would not be accepted as evidence in a court of law, but are often very
properly accepted by the court of history.

[4] *Cambridge Ancient History*, vol. i, p. 218.
[5] Herodotus, ii, 4.

In a fifth class we may place accounts obtained by
questioning people as to what happened a long time before, or accounts obtained at second or third hand. These
are often recorded as survivors' tales, conversations, memories, gleanings.

It should be quite clear that the first four classes are,
in varying degree, the only genuine sources of history.
The fifth class may be useful for reconciling discrepancies
or filling in details, but would not be accepted as a primary
authority for a fact otherwise unknown. Second-hand evidence is not accepted in a court of law because it is notoriously unreliable; it may be accepted by historians, but
only if it is given by persons especially well placed or
well qualified to obtain the facts. Nobody would accept a
fact on fourth-hand evidence alone, yet that is what tradition, supposing it to be historical, is at best.

"But," it may be said, "tradition is quite different.
"You are speaking of events which are known only to a
few people, but tradition is what is known to the whole
community." Tradition, certainly, is known to the whole
community, but what historical facts are known to the
whole community? How many people know at first or even
at third hand what blows the hero struck in the battle,
what the queen said to the king, or what passed between
the conspirators? Very few indeed, and the fact that a
rumor went through the crowd has no evidential value
whatever; a garbled account becomes more garbled every
time it is repeated. The loss of a battle or the destruction
of a city may be known to many, and if tradition were
wholly or even chiefly made up of such incidents, it might
be possible to make out a case for regarding it as founded
upon fact. Such incidents, however, play but a small part
in tradition, which consists chiefly of incidents in the lives
of kings, queens, and heroes. Now, the stories of court
life that get abroad today are always inaccurate and often
quite untrue, and we have no reason to believe that things
were different a thousand or five thousand years ago. It
is tedious to continue with generalities, so let us take a
concrete case, that of King Alfred and the cakes. Supposing it to have been a true story, how could it have become

public property? Even if the old woman had dared to whisper it to her cronies, they would not have believed her, and the King would never have recounted a story that would have exposed him to ridicule and lowered the prestige upon which his success depended. The story is really a myth, which seems to have been first attached to King Alfred in the twelfth century.[6]

Sir E. K. Chambers tells us that in such tales the names are the least permanent feature. He instances the story of how a horseman leaped over Bodrugan Head, in Cornwall, to escape from his pursuers. This story was once told of Tristram, later of Sir Bors, and has recently been transferred to one Henry of Bodrugan, who took the wrong side at Bosworth. "The lapse of folk-memory," he says, "is as characteristic as its tenacity. When I passed Athelney last year, a Glastonbury car-driver called my attention to a farmhouse in which 'Arthur' burnt the cakes." [7]

I shall discuss "folk-memory" presently; let us first consider the question of how long an incident that is not recorded in writing can be remembered. After much consideration I have fixed on the term of one hundred and fifty years as the maximum. I have arrived at this figure, which is of course approximate, in various ways.[8] A careful study of what is known of my grandparents and great-grandparents has convinced me that any fact about a person which is not placed on record within a hundred years of his death is lost. Giving a person about fifty years of active life, we get one hundred and fifty years as the limit. Among ourselves the names of the dead are recorded in various ways, but I believe that, among the illiterate, anyone who has been dead a hundred years is completely forgotten. Again, I have known cases in which old men have succeeded in impressing incidents of their own lives upon children in such a way that the children remember them; but they cannot impress in this way incidents that

---

[6] R. W. Chambers, op. cit., p. 202.

[7] E. K. Chambers: *Arthur of Britain*, pp. 193–4.

[8] A. van Gennep, op. cit., p. 164, fixes upon two hundred years, but makes a number of exceptions.

have not made an impression upon themselves. Matter
that is not part of the group tradition thus dies out in the
second generation. A study of the facts that survive, and
of the processes by which facts are transmitted, gives a
maximum period of about one hundred and fifty years in
both cases.

This is easy enough to check in Europe, but among
savages is very difficult because it is seldom that we have
any idea of what did take place one hundred and fifty
years ago. We often find, however, chiefs who are alleged
to be about fifth in descent from culture-heroes, and many
mythical events that are alleged to have occurred about
one hundred and fifty years before they are narrated or
first recorded. One hundred and fifty years ago, or even
less, we are in a period the events of which have been
completely forgotten, and which is therefore available for
the myths. These, being ageless, can be allotted to any
period.

Every incident begins to fade from the minds of both
actors and spectators as soon as it has occurred. As long
as some of them are alive, a record of the incident may
be preserved in their subconscious minds, even if they do
not consciously remember it. Of this we cannot be certain,
but what is quite certain is that facts cannot be transmitted
from one person to another by means of the subconscious
mind. The only facts that I can transmit to my children,
writing apart, are those of which I am conscious; these
require an effort on my part to transmit, and a greater
effort on my children's part to remember. Conceit may
lead me to transmit to my children, probably in a not
quite accurate form, certain selected incidents from my
own career, but what inducement have my children to
remember them and pass them on? And if people do not,
as in fact they usually do not, take the trouble to preserve
facts about their own immediate relatives, why should
they take so much trouble about more remote persons?
The only writer on tradition who has attempted to answer
this question, so far as I can learn, is Professor Chadwick,
who says:[9] "The existence of a poem or story which deals

[9] H. M. Chadwick: *The Heroic Age,* p. 273.

with reminiscences of tribal conflicts necessarily presup-
poses an absorbing interest in tribal history." He goes on
to suggest that this interest could be due only to patriotism,
but fails to realize that ardent patriots are notoriously
indifferent to historical facts; any fable which gratifies
their national pride is history to them. Professor Chadwick, then, does not take us very far in our search for
an answer, and none of the other writers whom I have
consulted attempt to deal with the question at all. They
seem to assume that the details of battles and floods, court
intrigues, and even domestic conversations, transmit themselves down the ages quite independently of human effort,
or even of human volition. They achieve this, it would
seem, by the aid of a mysterious agency that Sir E. K.
Chambers, as we have seen, calls "folk-memory." The
same term is used by Professor J. L. Myres,[1] while Professor T. H. Robinson calls it "race-memory." [2] He tells us
that the story of the Flood, as it stands in Genesis, is a
"race-memory of a remote historical event." Similarly
Professor Gordon Childe[3] assures us that "the ancient
Sumerian creation legend, wherein order is conjured out
of the primeval chaos by the separation of land from
water, preserves a vivid recollection of the tasks imposed
upon the first colonists." Professor Childe can hardly suppose that the writers of the legend had seen in real life
anything like what the legend describes, and if they had
not seen it, how could they preserve a vivid recollection of
it? Such terms seem to me to be quite meaningless; a
memory is an individual possession just as much as a hand;
I can pass on what is held in my memory as well as what
is held in my hand, but my memory itself dies with me.
Such terms as "race-memory" and "folk-memory" suggest
that there exists in every illiterate community something
analogous to our Public Record Office, and obscures the
fact that every unwritten tradition must be transmitted by
conscious individual effort at least once in each generation.
   Professor Hocart, it seems to me, falls into a similar

[1] *Journal of the Royal Anthropological Institute,* 1933, p. 295.
[2] *Myth and Ritual,* ed. S. H. Hooke, p. 189.
[3] V. G. Childe: *The Most Ancient East,* p. 124.

error when he says:[4] "Diversity of origin is, in my experience, one of the most tenacious memories a people can
have. If foreigners come and settle, whether peacefully
or by conquest, among another people, they will remember that, if nothing else. Even decayed rustics living a
precarious existence on the edge of the jungle remember
that, long ago, the people in the next hamlet came from
overseas under seven princes; yet all difference of language and custom has vanished." It is easy to show that
such migrations, when they are real and not mythical, are
soon forgotten. In the ninth and tenth centuries many
thousands of Danes settled in Yorkshire, Lincolnshire,
and other counties of north-east England, and the inhabitants of those counties must be largely of Danish descent,
yet, far from recognizing this descent, they regard the
Danes as enemies who came to plunder and then sailed
away. In the eleventh century a great part of Lancashire
and Cumberland was settled by Norwegians, and Nor-
wegian was for long the language of that area, yet the
fact is known only to students of history. In the sixteenth
there was a large influx of Protestant Flemings into south-
eastern England; they Anglicized their names, and within
a couple of generations were absorbed into the population.

The rapidity with which historical events are forgotten
shows how unlikely it is that what is remembered in the
form of tradition should be history. I shall now proceed
to examine various types of tradition, real or so called,
and shall show that, wherever they can be tested, their
lack of historicity becomes apparent.

[4] *Man* (1929), p. 102.

CHAPTER II

THE TRADITIONAL PEDIGREE

There are two forms of narrative which pass as traditional—that which has really been handed down by word of mouth from time immemorial, and that which, though it may sometimes pass from mouth to mouth, is derived from a literary source. The former I shall refer to as traditional, and the latter as pseudo-traditional. Since many people's belief in the historicity of tradition is based upon, or at any rate strongly supported by, their belief in the traditional pedigree, it may be as well to begin by showing that there is in England no such thing as a genuinely traditional pedigree at all.

It may be objected that the pedigree is not a narrative. As we are accustomed to see it, it is, of course, merely a collection of names and dates, connected by lines and mathematical signs. It is in fact, however, a series of potted biographies, and the lines and signs are too often employed to give a spurious appearance of mathematical certainty to statements that are unsupported by evidence or even demonstrably untrue.

There are, of course, many genuinely old pedigrees; these are always based on contemporary records, and get progressively fewer as we go farther back. There are one or two probably genuine pedigrees that go back to the eleventh century, but none that go back to the period of the Norman Conquest. The names of very few of the Normans who fought at Hastings and still fewer of the Saxons have been preserved, and of these hardly any of the former and none of the latter are known to have left descendants. There is no Englishman who can trace his family to the time of the Conquest by any evidence that would be admitted in a court of law.

Those, however, who claim Norman or Saxon ancestry
do not trouble about contemporary records; they rely upon
what they call tradition, and maintain that these alleged
traditions cannot be disproved, and are therefore entitled
to credence. That we are bound to believe what we cannot disprove is a misguided view, which, however, we
need not discuss here, since our so-called traditional pedigrees can always be disproved, for the most part quite
easily. The reason for this is that they are not really traditional at all, but are due either to the efforts of pedigree-
fakers or to the guesses of amateur historians. The former
have flourished at all times, but their golden age was the
reign of Queen Elizabeth, when, in order to satisfy the
new men, all of whom desired a Norman ancestry, "the
pedigree-maker stuck at nothing; he forged documents,
not only in Old Latin, but in Old English and Old French,
and these he showed to the heralds, by whom they were
easily swallowed." [1] These forgeries led to many innocent
blunders by amateurs, and were generally accepted until
towards the end of the last century, when a group of
students made an exhaustive study of all available documents bearing on the Norman period. As a result they
were able to throw much light upon some of the darker
aspects of our history, and incidentally to show that the
Norman England of Sir Walter Scott and his imitators
bears no recognizable resemblance to the genuine article,
and that our "traditional" pedigrees all contain blunders
that mark them out as fictions of a later age.

Many of the alleged ancestors occupied positions that
would involve their mention in Domesday, which omits to
mention them, or held manors that are known to have
been held by others, or not to have existed at all. Such
blunders, however, are only to be detected by the expert,
whereas anyone who is prepared to spend a little time in
the study of Norman and Saxon nomenclature can con-
demn most "traditional" pedigrees at a glance.

Let us start with the Saxons, and note without surprise
that they were called by Saxon names. Examples of such
names can be found in any history—Godwin, Stigand,

[1] J. H. Round: *Family Origins*, p. 5.

Siward, Leofric. The Saxons were not called William, Walter, or Robert, because these were Norman-French names, which were introduced into England by the Normans. A pre-Conquest Saxon would be no more likely to be called by a Norman-French name than would a modern Englishman to be called Marcel or Gaston, yet the Saxon "ancestors" of the pedigrees are almost always called by such names.

So much for the Christian names of the Saxons; now to surnames. The Saxons had no surnames. A Godric might be referred to as "the timberer," or "the son of Guthlac," but these were not his names; whether he was earl or churl he had one name, and one name only. This single name was never a place-name. Like the Scandinavians, Irish, and Welsh, the Saxons never used place-names as personal names. It is clear, then, that when a Saxon ancestor is alleged to have been called Bertram Ashburnham or William Pewse, he must be a fake, since no Saxon was ever called Bertram or Ashburnham or William or Pewse. Stanley of Stanley, who is alleged to have flourished fifty years before the Conquest, "Wynkfelde the Saxon," the alleged ancestor of the Wingfields, and many another, proclaim themselves by their very names to be creatures of fiction. The fact that not a single Saxon ancestor can be supported by evidence merely confirms what was in most cases a foregone conclusion.

The case of the Normans is different, since there are in existence several families with genuine Norman pedigrees, though these do not go nearly so far back as is popularly supposed. Here again it is necessary to study the names. During their residence in France the Normans had almost completely dropped their Norse names, and had adopted such Frankish names as Richard, Hugh, and Baldwin, besides those mentioned above. William's army contained many Frenchmen and Flemings, as well as Normans, but their names were much the same. There was also a large contingent of Bretons, who had some names of their own. Of these Alan was the commonest, though the ancestor of the FitzAlans (once famous but long extinct) did not come over till the next century. In that

century a few Biblical names began to creep in, probably
under the influence of the Crusades; previously such
names as John and Thomas are not found among either
Normans or Saxons. The range of Norman names was not
wide; no Norman was ever called Hildebrand, the alleged
Norman ancestor of the Alingtons, and such names as
Titus and Theophilus, which appear at the head of some
"Norman" pedigrees, are equally absurd. Nor did the
Normans have double Christian names, which are rare
before the eighteenth century, and unknown before the
sixteenth.

Unlike the Saxons, the Normans had surnames, but before about 1150 these were personal and not hereditary.
William, son of Hugh and lord of Dinard, would be called
William FitzHugh or William de Dinard, or both. His son
would be called Richard FitzWilliam, and would be called
de Dinard only if he actually owned it. If we find Robert
de Dinard succeeding Richard de Dinard, it by no means
follows that they were relatives; Richard might have sold,
or died without heirs, or been dispossessed.

We know that Robert de Belesme was the son of Roger
de Montgomery; that Richard de Réviers was the son of
Baldwin de Meules, and that Roger de Bréteuil was the
son of William FitzOsbern, but these were great nobles,
and for lesser men such evidence is, before 1150, extremely rare. By 1200 most of the nobles had settled
down to hereditary surnames, but as late as 1245 we find
Robert FitzRoger succeeding his father, Roger FitzJohn,
as lord of Clavering. Among the commoners the custom
of passing on surnames from father to son spread more
slowly still, and is hardly yet established in the wilder parts
of Wales.

About 1400 place-names began to be borne as surnames without *de* or *of* before them, and it was then, and
not till then, that it became possible for men to be called
Bertram Ashburnham or William Pewse.

It is to be noted that the Norman nobles whom I mentioned above have today no descendants, and the same
applies to their successors. Of the families in which earl-
doms were created from 1066 until 1442, when John,

Lord Talbot, became Earl of Shewsbury, in two only, Courtenay and Nevill, is there a legitimate descendant in the male line. Bigod, Bohun, Clare, Valence, Vere, Warenne, and many others whose deeds once made English history, all are gone. A few lesser families are known to have survived from the twelfth century, but so many more are known to have died out that the probabilities are always strongly against survival. It is, in fact, hardly an exaggeration to say that the Normans have left no legitimate descendants at all.

As we have already noted, the early Normans, de Belesme and the rest, came from France, and their surnames were therefore, like their Christian names, French. They thereby differ from the "Norman ancestor," who usually lands at Pevensey already equipped with the English surname, de Alington, de Burton, or whatever it may be, which his descendants will subsequently assume. He also styles himself "sir," unaware that knights were not so styled till the thirteenth century, and often makes the future mistake of bearing his family arms, unaware that family arms had not yet been invented. The origin of heraldry is involved in obscurity, but there seems no doubt that the first coat of arms of those that are still borne was that of the three golden leopards on a red field which was adopted by King Richard I in 1198. This coat is that of our sovereign, and anyone who seeks to take precedence of him should be regarded with the gravest suspicion.

In the matter of building, also, the "Norman ancestor" was apt to be before his time. Usually the first thing he did after settling in England was to build a stone castle. The early Norman castles, however, were wooden structures on a mound of earth, and stone castles were not, with one or two well-known exceptions, built until well on in the twelfth century.

Even in the matter of dress the "Norman ancestor" may go wrong. The "traditional" ancestor of the Fitzwilliams, Sir William FitzWilliam, received for his bravery at the Battle of Hastings a scarf from the Conqueror's own arm, which is still an heirloom. But the real founder of the family was a London tradesman of the thirteenth century, and such scarves were not worn until the six-teenth.[2]

An interesting example of the "traditional" pedigree is that of the Wakes. The family of Wake is one of the old-est in England, and its present head is Sir Hereward Wake, thirteenth baronet. The family "tradition" is that it is de-scended in the direct male line from the famous Saxon hero Hereward the Wake. The facts appear to be as fol-lows: in 1166 a Norman named Hugh Wac came over from Normandy, and married the heiress of the Norman FitzGilbert, lord of Bourne in Lincolnshire. About two hundred years later the family of Wake, as it had then become, having attained to wealth and importance, thought itself entitled to a more high-sounding pedigree, and hav-ing discovered that a Saxon called Hereward had in the eleventh century owned a small part of the lordship of Bourne, decided to adopt him as ancestor and to identify him with the famous hero. For this purpose a pedigree was forged conferring titles, ancestors, and descendants upon the Hereward who had lived at Bourne, and to make this pedigree more convincing there was conferred upon Here-ward the hero the hitherto unheard-of cognomen of "the Wake." There are some obscurities in the story, but the following facts seem certain: that Hereward was never called "the Wake" till he was adopted as ancestor by the Wakes about the middle of the fourteenth century; that the Wakes have no traceable connection with Hereward or any other Saxon; and that the first Wake to be chris-tened "Hereward" was born in 1851.[3] Hereward the Saxon hero *may* have been a real person, but the fact that among his exploits are narrated the slaughter of a gigantic bear in Scotland, and of a great champion, the lover of the King's daughter, in Cornwall, with other obviously mythical feats in Ireland and Flanders,[4] suggests that he

[2] *The Ancestor,* vol. i, p. 237.

[3] These facts are to be found in the *Dictionary of National Biography,* s.v. "Hereward"; J. H. Round: *Feudal England,* p. 161; *The Ancestor,* vol. ii, pp. 109–13.

[4] G. L. Gomme: *Folklore as an Historical Science,* p. 36.

was a mythical hero after whom Hereward of Bourne and other Saxons were named.

"The study of genealogy," says Dr. Round,[5] "is rich in illustration of the mental perversity of man, of his mis-directed toil, of his self-deception." It is astonishing how many distinguished men have not merely employed pedi-gree-fakers, but have taken a hand in the game themselves. Thus we find even Lord Burghley, perhaps England's greatest statesman, tampering with documents in the hope of inducing people to believe that his great-grandfather, whose name and identity were and still are unknown, was the scion of an illustrious line, and Mr. Oswald Barron[6] has amusingly shown how prone literary men have been to boast of fictitious pedigrees and to assume coats of arms to which they had no shadow of a claim. His list of offenders includes Montaigne, Spenser, Browning, Carlyle, Dickens, Victor Hugo, and Tennyson.

Dr. Round sums up the question by saying that "to the advocates of historical methods the word 'tradition' excites no reverence, for we know that those who appeal to it do so in default of any proof for the origin they seek to claim . . . there is, perhaps, no 'authority' so unworthy of credit."[7]

It is to be regretted that the works of Dr. Round seem totally unknown to our classical scholars. No one who had read even a few pages of them could write, as Pro-fessor Myres writes:[8] "As long as personal names succeed each other in a pedigree . . . there is a presumption that the family itself knew what it was talking about." Even the feeblest of the hundreds of pedigree-fakers whose efforts have been exposed by Dr. Round and his colleagues never failed to make personal names, of a sort, succeed one another. In his attempt to deduce a system of chro-nology from the Greek "traditional" pedigrees, Professor Myres has compared them to the English pedigrees going

[5] *The Ancestor,* vol. ii, p. 165.
[6] Ibid., pp. 187–90.
[7] J. H. Round, op. cit., pp. 12–13.
[8] J. L. Myres: *Who Were the Greeks?* p. 299.

back to those who came over "with the Conqueror," [9] and
has thereby shown clearly that his theories have no foundation in fact. He has, however, carried the art of believing just so much as theory requires less far than Mr. Burn,
who tells us that "we have five apparently trustworthy
pedigrees claiming to go back to the Heroic Age, and
though we may feel compelled to doubt their claims in
one case to descent from a god and in the other four from
famous legendary heroes, the number of generations in
each pedigree may give us a clue to the date at which
settled life began again after the migrations." [1] To doubt
a man's claim to divine descent and at the same time to
regard his pedigree as trustworthy is really an amazing
feat. That pedigree-faking was not unknown to the Greeks
is the opinion of Professor Halliday, who says that "there
is not a great deal of history to be got out of the Argive
genealogies. There are many alternative versions, and, as
I think is clear from the second book of Pausanias, a good
deal of manipulation was applied to them in antiquity." [2]

If Dr. Farnell is right, the ancient Athenians had no
genuine genealogy, or idea of genealogy, at all. Discussing
the cult of the *Tritopatores,* he tells us that their name
clearly reveals them as "fathers of the 'third degree back,'
and thus bears the stamp of primitiveness upon it, for
'third degree' was an early expression of an indefinite re-
moteness of ancestral affinity. Inscriptions suggest that
each Attic phratry, kinship being in each the nominal
bond of association, sacrificed to their own Tritopatores,
as a vague group of fathers of the kindred." [3]

However this may be, we need go no farther than Wales
to see the futility of basing any chronological scheme upon
traditional pedigrees. Thus "the date of Teithfallt, the
seventeenth descendant from Llyr Llediath in one line, is
A.D. 430; while that of Cystennin Goronog, the *ninth*

[9] Ibid., p. 300.
[1] A. R. Burn: *Minoans, Philistines, and Greeks,* p. 49.
[2] W. R. Halliday: *Indo-European Folk-tales and Greek Legend,* p. 122.
[3] L. R. Farnell: *Greek Hero Cults,* p. 333. It must be added
that this explanation of the tritopatores is regarded as extremely doubtful by Professor H. J. Rose.

descendant in another line, is A.D. 542." Similarly the date
of Iorwerth Hirflawdd, *ninth* in descent from Aflech, is
A.D. 430, while the date of Cunedda Wledig, *seventeenth*
in descent from Aflech in another line, is A.D. 400.[4] If in
the first case we take an average of thirty years to a generation for one pedigree, we have our choice of nine or
sixty-nine years to a generation for the other!

It is not only in the matter of chronology that Welsh
pedigrees show themselves to be fictitious. One of the most
celebrated is that of Brychan, eponym of Brecon. He is
alleged to have had twenty-four sons and twenty-six daughters, of whom all the former and half the latter were
saints. Many of them founded churches in various remote
parts of the Celtic world, and several were martyred by
pagan Saxons at places which, so far as is known, pagan
Saxons can never have reached. In addition to this Welsh
family, he had another large family of saints in Devon
and Cornwall.[5] The most determined efforts have failed to
give Brychan and his progeny the remotest appearance of
historical probability.

The Saxon pedigrees are equally unreliable. Thus that
of the West Saxon kings would make Woden a real man
who flourished about A.D. 200; while that of the kings of
Kent would bring him down to about A.D. 350. The name
of the Kaiser—that is, the Roman Emperor of the East—
became so famous that the East Anglian kings adopted
him as their ancestor and made him the son of Woden.[6]

Nor can we trust the Icelandic pedigrees. The *Landnamabok* professes to give an accurate account of the
settlement of Iceland and of the early settlers, yet Koht
tells us[7] that "in several cases we are able to prove that
the pedigrees given by the *Landnamabok* are absolutely
fictitious."

How this may have come about is explained by Professor Gronbech, who shows that among the early Teutons
any person, whether real or mythical, whose luck the clan

[4] R. Rees: *Welsh Saints,* p. 91.
[5] Ibid., pp. 136 ff.
[6] For this fact see R. W. Chambers: *Widsith,* p. 192.
[7] *The Old Norse Sagas,* p. 35.

believed itself to have acquired, by marriage with or adoption of a descendant of the lucky one or in any other way, was regarded as a clan ancestor, and concludes that "to understand the clan feeling and clan system of ancient times we must revise our ideas of kinship altogether, and replace our genealogical tree by other images. . . . We cannot get history in our sense by comparing related genealogies and synchronizing their data into our chronological system." [8] This impossibility is just what the early investigators in Polynesia thought that they could achieve. The Polynesians, and especially the Maoris, have enormously long traditional pedigrees, and by the aid of these a pseudo-history of Polynesia, extending back for thousands of years, was built up by Percy Smith and others. This pseudo-history, however, is now beginning to be recognized as such. Even Professor P. Buck, who is a Maori with a long traditional pedigree of his own, is constrained to admit that "interruptions by conquest and death, varying academic knowledge and ability, and the limitations of human memory, diminish the scientific value of orally transmitted genealogies and traditions as means of obtaining exact dates." [9]

But the would-be chronologist has still other dangers to guard against. In China, so Mr. Waley tells us, "So long as the Ancestors . . . were conceived of as former kings of a particular tribe, they could exist in popular imagination side by side, floating in a vague past. But when the idea of Empire arose, and it was asserted as a justification of an Imperialist policy that the Chou, for example, once ruled over everything under Heaven, having conquered the Yin, who also ruled the world, it was no longer possible to place a mighty and venerated ancestor such as Yao at the same period as the Yin or Chou 'empires,' and thus make him a subject of Yin or Chou. To bring him down to the historical period was obviously impossible, and the only alternative was to give him the vacant space previous to the dominance of the Yin. . . . The Yellow Ancestor was an even later comer, and had consequently to be

---

[8] W. Gronbech: *The Culture of the Teutons*, pp. 374–5.
[9] *Man*, 1933, p. 136.

accommodated 'behind' Yao, in an even more remote corner of prehistory. Thus the chronology was built up backwards, and has no relation whatever with an actual time sequence." [1] We may probably detect a similar process—namely, the combination of independent tribal heroes into a single genealogical scheme—in the Old Testament, and in ancient Greece and ancient Ireland.

Some pedigrees drawn up on these lines are obviously fabulous. Thus Miss Durham cites an Albanian tribe, three of the five sub-tribes of which claim descent from three brothers who fled from the east. One had a saddle (*shala*) and became ancestor of the Shala tribe; another had a winnowing sieve (*shoshi*) and became the ancestor of the Shoshi tribe; the third had nothing, so he said: *"Mir dit"* (good-day), and went off to become the ancestor of the Mirdita tribe (or three fifths of it). [2]

I must now discuss briefly the question whether the modern savage can remember his pedigree for more than four generations back. Sir William Ridgeway believed that he could. He says[3] that "the natives of the Torres Straits keep a kind of diary or record by means of cords or knots. By such artificial contrivances it was possible to keep an exact account of the number of generations, even though the name of one ancestor might be forgotten or blundered, a thing not very likely among people who had no other literature to distract their thoughts." He does not say for how long or what purpose these pedigrees were kept, and when he assures us later[4] that "pedigrees can be remembered with extraordinary accuracy by primitive people," he omits to mention that no such pedigree has ever been checked.

Professor Lévy-Bruhl, on the other hand, believes that savage ancestors may be divided into two classes: the real

---

[1] A. Waley: *The Way and its Power*, p. 134.

[2] M. E. Durham: *Some Tribal Origins . . . of the Balkans*, pp. 25, 29. Yet she says (p. 27) that certain Albanians have no tradition of descent from the ancient Dalmatians, and must therefore be later immigrants; by this argument people with no traditional pedigree can have no ancestors at all!

[3] W. Ridgeway: *Early Age of Greece*, vol. i, p. 130.

[4] Ibid., p. 151.

ancestors, consisting of the last four generations, and the mythical ancestors, a body of superhuman, partly animal beings, who are the creators of all species and all rites.[5] This view is confirmed, so far as Australasia is concerned, by what Dr. Fortune tells us of the islanders of Dobu, three hundred miles east of the Torres Straits. It appears that the inhabitants of each Dobuan village trace their pedigree back to a common ancestress, who is not a human being, but a bird. None know their pedigree for more than four generations back, and an informant said that his great-great-grandmother was hatched from a parrot's egg.[6]

While the beliefs of the Africans may not be quite the same, I am convinced that their genuine pedigrees are no longer. Sir Samuel Baker visited the Lotuko of the Upper Nile in the early 1860's, and in his account of them given in his *Journey to the Albert Nyanza* he mentions a number of chiefs and incidents. When I was there fifty years later I tried to identify these, and though I could not get the names as given by Baker, I managed to identify them in what at the time I considered a satisfactory manner.[7] But when some years later Professor and Mrs. Seligman visited the district and produced quite different identifications,[8] I considered the facts more carefully and came to the conclusion that the events we had attributed to Baker's time really happened much later, probably in the 1890's, and that Baker and the events of his time were completely forgotten. I may add that Ngalamitiko, a hero whose name is associated with myths and miracles, is said to have lived only four or five generations ago. My opinion is confirmed by what Mr. Huntingford says of the not far distant Nandi, namely, that the first date in their history which can be fixed is 1890, and that a chief who is supposed to have ruled as recently as 1870 is now "a somewhat shadowy figure," which I take to mean that it is doubtful whether he really existed or not.[9]

[5] *Congrès International*, 1934, p. 269.
[6] R. E. Fortune: *The Sorcerers of Dobu*, p. 31.
[7] *Sudan Notes and Records*, vol. i, p. 154.
[8] Ibid., vol. viii, p. 4.
[9] *Man*, 1935, p. 158.

That fictitious pedigrees are common in Africa there
can be no doubt. Dr. C. K. Meek tells me that in west
Africa the inhabitants of a village group often claim that
the inhabitants of the various villages are in each case
descended from a son of the first settler, but that an
examination shows that many of them came from various
foreign localities in quite recent times. "The legend of a
common ancestry is pure invention to promote a feeling
of solidarity or in some cases to explain the fact that the
group is an exogamous unit." The Nuers and Dinkas are
Nilotic tribes of the Sudan, and Dr. Evans-Pritchard found
that Dinkas who have been adopted into the clans of their
Nuer conquerors give pedigrees showing pure Nuer descent.[1] The process is similar to that by which converts to
Judaism become pure-blooded descendants of Abraham.

We thus see arrayed in defence of false genealogy the
powerful forces of religion and patriotism; of custom and
tradition; of family pride and individual vanity; and of
euhemerism and rationalization; not to mention the popular love of the marvellous and the romantic. On the other
side are only the puny and disunited columns of critical
investigation. It is not surprising that, although hundreds
of them have been proved false and none has ever been
proved true, the traditional pedigrees still hold the field.

[1] *S.N.R.*, vol. xvi, p. 52.

CHAPTER III

LOCAL TRADITION

The local tradition is, perhaps, less a matter of faith than the traditional pedigree, but it supplies even more evidence than the latter of the indifference to fact, and the complete lack of any critical faculty, which characterized most people, even those who are supposed to have been educated.

There are various ways in which a local tradition, so called, comes into existence. In the first place there is to be found in most rural areas some clergyman or schoolmaster with a smattering of history or archæology who enjoys speculating about the past and invariably ends, if he does not begin, by regarding himself as a more than sufficient authority for his own statements. He is regarded as the expert, and nobody dreams of questioning what he says, or of checking it with even the most readily accessible works of reference.

Then there is the person who seeks to add interest and romance to a house or a neighbourhood by transferring to it some story which he, or more often she, has heard or read in some other connection. The lady's story or the vicar's statement may gain a temporary vogue and, being taken down from the lips of some rustic by a collector of folklore or local historian, be accepted as a piece of genuine "folk-memory."

Then there is the snowball type of story, which grows as it goes. The process is somewhat as follows:

Stage I.—"This house dates from Elizabethan times, and since it lies close to the road which the Virgin Queen must have taken when travelling from X to Y, it may well have been visited by her."

Stage II.—"This house is said to have been visited by Queen Elizabeth on her way from X to Y."

Stage III.—"The state bedroom is over the entrance. It is this room which Queen Elizabeth probably occupied when she broke her journey here on her way from X to Y."

Stage IV.—"According to a local tradition, the truth of which there is no reason to doubt, the bed in the room over the entrance is that in which Queen Elizabeth slept, when she broke her journey here on her way from X to Y."

A man whom I asked how he knew that Queen Elizabeth had slept in his house asked in return, in a surprised and indignant tone: "Why shouldn't she have?" The idea that it might be desirable, or even possible, to verify the statement had obviously never occurred to him.

To make a pageant at Cardiff more interesting, the promoters brought the Emperor Constantine to Cardiff. I remarked to a friend, an exceptionally well-read man, that of course the Emperor Constantine was never there, to which he replied: "Oh, I expect he was if they say he was!" The visit of Constantine to Cardiff may now be becoming a "tradition."

I recently met with another possible "tradition" in the making. A friend bought a house that is said to have been the scene of a fight in the Civil War. The only authority, a doubtful one, gives no description of the fight, yet my friend had not been long installed before he was able to describe to us how the Royalists attacked, and how they were repulsed.

I had a similar experience in my own house, which was visited by Sir Thomas Fairfax during the siege of Raglan Castle. Returning after it had been let for a number of years, I found that a "tradition," quite unknown to my family, had grown up to the effect that Lady Fairfax had crept out of a certain window to warn the defenders of Raglan Castle of an impending attack. There is, in fact, no tradition about the house at all. Charles Heath, the local antiquary, who visited it about 1800, when it was used as a farm, says: "The Writer has endeavoured to obtain in the neighbourhood 'Some Anecdote of the conclusion of this business, as well as of the parties who met here, and signed the Treaty;'—but such is the oblivion in which the transactions are involved, that even the Mansion House is little known in the county; and, with regard to its *eventful history,* many otherwise well-informed persons, of whom he made inquiry, seemed *surprised* when acquainted with the *motives* for his curiosity." [1] So much for "folk-memory." I may add that the window through which Lady Fairfax is alleged to have crept is in a part of the house which was built about 1860.

At a house between Hereford and Abergavenny is shown a room in which King Charles I is alleged to have slept. The itineraries show, however, that on the only occasion on which he travelled from Hereford to Abergavenny he completed the journey in the day, and dined at a house the way to which must have taken him far from the house in question.

At Monmouth is shown the window at which Geoffrey of Monmouth wrote his history. It is highly improbable, however, that he wrote anything at Monmouth,[2] and anyhow the window dates from the fifteenth century, whereas Geoffrey died in the twelfth.

Some time in the nineteenth century a local antiquary identified the motte of the Norman castle at Trelleck as a Roman signal mound. There seems to be no doubt whatever that the mound is not older than the eleventh century, or the story of its Roman origin than the nineteenth, but nevertheless the latter has become a well-attested local tradition, and on it have been based elaborate and purely fictitious accounts of the Roman campaigns against the Silures.

Wherever such stories are told and can be checked, they prove to be fictitious. A bed in Cardiganshire, traditionally that in which King Henry VII slept on his way to Bosworth Field, proved to be of the eighteenth century.

The room in Fyvie Castle, Aberdeenshire, allotted by

[1] C. Heath: *Historical and Descriptive Accounts.*
[2] E. K. Chambers: *Arthur of Britain,* p. 24.

tradition to King Edward I, is in the Preston Tower, which was built in the fifteenth century.[3]

To go farther afield, Dr. C. K. Meek tells me that "the sacred sword of the Bolewa chiefs (of Nigeria) was, according to tradition, brought by the tribal leaders from the Yemen many hundreds of years ago. The sword was shown to me secretly and permission given to remove the rust. It had a Prussian stamp!" With this may be compared the chain armour of the Sudanese Arabs, traditionally captured from the Crusaders, but really imported from Germany in the eighteenth century.[4]

Sometimes the anachronism is the other way round; that is to say, tradition associates local features with people who lived long after their construction. It is, for example, universally believed by the Irish peasants that the raths or hill forts are the work of the Danes, though they really date from a much earlier period.[5] The inhabitants of southern India[6] refer everything prehistoric to Tippoo Sultan, who was killed in 1799, and in many parts of the continent of Europe buildings, ruins, weapons, bones, etc., of earlier date are referred to the armies of Napoleon.[7]

There is near Megara a peak from which, according to local tradition, Xerxes on his throne watched the Battle of Salamis. An investigator found on the top of the peak a rock-cut throne, but so placed that anyone sitting in it would have his back to Salamis.[8] The author of the "tradition" had obviously heard of, but not seen, the throne.

Another type of anachronism appears in the Westphalian legend which tells how the Catholic Charlemagne, with the aid of a big iron cannon, defeated the Lutheran Swedes.[9]

Local tradition is not merely anachronistic. Miss M. E. Durham tells me that on Highgate Hill there is a stone at

[3] D. MacGibbon and T. Ross: *The Architecture of Scotland,* vol. ii, p. 355.

[4] A. E. Robinson, in *Man,* 1935, p. 74.

[5] W. G. Wood-Martin: *Pagan Ireland,* p. 200.

[6] According to Mr. F. J. Richards.

[7] A. van Gennep, op. cit., p. 168.

[8] A. B. Cook, op. cit., vol. i, p. 145.

[9] A. van Gennep, op. cit., p. 167.

which Dick Whittington is supposed to have heard the
bells and turned again, but that *Dick Whittington* has been
locally corrupted into the *Duke of Wellington*, and that
someone was recently told that the stone marked the place
where the Duke of Wellington had said: "Turn again!"
and won the battle! One can imagine a historian of the
future, if his mentality resembled that of many historians
of the past, getting hold of this "tradition" and basing
upon it an account of a previously unrecorded campaign
of the Duke against the Chartists.

Where tradition does not arise from such blunders, it is
usually the result of ignorance and superstition. Thus
Krappe tells us that "the dolmens of France and the
British Isles are the work of fairies; the remains of the
Roman limes are attributed by German peasants to the
Devil, who divided the earth with Our Lord, and erected
the wall to mark the boundary. The ruins of the Roman
amphitheatres of Southern France are called the 'palais de
Gallienne,' Gallienne being a powerful Moorish princess
and the wife of Charlemagne. To the fellahin of modern
Egypt the pyramids are the work of the jinn." [1]

Those who believe that Cæsar's Camp was constructed
by Cæsar are morally bound to believe that the Devil's
Dyke was constructed by the Devil. Cæsar's Camp in Sussex, excavated by General Pitt-Rivers, proved to be of
Norman origin.[2]

It is not merely peasants who believe in fables. Miss
Caton-Thompson has proved conclusively[3] what was not
really in doubt: namely, that the ruins of Zimbabwe, in
Rhodesia, are not older than the ninth century of our era,
and there is much evidence to connect the culture of its
builders with that of Java.[4] Many educated people, however, continue to believe in its fabled construction by King
Solomon, merely because they like to do so, and because

[1] A. H. Krappe: *The Science of Folklore*, p. 75.
[2] H. St. G. Gray, in *Handbook to the Pitt-Rivers Museum,
Farnham*, p. 20.
[3] G. Caton-Thompson: *The Zimbabwe Culture*.
[4] J. Hornell, in *J.R.A.I.*, 1934, pp. 305 ff.

the truth is "so dull," an expression that I have often heard applied to it.

Even archæologists are not above reproach. The most elaborately carved rock dwelling at Petra is known to the local Arabs as Pharaoh's Treasury, but since Petra is notoriously post-Pharaonic, this tradition is quietly ignored. A similar tradition is, however, called in to support the identification of Ahab's Palace at Samaria.[5]

"History's greatest foe," says a writer in the *Sunday Times*,[6] "is not science, but that form of local tradition which supplies gaps in our knowledge with the wildest guesses, which too frequently deceive with a plausible tale." The writer is referring to *Erinus Alpinus*, a plant which the local historians allege to have been introduced to the region of the Roman Wall by Spanish soldiers in the Roman army, but which was in fact introduced by a nineteenth-century vicar.

It is not only local historians who make guesses. Sir Laurence Gomme says that "perhaps the 'White Horse Stone' at Aylesford, in Kent, the legend of which is that one who rode a beast of this description was killed at or about this spot, may take us back to the great battle at Crayford, where Horsa was killed." [7] We may believe that Horsa never died, since he never lived, or we may, if we think fit, believe that he fell at "Aegelesthrep," as the *Chronicle* says, but for such guesses there is no justification. Dozens of kings, and hundreds of other eminent men, have met their death in various parts of England; Harold fell on the field of Hastings, Simon de Montfort at Evesham, Richard III at Bosworth Field; their deaths marked epochs in our history, yet who knows the spot where they fell? Nobody, since tradition never preserves historical facts. Anyone who attempted to supplement our knowledge of the Civil War by making inquiries among the inhabitants of Marston Moor or Naseby would be foredoomed to failure, yet Gomme and many others can

[5] *Man*, 1932, p. 249.
[6] December 31, 1933.
[7] G. L. Gomme: *Folklore as an Historical Science*, p. 43.

believe that while the memory of events three centuries old is completely lost, that of events fifteen centuries old is miraculously preserved.

The fact is that all history, except in so far as it has been recorded, or as it can be recovered by archæologists, is completely lost. "Wales," says Sir John Rhys, "is dotted with many a *caer* and many a *dinas*, the ancient name of which is now unknown." [8] If even the names are lost, can it be seriously supposed that the facts have been preserved? In Monmouthshire nearly all the castles have names, but of most of them very little is known, and nothing that has not been placed on record.

Asked if he knew anything about a certain dolmen, a native of East Africa told the inquirer that "the people say that it is the work of spirits. It has been like that for a long, long time. Even the oldest man cannot remember the time when it was not there." [9]

Caldicot Castle has been for six centuries the most conspicuous feature of the landscape of south Monmouthshire. According to Mr. Wheatley Cobb,[1] it belonged to Edward Stafford, Duke of Buckingham, executed in 1521, and was probably sacked and dismantled after his fall; yet in 1613 a jury at a Court of Survey presented that "there is an old ancient castle at Caldicot and that it is in ruin and decay, but the cause of the decay thereof they cannot present, for it was before the memory of this jury or any of them." In Europe and in Africa the story is the same: "We know nothing about that. It happened before our time."

Near Nemi, in Italy, of *Golden Bough* fame, formerly stood a colossal oak, which was said to have been planted by Augustus, and the hollow trunk of which was large enough to hold twenty-five persons. It is mentioned by several writers of the seventeenth and eighteenth centuries and was then apparently one of the wonders of Italy. It was cut down about 1790, and in 1912 an inquirer found that the local inhabitants had lost all memory of it.[2]

[8] *The Arthurian Legend,* p. 351 n.
[9] Quoted by E. Evans-Pritchard in *Antiquity,* 1935, p. 159.
[1] *The Story of Caldicot Castle,* p. 30.
[2] A. B. Cook: *Zeus,* vol. ii, p. 419.

From time to time there have been discovered in the forests of south-eastern Asia deserted cities, temples, etc., and it has frequently been found that the nearest local inhabitants were completely ignorant, not merely of their history, but even of their existence. A striking example is given by Mr. Hornell, who tells us[3] that "The schist belt that runs through the Raichur Doab in Hyderabad State is honeycombed with the ramifications of ancient shafts and tunnellings made by miners in extracting gold . . . the amount of gold extracted must have been enormous. Strangely enough, no memory survives in the district of aught pertaining to these old gold mines, of whose existence the local people were actually unaware until they were discovered by European prospectors." Mr. Hornell tells me that these workings reach, in places, a depth of 640 feet, and must, according to the experts, have taken an incalculable period, many centuries at least.

Such evidence as I have been able to collect, then, shows firstly that the alleged historical facts embodied in local tradition are not facts at all, and secondly that the real facts of history are never preserved by local tradition. Some distinguished writers have, however, attempted to prove the contrary, and it is interesting to compare Gomme's tale of buried treasure with the facts about the old gold workings which I have just quoted. He tells us[4] that there was a tradition of buried treasure in the valley of the Ribble, in Lancashire, and that this treasure was found at Cuerdale in 1840. He goes on to say that it was the treasure-chest of the Danes, who raided Mercia in 911, but were followed up by the English King and thoroughly defeated. This story received the blessing of Andrew Lang, who wrote that "the theory . . . quite accounts for the presence of the hoard where it was found. The Danish rearguard defending the line of the Darwen would know that their treasure was hurried forward and probably concealed, but would not know the exact spot." Yet the story is demonstrably untrue. It is not merely that the *Anglo-Saxon Chronicle* gives us no reason to suppose

---

[3] *J.R.A.I.*, 1934, p. 331 n.
[4] Op. cit., p. 30.

that the fight took place in Lancashire and that the
Chronicle of Ethelwerd places it on the Severn,[5] at least
eighty miles from Cuerdale; Gomme's eagerness to believe
was such that it caused him to overlook a fact which he
himself mentions: namely, that more than a third of the
hoard consisted of coins of Canute, who did not come to
the throne until more than a century after the fight in
question.

Another firm believer in the historicity of tradition was
Sir William Ridgeway, who gives the following as an
example: "In 1884 two of the descendants of Prittie's
troopers sought a reduction of rent from Lord Dunalley,
Prittie's descendant. In the Land Court an old farmer
named Armitage gave evidence of the customs, etc. of the
estate. He stated that he was 92, that he remembered his
grandfather, and that his grandfather had talked with some
of the men who came with Cromwell. He was cross-
examined, but the Court was convinced of his veracity.
There was thus but one step in oral tradition between 1651
and 1884. Although these troopers were mostly young
men when they settled in Ireland, yet each of them must
have known in his English home those who were old
enough in 1588 to remember the coming of the Spanish
Armada. . . . Thus between 1588 and 1884, that is nearly
three centuries, there were but two steps in the tradition.
But at Rome the same space of time would take us back
to 690 B.C., that is to the traditional reign of Numa
Pompilius." [6] Sir William failed to note that the court was
not concerned with the Spanish Armada, and that we are
given no reason to believe that Mr. Armitage, or his
grandfather, or even Prittie's troopers, had ever heard of
it. From the historical point of view the story proves nothing whatever, and both it and the previous story suggest
that a belief in the historicity of tradition is the outcome
of a wish to believe rather than of a critical study of the
facts.

I shall now consider local traditions of a different type
—the type, that is to say, where a story is told over a

[5] J. A. Giles: *Six Old English Chronicles,* p. 38.
[6] W. Ridgeway: *The Early Age of Greece,* vol. ii, p. 231.

wide area, but is localized at various places. Let us begin
with the "Faithful Hound." The Faithful Hound is best
known in this country from its association with Beddgelert,
in Carnarvonshire. The name "Beddgelert" seems to mean
"the grave of Celert," Celert being a legendary saint.
There was, however, an English version of the story in
which the Faithful Hound was called "Kill-hart," and it
would seem that some etymologist of the eighteenth century, probably influenced by a local legend which told
how the inhabitants had cheated the Devil by substituting
a dog for a man,[7] identified Kill-hart with Gelert. The
story thus started was reinforced by the enterprise of an
innkeeper, who about 1830 set up a tombstone at a suitable spot, and grew rapidly into a tradition which was
accepted as genuine by thousands, not merely of the ignorant but of the learned.[8] Baring-Gould [9] traced this story
in various forms to many parts of Europe, Asia, and
Africa, and more recently Mr. A. H. A. Simcox[1] found,
installed in a temple in central India, an idol in the form
of a dog which was explained by a similar story.

In case, however, it might be supposed that the story of
the Faithful Hound, though false at Beddgelert, was probably true somewhere else, I shall now consider another
wide-spread form of local tradition, and one that could not
possibly be true anywhere—the story of the Sleeping
Warriors. The story, as told in many parts of Europe, is
that beneath a neighbouring mountain there is a cave, and
that in the cave a number of armed men are lying asleep,
waiting for the day when they shall be called upon to rise
and deliver their country from some enemy. A man entering the cave by chance rings a bell or makes some other
noise, whereupon the warriors spring to their feet, exclaim-
ing: "Is it time?" "The time is not yet," replies the leader,
whereupon they all lie down again.

The leader, in Wales, may be Arthur, Owen Lawgoch,

[7] G. L. Gomme, op. cit., p. 26.
[8] J. Jacobs: *Celtic Fairy Tales,* pp. 261–4.
[9] S. Baring-Gould: *Curious Myths of the Middle Ages,* pp.
134 ff.
[1] *Man,* 1932, p. 9.

or Owen Glendower; in Scotland he may be Finn, Bruce,
or nameless; in Ireland, Garry Geerlaug, Earl Garald, The
O'Donoghue, or nameless. In Germany he may be Odin,
Dietrich, Siegfried, Charlemagne, Frederick Barbarossa,
or the Emperor Otto; in Bohemia King Wentzel, in Serbia
King Marko, in Spain the Cid. There are many others,
both in Europe and beyond; most if not all of them have
been found by a chance intruder, but the latter has never
succeeded in finding the entrance to the cave a second
time.[2]

Sir John Rhys attempts to rationalize some of these
stories, and in so doing misses their point. "To take Garry
Geerlaug, for instance, a roving Norseman as we may suppose from his name, who may have suddenly disappeared
with his followers, never more to be heard of, in the east
of Ireland. In the absence of certain news of his death, it
was all the easier to imagine that he was dozing quietly
away in an enchanted fortress." It is, I should have
thought, much easier to imagine that someone who has
disappeared is dead, rather than that he is dozing away in
an enchanted fortress, but the point is that the story is not
told in Norway or Iceland, where Garry's disappearance
may be supposed to have caused regret, but by Irish peasants in the neighbourhood of Ardee, County Louth, where
Garry is believed still to lie asleep in his enchanted fortress. Sir John later admits, however,[3] that in the story of
how Arthur lies asleep at Caerleon and elsewhere "Arthur
has taken the place of some ancient divinity," and that the
story is linked with "the beliefs of the Latter-day Saints
as to the coming of Christ to reign on earth."

Two things are clear: the first is that these stories cannot have any basis in historical fact, and the second is
that since the versions told in the various countries are
almost word for word the same, they cannot possibly
have arisen in the places where they are now told, but
must be derived from a common source. This applies to

[2] S. Baring-Gould, op. cit., p. 105; J. Rhys: *Celtic Folklore,*
vol. ii, p. 492; E. K. Chambers: *Arthur of Britain,* p. 225; A.
van Gennep, op. cit., p. 196.

[3] J. Rhys, op. cit., p. 493.

the Faithful Hound no less than to the Sleeping Warriors.

And now, what is the explanation of these stories? I shall try to show as this book goes on that all traditional narratives originate in ritual, and shall discuss in detail many aspects of the question. Here I shall be content to suggest lines along which the solution of these two particular problems may perhaps be found. I am inclined to believe that the story of the Faithful Hound is a reminiscence of a rite, similar to that described in Genesis xxii, by which a pretence is made of sacrificing a child, and an animal substituted at the last moment. The mourning for the dog, and the praise lavished upon it, may be part of a ceremony intended to identify it with the child, or to convince the powers-that-be that although they are not getting a child they are really getting something just as valuable.

The Sleeping Warriors are more difficult to explain, yet the features of the story—the recumbent warriors, the enthroned leader, the concerted movement and chorused question—all suggest ritual. Is there any known ritual with which we can compare them? In the highlands of Fiji, so Sir James Frazer tells us,[4] there was a point in the boys' initiation ritual at which the novices were taken to the sacred enclosure. There they saw a row of men lying on the ground, covered with blood, and with their entrails protruding. The novices had to crawl over these bodies till they reached the High Priest, who sat at the far end. The High Priest suddenly uttered a yell, whereupon the corpses sprang to their feet and ran down to the river to wash off the pigs' blood with which they had been smeared. This rite has at least four features in common with the story of the Sleeping Warriors: the recumbent men, the seated leader, the frightened intruders, and the sudden resurrection. Elsewhere in Fiji "the novices also go and visit the cave where the dead nobles are buried to find a conch which is hidden there."[5] Here we have the cave and also the horn, which, as we shall see, is a feature of several of the Sleeping Warrior stories. Professor Hocart tells us that the object of the whole ritual is to enable the novices to

[4] *Golden Bough,* vol. xi, p. 245.
[5] A. M. Hocart, *Kingship,* p. 137.

impersonate the departed ancestors.[6] He also shows that all initiation rites are more or less degenerate forms of coronation rites—that is to say, rites attendant upon the installation of a king or queen.[7] If that is so, and if our comparison is justified, then the story of the Sleeping Warriors is connected with a coronation ritual, a ritual intended to qualify the new king to impersonate the old king. Is there anything in the stories to suggest any connection with coronation? Beneath the castle of Sewing-shields, in Northumberland, sleeps King Arthur with all his court, until someone blows the horn that lies ready on a table and cuts a garter placed beside it with a sword of stone. Once a farmer, knitting on the ruins, followed his clew of wool, which had fallen into a crevice, and found the vault. He cut the garter and Arthur woke, but, as he sheathed the sword, fell asleep again with the words:

> *"O woe betide that evil day*
> *On which this witless wight was born,*
> *Who drew the sword, the garter cut,*
> *But never blew the bugle horn."*

In another version Arthur says that if the visitant will blow the horn and draw the sword, he will "confer upon him the honours of knighthood, to last through time."

A similar adventure befell one Potter Thompson in the ruins of Richmond Castle, in Yorkshire. He was dismissed by King Arthur with the words:

> *"Potter Thompson, Potter Thompson, hadst thou blown*
> *the horn,*
> *Thou hadst been the greatest man that ever was born."* [8]

What is suggested in the first story, and stated in the second, is that the intruder, if he performs the ritual correctly, will himself become king. The whole story of the Sleeping Warriors, then, taken in conjunction with the material from Fiji (and certain facts that we shall come

---

[6] Ibid., p. 135.
[7] Ibid., p. 152.
[8] E. K. Chambers, op. cit., p. 224. The clew of wool is reminiscent of the Labyrinth.

to in Chapter XIV), suggests a ritual in the course of which the candidate for kingship entered a cave, in which the courtiers were lying in feigned death about the corpse of the late king, and, after certain rites had been performed, emerged in the character of the old king resurrected.

There is no reason to suppose that such a ritual was ever performed in Europe. It seems far more probable that the belief was imported, and localized wherever there was a suitable site and a suitable hero. It seems to have influenced Christian ideas, since in mediæval pictures of Christ's resurrection the sepulchre is often surrounded by sleeping warriors, in defiance of the story as told in the Gospels.

As this book goes on, I shall deal with a large number of traditional stories, and shall try to show that all of them, in so far as they are really traditional, are of ritual origin. Of most of these stories it is alleged that they are founded on fact, the theory apparently being that if only nine tenths of a story can be shown to be untrue, we are bound to accept the remaining tenth as genuine history. Here we have a story for which nobody can claim a basis in fact. No rational person can believe that kings who lived centuries ago are really sleeping in caves, or that anyone ever met with an adventure such as that attributed to Potter Thompson. If one traditional tale, told as a tale of fact, is completely devoid of fact, then the belief that such stories must have a historical basis is clearly ill-founded. I do not suggest, of course, that such stories as that of the Roman signal mound are based on ritual. That is a mere blunder, and many so-called traditions are, as I have tried to show, the result of such blunders or of deliberate fiction. It is not easy to tell the sham from the genuine, since both speculation and fiction tend to move along traditional lines, and since, as Professor Halliday has shown, "even legends of known antiquity may ultimately be derived from a laborious invention based on garbled documents." [9] There is one test that may be applied, though it is not infallible; it is to ascertain whether

[9] W. R. Halliday: *Folklore Studies,* p. 72.

the story is connected with a living superstition. To know whether Queen Elizabeth really slept at a certain house is of interest only to a handful of historians and antiquaries, but the idea of meeting Queen Elizabeth's ghost on the stairs will cause a thrill to millions. What interests them is not whether Queen Elizabeth *was* there, but whether she *is* there. A large proportion of traditional stories are ghost stories, and though many of them are modern inventions, yet the latter are mere imitations of the genuine ones. Here again no rational person can believe that the stories have any foundation in fact, and here again I suggest a ritual origin. It may be that these stories go back to a time when the initiated men dressed up in white to represent the ancestral spirits, and it may be that this is the reason why the belief in ghosts is so prevalent among women. However this may be, there can be no doubt that traditional stories are very often told of places associated with supernatural beings, and also of wells, lakes, trees, rocks, megaliths, and other places and objects, natural or artificial, to which people are, or were, wont to resort for magical purposes of one kind or another. It seems at least doubtful whether any local tradition can survive without its associated superstition. The connection of local tradition with cult is well attested; its connection with historical fact is not attested at all.

CHAPTER IV

ROBIN HOOD

Having tried, I hope with some success, to show that the world of tradition is quite a different one from that of history, I shall next take a series of well-known traditional figures and shall show that there is no good reason to believe that any of them had a historical existence. The belief in their historicity is due partly to the false theories of tradition and history with which I have already dealt, and partly to the fact that, so far as I can learn, no previous writer has ever attempted to survey the field as a whole. Every writer on a particular tradition, or group of traditions, has always assumed the historicity of all the traditions that he has not studied; a writer on King Arthur will tell us that he is as historical as Achilles, and a writer on the *Iliad* that Achilles is as historical as the saga heroes. We are thus in a vicious circle. It is impossible to break this circle; it is impossible to show that King Arthur is a myth, as long as the numerous other heroes with whom he can be compared are regarded as historical, and the same applies to every other hero considered individually. The only method open is that which I propose to adopt: namely, to make a simultaneous 'tack upon all the heroes of tradition. In so doing I shall nave to discuss questions with which it is impossible to be thoroughly acquainted without long specialized study. I shall therefore have to expose myself to the scorn of the pedants, who, as I know by experience, will regard the detection of some minor inaccuracy as a triumphant refutation of my case.

The traditional hero with whom I shall deal in this chapter is Robin Hood. I begin with him because he is supposed to have lived within historic times, so that in his case we are in an exceptionally favourable position to

trace the processes by which a hero of tradition becomes
endowed with pseudo-historicity.

Robin Hood is alleged to have lived at various dates,
from the twelfth to the fourteenth century. According to
the most popular version of his career, he was a Saxon
who fled into Sherwood Forest to escape the tyranny of
the Normans. There he gathered about him a band of
stout Saxons in like case, and lived a life of chivalrous
adventure, robbing the rich and brutal Normans, and
giving the proceeds of his robberies to the poor, oppressed
Saxons. Endless attempts were made by the Sheriff of
Nottingham to capture him and disperse his band, but all
his attempts ended in failure, and Robin finally received
a pardon from the King in person. According to this
version, the King was Richard I, and Robin was born at
Locksley in 1160, and died in 1247.

Let us consider this story before we turn to other versions. We may first note that Locksley, Robin's birthplace,
is said to have been either in Nottinghamshire or in Yorkshire, but there seems to have been no place of that name
in either county. Now to the personal names. The name
"Robin" is, of course, a diminutive of "Robert"; I shall
have more to say about this name presently, but here we
may note that it is, so far as England is concerned, a
purely Norman name. We come next to Little John; the
name "John," though, of course, not of Norman origin,
was introduced by the Normans, and *little,* in its Saxon
form, means, we are told, "mean, deceitful."[1] Little John
is, then, a strange name for a Saxon hero. "Much" might
be a Saxon name, but the names of Robin's other hench-
men, "William," "George," "Allen," "Gilbert," are such
as could never have been borne by Saxons while there was
any distinction between Saxons and Normans. Another
companion of Robin's was Friar Tuck, but the first friar
did not land in England till 1224.

Then there is the long-bow. Robin and his men are all
experts with this weapon, and the "clothyard shaft" figures
in almost every story. But Sir Ralph Payne-Gallwey tells
us that though the Saxons knew the *short* bow, they made

[1] W. W. Skeat: *Etymological Dictionary.*

little use of it, and the Normans, though they used both the short bow and the crossbow, did not know the long-bow. The latter did not come into use in England till the last quarter of the thirteenth century, and was first successfully employed in battle at Falkirk in 1298. "In the assize of arms fixed by Henry II in 1181, bows, whether short or long, are not alluded to as weapons of the period." [2] And this when Robin Hood was twenty-one!

According to another version of the story, Robin was not a Saxon but a Norman nobleman, who either was by birth Earl of Huntingdon, or was so created by Richard I. Anyone who consults a work of reference, however, will see that the earldom of Huntingdon was held from 1185 till 1216 by David of Scotland, brother of King William the Lion.

The attempt to give a date to Robin Hood seems not to be earlier than the sixteenth century. One of the earliest published poems, the *Mery Geste,* of Wynkyn de Worde, printed about 1500, associates Robin Hood not with King Richard, but with a King Edward, and another early ballad associates him with King Henry and Queen Catherine;[3] I shall come back to these facts later. The attribution to Robin of a date later than the reign of Richard I, though it has often been made, and though it makes the friar and the long-bow possible, is rendered difficult by the fact that by the beginning of the thirteenth century Robin Hood's name seems to have been already proverbial.[4]

Nor is his place of residence more certain than his date, since though bows, chairs, caps, and slippers said to have belonged to him are, or were, shown at various places in Nottinghamshire and Yorkshire, yet his traditional activities were by no means limited to those counties. He owns hills, rocks, caves, and wells in Lancashire, Derbyshire, Shropshire, Gloucestershire, and Somerset. His story has been localized not only in Sherwood Forest and in Yorkshire, but in Derbyshire, Cumberland, and also in Scotland. The place of his death, called variously Kirkley,

[2] Sir Ralph Payne-Gallwey: *The Crossbow,* pp. 31–2.
[3] J. Ritson: *Robin Hood,* p. 170.
[4] Ibid., p. xxxiv.

Bricklies, etc., is located in Yorkshire and in Scotland, and his chief henchman, Little John, is said to have been buried at Hathersage in Derbyshire, at Pette in Moray-shire, and at Dublin.

"In the parish of Halifax is an immense stone or rock, supposed to be a druidical monument, there called *Robin Hood's Penny-stone*, which he is said to have used to pitch with at a mark for his amusement. There is likewise another of these stones, of several tons weight, which the country people will tell you he threw off an adjoining hill with a spade as he was digging. Everything of the marvellous kind being attributed here to Robin Hood, as it is in Cornwall to King Arthur."[5] "As proofs of his universal popularity," says the same writer,[6] "his stories and exploits have been made the subject as well of various dramatic exhibitions, as of innumerable poems, rhymes, songs and ballads; he has given rise to divers proverbs, and to swear by him, or by some of his companions, seems to have been a usual practice; he may be regarded as the patron of archery; and though not actually canonized (a situation to which the miracles wrought in his favour, as well in his lifetime as after his death, and the supernatural powers he is, in some parts, supposed to have possessed, give him an indisputable claim), he obtained the principal distinction of sainthood, in having a festival allotted to him, and solemn games instituted in honour of his memory, which were celebrated to the latter end of the sixteenth century; not by the populace only, but by kings or princes and grave magistrates, and that as well in Scotland as in England; being considered in the former country as of the highest political importance, and as essential to the civil and religious liberties of the people, the efforts of the government to suppress them frequently producing tumult and insurrection."

At Aberdeen in 1508 it was ordered by the provost and baillies that all persons who were able should be ready with green and yellow raiment, bows and arrows, to go with "Robyne Huyd and Litile Johnne" whenever

[5] Ibid., p. lxi.
[6] Ibid., p. xiii.

these should require them,[7] and as late as 1577 the Scottish Parliament requested the King to prohibit plays of "Robin Hood, king of May," on the Sabbath.

Bishop Latimer, in his sixth sermon before King Edward VI, stated that he had given notice of his intention to preach at a certain church on the following day, being a holy day, but when he came there found the door of the church locked, and one of the parish said to him: "Sir, this is a busy day, we cannot hear you; it is Robin Hood's day. The parish are gone abroad to gather for Robin Hood, I pray you let them not."

Robin Hood's day, then, was observed as a religious festival, yet he certainly was not a saint. Not only was he, according to tradition, a robber, but the victims of his robberies were usually ecclesiastics; in fact, as Ritson says,[8] he "seems to have held bishops, abbots, priests and monks, in a word, all the clergy, regular and secular, in decided aversion."

Who, then, was he? The answer is that he was the hero of a ritual drama. In the fifteenth century, and later, the May-day celebration was called "Robin Hood's festival," and he was "one of the mythical characters whom the populace was fond of personating in the semi-dramatic devices and morris-dances performed at that season." [9] In Scotland, as we have seen, he was as popular as in England, and in France Robin des Bois and Marion are found in the thirteenth century as characters in the Whitsuntide *pastourelles,* "the earliest and not the least charming of pastoral comedies." [1] The facts that the name "Robin" is French in origin, and that we find "Robin des Bois" in France at such an early date, suggest that the name as a whole may have been imported from France, and that "Robin Hood" is merely a translation of "Robin des Bois";[2] *hood* and *wood* are interchangeable in several English dialects.

[7] E. K. Chambers: *The Mediæval Stage,* vol. ii, p. 334.
[8] Op. cit., p. x.
[9] *D.N.B.,* s.v. "Robin Hood."
[1] E. K. Chambers: *The Mediævel Stage,* vol. i, p. 172.
[2] Not, as Miss Murray suggests, Robin with a hood; M. A. Murray: *The God of the Witches,* p. 36.

Now what was this May-day festival at which Robin
Hood played such a prominent part? There can be no
doubt that it was of pagan origin—that it was, in fact, the
spring festival which was theoretically superseded by the
Christian Easter. We should expect a pagan festival to be
associated with a pagan deity, and we should not be disappointed. We have in Robin Hood a deity particularly
associated with spring and vegetation. He was the King of
May, and Maid Marian was the Queen of May. As such
she wore a golden crown,[3] and it seems that it was the
custom in every town and village of England for a young
man and a girl or pretty boy to be dressed in royal costume in order that they might play the parts of Robin
Hood and Maid Marian, otherwise the King and Queen
of May, in the May-day festivities.

All classes took part in these festivities, and the belief
that Robin Hood was particularly the hero of the poor is
quite unfounded. In 1473 Sir John Paston complains that
the man whom he has kept to play St. George and Robin
Hood has left him,[4] and the household book of the Earl of
Northumberland, *circa* 1520, makes provision for "liveries
for Robin Hood."[5] It is recorded that in the reign of
Henry VI the aldermen and sheriffs of London dined on
May-day in a wood at Stepney, and in 1515 King Henry
VIII spent May-day with his court in a wood near Green-
wich, the courtiers all dressed in green and carrying bows.
That in so doing he was following an established custom
seems clear from Malory, who tells us that in the month
of May, Queen Guinevere warned the Knights of the
Round Table to be ready early in the morning, well horsed
and clad in green, to accompany her on maying into the
woods and fields beside Westminster.[6] On these occasions
there was probably a masque at the conclusion of which
the player who had taken the part of Robin Hood, King
of May, made a graceful apology to the King for having
usurped his title, and received a gracious pardon. Wynkyn

[3] W. C. Hazlitt: *Faiths and Folklore,* vol. ii, p. 383.
[4] J. Gairdner: *Paston Letters,* vol. iii, p. 89.
[5] E. K. Chambers: *Mediæval Stage,* vol. i, p. 177.
[6] *Morte Darthur,* xix, i.

de Worde's *Mery Geste,* in which "King Edward" appears, may well have been performed for King Edward IV. When the festivities were no longer held, references to some such little ceremony were taken to mean that a real Robin Hood had once been really pardoned by a king. This, in my view, is how myths often arise.

The May-day ceremonies of medieval England must have been very different from their prehistoric prototypes, but we can perhaps gain some idea of the latter from an analysis of the stories. They fall into three classes: stories of single combat, stories of feats with the bow, and tricky stories. To take the first class, Robin Hood fights single combats with Little John, Will Scarlet, Friar Tuck, Arthur-a-Bland, the beggar, and the potter. In all these combats he is worsted, and in several is knocked out. They all seem to be variants of a type story that goes as follows: Robin Hood is alone in the forest and meets a stranger; after a great deal of boasting, challenging, and, in the older versions, coarse abuse, they fight, and Robin is knocked out. Recovering himself, he sounds his horn, and his men, who are close at hand though unseen, rush onto the scene. The stranger is then acclaimed a member of the band. In some versions Robin hands his lady over to the victor, who receives her with coarse delight.[7] It is interesting to compare with this the story told in the *Mabinogi* of Kulhwch and Olwen, of how two warriors quarrelled over Creidylad or Cordelia, daughter of Lud of the Silver Hand. The judgment of Arthur was "that the two suitors fight every First of May for ever henceforth till the Day of Doom; and he who then proves victorious—let him take the damsel." [8]

All these stories are suggestive of an ancient system by which the king reigned from one May-day till the next, when he had to fight for his title, if not for his life, and in which the queen became the wife of the successful combatant. There is a great deal of evidence for the existence of such systems in many parts of the world, and I shall discuss some of it in Chapter XVI.

[7] Malone Society Collections, vol. ii, p. 132.
[8] Quoted by J. Rhys: *The Arthurian Legend,* p. 319.

The only combat in which Robin Hood is victorious is that with Guy of Gisborne, who is disguised as a horse, and Robin, having killed and mutilated him, assumes his horse disguise. This seems to go back to a somewhat different type of tradition, that of men in animal form, with which I shall deal in Chapter XXIV.

The second class of Robin Hood stories, the stories of feats with the bow, may be due partly to the fact that by the fifteenth century the long-bow had become the traditional weapon of Englishmen, and partly to borrowings from the cognate myth of William Tell. It is interesting to note that whereas a century ago all scholars believed as firmly in the historicity of William Tell as most of them now do in that of Achilles or King Arthur, Tell is now recognized as a purely mythical figure, a member of a widespread group.[9] Robin Hood is as clearly related to William Tell as is the Sheriff of Nottingham to Gessler.

As regards the tricky stories, they may be due to a confusion between Robin Hood and Robin Goodfellow. Perhaps the two were never very clearly distinguished.

It is probable, as we have seen, that Robin Hood is Robin of the Wood. Now, according to Skeat the original meaning of *wood* was "twig," and hence a mass of twigs or "bush"; if this is so, then Robin Hood is Robin of the Twigs, or the Bush, which suggests connections with another well-known figure of the spring festivities, Jack-in-the-Green, and with the carved faces, with twigs protruding from their mouths, which are a feature of so many of our old churches. Robin's relations with the Church are obscure. His festivities, like many pagan survivals, seem to have been tolerated, and in 1499 the churchwardens of Reading received xix *s.* on account of the "gaderyng of Robynhod," while as late as 1566 the churchwardens of Abingdon paid eighteen pence for setting up Robin Hood's bower.[1] Yet he was, as we have seen, the professed enemy of all clergy. It may be that the incidents in which ecclesiastics cut such a poor figure were aimed at individuals who tried to suppress the festivities, or it may be that in

[9] S. Baring-Gould: *Curious Myths of the Middle Ages,* ch. v.
[1] W. C. Hazlitt, op. cit., p. 529.

the sixteenth century bishops and abbots were fair game. Anyhow, there can be little doubt that these incidents, like all the features of the Robin Hood stories which are not purely mythical, represent the customs and ideas of the late fifteenth or early sixteenth century rather than those of any period at which Robin Hood can be supposed to have lived.

We may then summarize the results obtained in this chapter as follows:

1. There is no evidence for Robin Hood as a historical character, or for any attempt to set him up as such within at least three centuries of his alleged lifetime.

2. There is abundant evidence, in many parts of England and Scotland, for Robin Hood as the name given to the principal actor in the May-day dramatic performances and revels.

3. The attempt to make Robin Hood a historical character not merely involves us in endless anachronisms and other absurdities, but renders the known facts of his cult completely inexplicable.

4. The alleged incidents of his career are analogous to those of many other heroes of tradition, especially William Tell, who is admittedly mythical.

We may conclude with a quotation from Dr. Johnson, who, having commented on the readiness with which the poems attributed to Ossian were accepted in Scotland as genuine, admitted that the same kind of ready belief might be found in his own country. "He would undertake," he said, "to write an epic poem on the story of Robin Hood, and half England, to whom the names and places he should mention in it are familiar, would believe and declare they had heard it from their earliest years." [2]

[2] J. Boswell: *The Journal of a Tour to the Hebrides with Samuel Johnson*, p. 324.

CHAPTER V

THE NORSE SAGAS

The task of proving a negative is always a hard one. To prove Robin Hood unhistoric is rendered comparatively easy by the fact that we can meet him in print when he is still a character in the popular drama and has as yet made no serious claim to historicity. I shall try to show that the heroes of the sagas were originally dramatic characters, but this task is far more difficult because the saga heroes were recruited, not from contemporary drama, but from the traditions of a drama which had long been extinct.

The Icelandic or other Norse narratives derived from traditional sources may be divided into three classes. The first consists of tales of the gods; the second of tales of Sigurd the Volsung and other heroes who are supposed to have lived in the period A.D. 350–550; and the third of the Icelandic and other sagas which deal with heroes who are supposed to have lived in the period A.D. 850–1050.

It is now generally recognized that the tales of the gods are purely mythological, but there are still a few incorrigible euhemerists who believe that Odin, Woden, or Wotan, the northern Zeus, was a real man, a hero who led the original Swedes to Sweden, or the original somebodies to somewhere. A reference to the *Edda* should suffice to dispel this illusion. We are told [1] that Odin was the son of Fridleif and a descendant of Thor, and later[2] that he was the son of Borr and the father of Thor. In both versions Odin's wife is Frigg, but Thor is not the son of Frigg but of Ertha, who is Odin's daughter and wife, though in the next paragraph Ertha is the daughter of Annar.

Baldur, again, lives in Heaven, and is the wisest of the

[1] A. G. Brodeur: *Prose Edda,* p. 7.
[2] Ibid., pp. 19, 22.

gods, but he was killed and burnt, and now resides with
the dead. He is young and fair, but has a grown-up son.[3]

Such discrepancies, of course, never occur in connection
with historical personages, and the fact that the compilers
of the *Edda* made no attempt to reconcile them shows
that they did not regard Odin and Baldur as historical
personages, even if they had any idea of history at all,
which is improbable.

Nevertheless, Mr. Hodgkin, following previous writers,
tells us that "the Scandinavian traditions tell of a war between the Njorth-Frey family ('the Vanir') and the family
of Odin ('the Anses'). Here we have a true reminiscence
of rivalry between competing cults." [4] This is equivalent
to maintaining that *Paradise Lost* embodies a true reminiscence of a conflict between Christians and pagans.

We will now pass to the second group of tales, of which
Sigurd is the central figure, and consider what Professor
Chadwick has to say about them. He tells us that "apart
from the last cycles embracing Harald Hilditonn and
Ragnar Lodbrok, which are entirely confined to Northern
literature, all the historical personages whom we have
been able to identify belong to a period extending over
barely two centuries. . . . In the stories which form the
common theme of English, German, and Scandinavian
poets we find no mention of historical persons who lived
after the middle of the sixth century. . . . This period
coincides with the Age of National Migrations, the conquest of Roman provinces, and the conversion of most of
the Continental peoples to Christianity. Yet Danish characters figure more prominently than those of any other
nation in the stories, though the Danes took no part, col-
lectively at least, in the movements against the Roman
Empire, and were not converted to Christianity till much
later. Some of the chief characters, such as Attila, were
heathens, and some, such as Theodric, Christians, yet the
change of faith plays no part in the stories." [5] Nor does
the Roman Empire play any part in the stories, in which

[3] Ibid., pp. 36, 41, 74.
[4] R. H. Hodgkin: *History of the Anglo-Saxons,* vol. i, p. 28.
[5] H. M. Chadwick: *The Heroic Age,* pp. 25–9.

all the characters are represented as sharing a common
religion, language, and culture. Attila and Theodric were,
of course, historical personages, but they are never represented in the stories as doing anything that they can be
supposed to have done in real life. Their names were
probably put in as suitable names for important characters
at a time when they were vaguely famous, perhaps fifty
years after their deaths. According to Sir John Rhys, Attila takes the place of the king of the dead, and Theodric
or Dietrich is really a sun-hero.[6]

The case of Jormunrek or Ermanaric is different, since
he is said by Ammian not merely to have lived, but to
have done some of the things which the stories say that
he did. A good deal of capital has been made of this, but
when we examine Ammian's narrative[7] we see that he does
not speak of these incidents as happenings in his own
time or vicinity, but at some uncertain time in the past,
and in a region of which we are merely told that it was
beyond the Dniester. While we may give Ammian full
credit for reporting faithfully all that he saw and heard,
we cannot suppose him capable of distinguishing the history of eastern Europe from its mythology, or suppose
his barbarian informants to have been more capable than
other illiterates of transmitting historical facts. The fact
that Swanhild, Ermanaric's luckless Queen, is a Rosomo-
nian according to Jordanes, a Lombard in *Widsith,* a Hel-
lespontine in Saxo, and a Volsung in the *Volsunga Saga,*[8]
makes it pretty clear that she, at any rate, was not a historical personage.

The great central figure in this group of stories, however, is Sigurd or Siegfried, the dragon-slayer, and if we
can dispose of his claims to historicity, we may perhaps
disregard his fellows. As Sigurd he is the hero of the *Volsunga Saga,* the great Icelandic saga upon which all later
sagas are modelled, and from which, as we shall see, they
draw many of their incidents. It was composed, probably
in the twelfth century, out of elements drawn from a large

[6] J. Rhys: *The Arthurian Legend,* p. 266.
[7] *Ammianus Marcellinus,* ch. xxxi, p. 3.
[8] R. W. Chambers: *Widsith,* p. 23.

number of traditional poems and ballads. As Siegfried he is the hero of the *Lay of the Nibelungs,* which was composed in Germany about the same time. The two are versions of the same story, of which the main features are as follows: Sigmund (Siegmund) obtains from Odin (Wotan) a magic sword, with which he performs various feats. After his death in battle, the pieces of the sword, which had been shattered, are kept for his son Sigurd (Siegfried) and made by a cunning smith into a sword as good as before. With this sword he slays the dragon Fafnir (Fafner), which guards the hoard of gold. On cooking the dragon's heart and accidentally tasting it, he finds that he can understand the song of the birds, which warn him against the treachery of the smith.

The slaying of the dragon, and the roasting of its heart, seem to have been regarded in the north as the most important incidents in the story, to judge by the frequency with which they are represented on monuments.[9]

Having slain the smith and loaded the treasure onto his horse, the hero proceeds on his way, and comes to a hilltop upon which he finds Brynhild (Brunhilde) asleep within a ring of fire. They fall in love, but by spells and shape-changings are tricked into marrying others. Eventually Brynhild's jealousy causes his death, which is avenged upon his slayers. One of them, Gunnar (Gunther), is thrown bound into a snake-pit, but charms the snakes by playing upon a harp with his toes. This incident also is often represented on monuments.

The usual method of dealing with such stories may be expressed in the words of Mr. Gray, who tells us[1] that "the saga constitutes the earliest type of history, and it is possible, in great part, to reconstruct a large portion of real history by the excision of material obviously fictitious." We are apparently to suppose that the story-tellers could, and often did, lie when they spoke of giants and dragons, but that they were incapable of diverging a hair's breadth from the truth when dealing with purely human

[9] B. S. Phillpotts: *The Elder Edda and Ancient Scandinavian Drama,* p. 49; P. M. C. Kermode: *Manx Crosses,* pp. 172–4.
[1] L. H. Gray, in *Hastings' Encyclopædia,* vol. vi, p. 1.

activities. How much of the narrative that I have just
sketched would be regarded as history by Mr. Gray is
uncertain. It would no doubt depend on whether he regarded harp-playing with the toes as "obviously fictitious." In any case, the criterion is purely subjective, and
therefore quite valueless. Professor H. J. Rose is driven to
admitting that "we have not yet an agreed and perfected
technique" for extracting history from saga;[2] obviously
not, since the only way of attempting to extract history from any narrative is to check it with facts known
from other sources, and tested in this way, the sagas break
down completely.

It is impossible to give Sigurd a date or a place. On one
view the wide distribution of his story in Teutonic lands
shows that he was a great hero of the still-undivided
Teutonic race; another view, as we have seen, would put
him somewhere about A.D. 450; that is to say, a thousand
years later. But even if we were to accept the latter date,
we should find it difficult to explain how his daughter
Aslaug came to marry Ragnar Lodbrog, the traditional
leader of the Viking army that looted Paris in A.D. 845.
And no amount of rationalization will explain how he
came to perform the same feats, and meet the same fate,
on the shores of the Baltic and the banks of the Rhine.

But there are still further difficulties. In the Saxon poem
of *Beowulf,* which is believed to have been composed in
the first half of the eighth century, and therefore gives us
much the oldest extant version of the story, we find that
Sigurd is not mentioned at all, but that the feats later
attributed to him are attributed to Sigmund, who gains
immortal fame by slaying the dragon and carrying off the
hoard.[3] The conclusion to which we are driven is that the
Volsunga Saga, far from being "the earliest type of history," is nothing but a novel based on myth.

The *Volsunga Saga* was the first of a long series of
sagas, most of which were composed in the thirteenth
century. They were almost unknown in England till about

[2] *Folk-Lore,* vol. xlvi, p. 22.
[3] T. Arnold: *Beowulf,* pp. xix, 220.

seventy years ago, when many of them were translated into English, and aroused by their literary qualities unstinted admiration. It was not only their literary qualities, however, that popularized them, but the belief that they contained genuine historical records of people who were either actually our ancestors or closely akin to them. A more critical study has shown, however, that like the *Volsunga Saga,* which they closely follow, they are really novels, and, what is more, novels written in a highly artificial and sophisticated literary style, so artificial that it would be difficult to adapt a true story to the saga form, even if the attempt were made. The sagas are great literature, and the belief that simple stories of fact, related by simple people, could be great literature can be held only by those who have never heard such stories related by simple people, and who have never studied the development of literature. Great literature is always the endproduct of a long process of experiment and evolution.

Koht gives us an idea of the manner in which this evolution occurred. He tells us that the first known saga, one about St. Olaf, of which only fragments are preserved, was written about 1160. It seems to have consisted largely of accounts of miracles. "The pioneer of secular sagawriting was a man named Eirek Oddson," who wrote, about 1170, an account of the civil wars in Norway which had taken place in his own lifetime. The subject, and in part the author, of the first royal saga was King Sverri, and the saga was written, about 1185, as a piece of propaganda. "The bishops' sagas . . . are devotional just as much as historical literature, and so, like King Sverri's saga, they belong to the field of propaganda." [4] Koht also tells us that "the writing of the family sagas does not constitute the beginning of saga-writing, but is a later product of it"; that "the pure Icelandic sagas still maintained the character of art and entertainment so strongly stamped upon them that they could not easily come to be considered as historical works before real historical sagas had come into existence"; and that the *Njalssaga* was one

[4] H. Koht: *The Old Norse Sagas,* pp. 49, 52, 61.

of the last to be written, about the end of the thirteenth century.[5] The English editor of this saga, Sir George Dasent, supposed it to have been written down about 1100.[6]

Olrik tells us[7] that "Iceland has its saga age, the age in which 'the sagas were made' as the saga language itself states, i.e., when the events described took place. This is the period from 930, the end of the settlement age, to 1030, the conclusion of the first generation after the introduction of Christianity." But it is impossible to believe that noteworthy events were limited to this period. The sagas were made, of course, when they were written down, and we have here one of many examples of the fact that traditional incidents are usually supposed to have happened about one hundred and fifty to two hundred years before they were first recorded in writing.

The so-called "family saga" really revolves round the life of a single hero, and follows a set form. The prologue gives the hero's pedigree and tells in brief some of the principal feats of his ancestors. In the first act we have the birth and upbringing of the hero and his youthful exploits; we have also an account of the rise and progress of the family feud through which the hero will meet his death.

The second act is an interlude, in which the hero leaves his home in Iceland (Orkney, Faroe) and goes to Norway, where he defeats and kills famous vikings, berserks, and giants, and becomes one of the leading men at the court of Olaf Tryggvason or Earl Hakon. A comparative study of these interludes has led Miss Danielli to conclude that they are descriptions of an initiation ceremonial.[8]

In the third act the hero is at home again and, though guiltless, is involved in feuds with powerful and unscrupulous neighbours. The toils gradually close about him, and eventually he is killed fighting bravely against enormous odds. An epilogue tells how his death is avenged.

[5] Ibid., pp. 48, 169.
[6] G. W. Dasent: *The Story of Burnt Njal*, p. xii.
[7] A. Olrik: *Viking Civilization*, p. 179.
[8] *Folk-Lore*, vol. lvi, pp. 229 ff.

It is impossible to believe that such a series of incidents formed the normal life-history of a Norseman, even of a Norse hero, so that when Koht says that "the family saga manifests a definite tendency to depart from history and approach the pure novel," [9] he is hardly stating the case correctly, since he implies that these sagas were originally historical. The common form in their framework seems to show quite clearly that this was not so. Even the so-called "historical sagas" are not really historical, since "scholars have been forced to discover in the historical sagas ? . increasing quantity of mistakes and misinformation." [1] The phrase "scholars have been forced" is significant as indicating the general reluctance of scholars to face the facts. Koht shows that the mistakes go much farther than the misrepresentation of incidents. Thus we learn that true history knows nothing of the duel as a legal remedy, though it plays a large part in the sagas; that Snorri's conception of the struggle between king and nobility, in which the plots of many of the sagas begin, is essentially false; and that, though the sagas profess to deal chiefly with heathen times, "it is remarkable how little they contain of really heathen thinking and practice." [2]

In spite of all this, however, Koht holds that the sagas contain many historical facts, and instances the discovery of America by Leif. I shall discuss this story later, but will note here that, like all the other sagas, it contains many supernatural incidents. Sir George Dasent, who translated many of the sagas and believed implicitly in their historicity, regarded these supernatural incidents as proofs of this, since they were in accordance with the beliefs of the age.[3] The age, with the beliefs of which they accorded, may well have been the thirteenth century. In any case the question is one not of local colour, but of actual fact, and it is difficult to see how the introduction of supernatural beings could make a story more credible than it would otherwise have been. The

[9] H. Koht, op. cit., p. 87.
[1] Ibid., p. 119.
[2] Ibid., pp. 69, 117, 138.
[3] Op. cit., p. xii.

appearance of the ghost in *Hamlet* does not convince us
of the play's historicity.

An analysis of the sagas shows not merely that their
framework is common form, but that their basis is mythological. The saga of Grettir the Strong is supposed to be
the true story of a man who died about the year 1030, and
was composed about two hundred years later. When we
examine it, we find that it has striking resemblance to the
saga of Beowulf, which is supposed to be the more or less
true story of a man who lived in Denmark about the sixth
century, and which was composed in England about two
hundred years later. Grettir, we are told, was "the strongest
man in the land of his age, and the best able to deal with
spectres and goblins." [4] His chief feats, like those of
Beowulf, were victories over supernatural beings, and
these are described in very similar language. Grettir's
struggle with Glam's ghost is closely parallel to Beowulf's
struggle with Grendel, and his fights with the troll-woman
and the giant under the waterfall to Beowulf's fight with
Grendel's mother. It is to be noted that the saga of Beowulf was preserved by the merest accident, and that but
for its existence Grettir would have a much more plausible
claim to historicity.

The chief apparent difference is that the saga of Grettir
is in prose, and that of Beowulf in verse, but this difference is less important than it seems at first glance. Though
most of *Grettissaga* is in prose, we find that on important
occasions the hero always bursts into verse. There are
some sixty stanzas in the saga, of which about two thirds
are spoken by Grettir himself, often on occasions, such
as the middle of a fight, when they come very oddly in a
prose narrative. There can, I think, be little doubt that
the saga was originally a mythological poem parallel to
that of Beowulf, and that it was reduced to prose by a
novelist who was unable to break away altogether from
the traditional form.

We are told that in the Irish traditional tales "not in-
frequently the fragments of verse introduced into a prose
tale are quotations from an older poetical version of the

[4] G. A. Hight: *The Saga of Grettir the Strong,* p. 238.

same tale; and hence it often happens that while the prose may be plain enough, the poetry is archaic and obscure." [5] Exactly the same applies to the sagas. The verses that we find in them are full of circumlocutions and obscure metaphors. The boastful and prolix Grettir of the verses is quite a different person from the laconic Grettir of the prose. Even a wet cloak, when it suddenly breaks out into verse,[6] cannot speak straightforwardly. In the *Njalssaga* the novelist has sometimes allowed the verse to remain next to his prose paraphrase,[7] and anyone who compares them can see clearly that the simplicity and directness, which has caused the "naturalness" of the sagas to be so highly praised, forms no part of the traditional narrative.

In the *Njalssaga* the culminating incident is the burning of Njal and his sons in their house, and the account of this incident and of the events that lead up to it bear a striking resemblance to the death of the sons of Usnach, as related in the Irish mythological tale. For example, when Skarphedinn and his brothers are shut up in the burning house, Gunnar, a man whose relatives Skarphedinn has slain, climbs up and looks over the wall. Sharphedinn throws a tooth at him, hitting him in the eye and causing his eyeball to fall out onto his cheek. Naisi and his brothers are shut up in a house, and before Conchobar orders his men to set fire to it, he sends Trendorn, a man whose relatives Naisi has slain, "to see whether her own shape and form remain on Deirdre." He peeps through a small window which had been left open, and Naisi throws a draughtsman at him, hitting him in the eye and causing his eyeball to fall out onto his cheek.[8]

Parallels with Irish myth are not confined to the *Njalssaga*. In the *Volsunga Saga*, Sigurd roasts the dragon's heart for Regin, who warns him not to eat it himself; happening to touch it, he burns his thumb and, putting it into his mouth to cool it, immediately understands the

[5] P. W. Joyce: *Old Celtic Romances*, p. v.
[6] R. Proctor: *The Story of the Laxdalers*, p. 209.
[7] E.g., pp. 42, 75, 115.
[8] G. W. Dasent, op. cit., p. 241; E. Hull: *The Cuchullin Saga*, p. 39.

song of the birds. In an Irish myth Finn Eges roasts the
heart of the Salmon of Linn Feic for Finn mac Cumhail,
who warns him not to eat it himself; happening to touch
it, he burns his thumb and, putting it into his mouth to
cool it, immediately becomes possessed of all knowledge.[9]

The description of Egil's grief in *Egilssaga* is "surely
but an echo of Cuchullin's rage in the Irish heroic poetry." [1] It may be noted that *Egilssaga* is one of the most
convincingly written, yet one series of incidents is described by Olrik[2] as "quite unhistorical," and another by
Koht [3] as "pure invention."

Of the *Laxdæla Saga,* Koht says that "it has even a
kind of historical setting, though it may be said that the
chronology is confused, and other pretended facts are
rather untrustworthy." [4] Olrik derives one of its leading
incidents from the *Volsunga Saga,*[5] while Professor Ker
describes it as a modern prose version of the "Niblung
tragedy." [6]

From the *Volsunga Saga* come also, according to Keary,
who describes them as "utterly fabulous," the stories of
Ragnar Lodbrok, including his death in the snake-pit;[7]
and from the same saga, according to Koht,[8] comes the
story told in Olaf Tryggvason's saga of Olaf and Queen
Sigrid.

Nor is it only from the *Volsunga Saga* and Irish myth
that the incidents of the later sagas are derived. "The death
of Skarphedinn," says Professor Ker,[9] "is like a prose
rendering of the death of Roland," and the epilogue to the
Grettissaga is derived from French romance.[1]

[9] Magnusson and Morris: *The Volsunga Saga,* p. 64; J.
Weston: *From Ritual to Romance,* p. 125.
[1] A. Olrik, op. cit., p. 188.
[2] Ibid., p. 186.
[3] Op. cit., p. 73.
[4] Ibid., p. 91.
[5] Op. cit., p. 188.
[6] W. P. Ker: *Epic and Romance,* p. 219.
[7] C. F. Keary: *The Vikings in Western Christendom,* pp. 257,
326.
[8] Op. cit., p. 155.
[9] Op. cit., p. 265.
[1] G. A. Hight, op. cit., p. x.

Sir Charles Oman, discussing the well-known story of the Battle of Stamford Bridge in the saga of Harald Haardraade,[2] shows that "the whole story is one tissue of mistakes"; it appears to be based on an account of the Battle of Hastings. The saga is composed largely of incidents and anecdotes derived from earlier sources, and is, in fact, a historical novel by one who has been at small pains to work up his subject.

It is possible that extracts from contemporary records may have been inserted in some of the royal sagas, and that these are therefore to that extent historical, but this possibility will but slightly affect our conclusions about the sagas as a whole, which are:

1. That their framework is common form.
2. That their principal incidents are mythological.
3. That their superficial appearance of realism is a literary artifice.
4. That the picture of pagan times which they present is a false one.
5. That when they can be checked with known facts, they prove to be quite unhistorical.

I shall later adduce evidence to suggest that the origin, not of the sagas themselves, but of the poems on which they are based, is the ritual drama.

EXCURSUS ON LEIF THE LUCKY

So much importance has been attached to the alleged discovery of Greenland by Eirek the Red, and that of America by his son Leif, that some discussion of them seems called for. Mr. Gathorne-Hardy, in his book *The Norse Discoverers of America,* collects all the references to the subject in the sagas and concludes that they are in the main statements of fact. I shall give as briefly as possible my reasons for believing the contrary.

For the Norse discovery of America there is no evidence outside the sagas, whereas there is proof, from his-

---

[2] C. W. Oman: *England before the Norman Conquest,* p. 640 n.

torical and archæological sources, that the Norse did, in
fact, discover and settle Greenland. This fact, however, no
more proves the historicity of Eirek than does the fact
that the Saxons conquered England prove the historicity
of Hengist and Horsa, or the fact that there are people in
the world prove that it was first settled by Adam and Eve.
All the evidence for Eirek is purely traditional, which
means, as I have tried to show, that it is no evidence at all.

The stories of Eirek and of Leif, in their original form,
seem to be derived solely from one Ari, called the Wise
or the Learned, who appears to have been born about
1067, and to have written, about 1130, a history of the
Icelanders, of which we have not the original, but a sum-
mary written at a later date by an unknown hand.[3] In this
we are told that Ari had received his information about
Eirek the Red, and also apparently about Leif, from his
uncle Thorkel, who had received it from one of Eirek's
men. The events described fall, according to Gathorne-
Hardy, "within a period bridged by one human memory
from the time of occurrence to the time when they could
be recorded in writing," but when we realize that the
interval was one of about a hundred and forty years, we
see that this is a misstatement. Eirek's man must have
kept the facts in his mind for about fifty years before he
passed them on to Thorkel, who again must have kept
them in his mind for about fifty years before he passed
them on to Ari, who did not write them down till about
forty years later. Even then, if we have Ari's own words,
which is doubtful, his evidence is merely third-hand evidence, and very bad third-hand evidence at that.

The only other alleged reference to the discovery of
America in any early document is in a description of the
North written by Adam of Bremen about 1070. He says
that King Svein, of Denmark, told him of an island in the
ocean, which many had discovered, and which abounded
in vines and corn, both growing wild.[4] Such stories, which
I shall return to presently, are a commonplace of myth,
but anyhow we have here no mention of Leif. The five

[3] Koht, op. cit., p. 130; Gathorne-Hardy, op. cit., p. 98.
[4] Gathorne-Hardy, op. cit., p. 98.

extant versions of Leif's story are all, so we are apparently invited to believe, derived from Ari, or rather from Ari's uncle's anonymous informant.

According to three of these versions, Leif goes from Greenland to Norway, where he is converted to Christianity and finds favour with King Olaf Tryggvason. The latter urges him to convert Greenland to Christianity, and sends him back there accompanied by a priest and some holy men. On the way Leif finds Wine-land the Good (no details given), and rescues a shipwrecked crew; and when he reaches Greenland succeeds in converting the inhabitants to Christianity. He is afterwards called Leif the Lucky, whether because he converted the Greenlanders or rescued the shipwrecked crew is not clear; anyhow it is not because he discovered Wine-land. A fourth account is similar to the three previously mentioned, but does not mention Wine-land at all.[5]

The fifth version of the story of Leif, which contains the detailed account of his discovery of Wine-land, is in the *Flatey Book*. It makes him start off on a voyage of discovery after his return to Greenland, and implies distinctly that he had not made any discoveries before.[6] The other detailed account of alleged American exploration is in the story of Thorfinn Karlsefni; of this there are two versions, both late, and one obviously copied from the other.[7]

The first four versions of the story of Leif are also obviously copied one from another, and it seems certain that whichever of these is the earliest contains the earliest version of the story. It seems impossible that they can be abridgements of the longer version, since they all differ from it in the same material points.

Now, if a man called Leif really discovered America, it seems to me quite absurd to suppose that three chroniclers could mention the fact without giving any particulars whatever, and that a fourth could mention Leif without mentioning his discovery at all. The only historical charac-

[5] Ibid., pp. 74–6.
[6] Ibid., p. 41.
[7] Ibid., pp. 52 ff.

ter mentioned in the story is Olaf Tryggvason, and as I have already suggested, association with him impels a suspicion of fiction. Apart from that, the story is strongly suggestive of a religious tract. The seeker after righteousness takes with him a priest as a companion and guide on his voyage through life, and is thereby enabled to steer clear of Sin (the fleshpots of the heathen) and Death (shipwreck), and to reach that Green Land where the Lucky (that is, the saved) enjoy eternal bliss. I suggest that some such tract, imported probably from Ireland, was, with other material of diverse but equally unhistorical origin, embodied by Ari, or someone else, in a quasi-historical narrative.

I further suggest that a little later, when saga-novels were all the rage, some novelist made the story of Leif the basis of a novel, to which that of Thorfinn formed a popular sequel, and that this novel found its way into the *Flatey Book* in much the same way as the romances of Geoffrey of Monmouth found their way into the history of England.

The novelist did not, of course, draw his materials from his inner consciousness, and his sources were, in the main, the Otherworld voyages of Irish mythology, those of Bran, of Maelduin, and of Tadg.[8] The resemblances to the voyage of Tadg[9] are particularly striking. In both stories there are salmon and whales, and the vines of Leif correspond with the large purple berries of Tadg. Tadg meets a large and fierce ram, while Thorfinn has a bull that goes wild and gives trouble. Tadg and his men find a plain with "a dew of honey over it," while Leif and his men "found dew on the grass, and put it into their mouths, and it seemed to them that they had never tasted anything so sweet as this dew."

Tadg's encounter with the woman of the Otherworld and with Connla the son of Conn are paralleled by the visit of the Otherworld woman to Thorfinn's wife, and by the conversation between the living and the dead Thor-

[8] The suggestion that Wine-land was the Otherworld has been made by Dr. Nansen; Gathorne-Hardy, op. cit., p. 154.

[9] Lady Gregory: *Gods and Fighting Men,* pp. 126 ff.

steins. Tadg has a man of the Otherworld who goes with
him as guide, and he corresponds with Leif's foster-father,
who recognizes the berries as grapes and gets drunk on
them. But the sagamen could never keep away from the
Volsunga Saga for long, and in the characteristics of this
foster-father, who was small and skilled in crafts and spoke
a strange tongue, we may recognize Regin, the foster-
father of Sigurd, who was small, and a skilled craftsman,
with a knowledge of many tongues.

The sagaman may have drawn upon the classics for
the curious uniped that figures in one of his stories, but
Ireland was his main source of inspiration. It is several
times mentioned, and some of Thorfinn's men, meeting with
a storm off "Keelness" in Wine-land, are cast ashore in Ireland.

The stories contain many more improbabilities and
supernatural events, but I will only add that, as in the
Irish Otherworld, there is no frost in Wine-land. This fact
has been carefully overlooked by those who would find
Wine-land in America.

CHAPTER VI

KING ARTHUR

It should be an easier task to prove the mythical character of King Arthur, since the literature that has grown up round his name is admittedly a literature of pure fiction. Nobody mistakes Chrestien de Troyes, Malory, or nowadays even Geoffrey of Monmouth, for historians, and Arthur should therefore be in a different category from the heroes created, or rather adapted from myth, by the anonymous genius who composed the prose version of the *Volsunga Saga,* and his successors and imitators.

That he is not so is due to two causes. The first is the extreme lengths to which euhemerism has been carried by modern scholars. Whereas Euhemeros was content to claim that the gods had once been great men, it now seems to be generally held that such a thing as a purely mythical character has never existed. The second cause is that Arthur is supposed to have lived among the post-Roman Britons, a people of whom we know almost nothing, and about whom, therefore, those who attach little weight to evidence can speculate with considerable freedom.

The evidence for Arthur's historical existence is almost nil. The only extant writer of the time when he is, according to the more fashionable theories, supposed to have lived, is Gildas, a monk of British origin, who probably composed in Brittany, between 550 and 570, his *De Excidio et Conquestu Britanniae (The Destruction and Conquest of Britain).* Gildas makes little claim to historicity: "If there were any records of my country," he says, "they were burned in the fires of the conquest, or carried away on the ships of the exiles, so that I can only follow the dark and fragmentary tale that was told me beyond the sea." He deals in a highly dramatic and rhetorical manner

with the defeat of the Britons, but tells us that "a remnant
. . . take up arms and challenge their victors to battle
under Ambrosius Aurelianus. . . . To these men, by the
Lord's favour, there came victory. . . . From that time,
the citizens were sometimes victorious, sometimes the
enemy. . . . This continued up to the year of the siege
of Badon Hill, and of almost the last great slaughter in-
flicted upon the rascally crew." [1]

"Gildas," says his editor, "would never have regarded
himself as a 'historian'; he is a preacher, a revivalist, who
will 'attempt to state a few facts' by way of illustrating his
message that divine anger must visit with punishment a
sinning people and priesthood." [2] His material seems to
have been derived chiefly from the prophet Isaiah,[3] and
from classical sources,[4] so that although he places the
siege of Badon Hill in the year of his own birth, we cannot be sure that it ever took place at all. Anyhow, he
knows nothing of Arthur. "We must admit that there is
no echo of Arthur in Gildas," says Chambers,[5] and describes this fact as odd, but it is odd only on the assumption, which, as I shall show, is unwarrantable, that Arthur
was a real man, Gildas's contemporary.

There is no mention of Arthur in Beda or in the
Anglo-Saxon Chronicle, but this is unimportant, since
these writings are quite unhistorical for the period before
about A.D. 600. We pass on to Nennius, in whose *Historia
Britonum* the first mention of Arthur occurs. Who Nennius
was is uncertain, but he is believed to have lived, somewhere on the borders of England and Wales, about the
end of the eighth or beginning of the ninth centuries. His
sole written authorities, apart from certain of the classics,
seem to have been Gildas, a fabulous life of St. Ger-
manus, and perhaps Beda. His "history" consists so largely
of miracles, anachronisms, and other absurdities that it is

---

[1] H. Williams: *Gildas,* pp. 61–3.
[2] Ibid., p. vii.
[3] C. Elton: *Origins of English History,* p. 364.
[4] C. B. Lewis: *Classical Mythology and Arthurian Romance,*
p. 248.
[5] E. K. Chambers: *Arthur of Britain,* p. 181.

obviously unworthy to be regarded as an authority for any fact whatever. "To-day, at any rate," says Dr. Wheeler, discussing the story of Vortigern, "the absolute, basic value of Nennius to the historian of the fifth century is precisely nothing." [6] What applies to the fifth century applies equally to the sixth. Yet this farrago of myths and absurdities, written some three hundred years after the alleged event, is the sole evidence for Arthur's historicity.

Nennius credits Arthur with twelve glorious victories, of which the last was at Mount Badon, "wherein fell 960 men in one day at a single onset of Arthur; and no one overthrew them but he alone, and in all the battles he came out victorious." He does not speak of Arthur as king, but as "war-leader" (*dux bellorum*) to the kings of Britain.

And where was Mount Badon? The old writers all identified it with Bath, but the moderns, who accept "tradition" when it suits them, but have no hesitation in throwing it over when it does not, have rejected Bath, though they are not agreed upon a substitute. One school places it at Badbury, in Dorset, and places the other eleven battles in various parts of southwestern England. Another school equates Badon with Bouden, in Linlithgowshire, and finds sites for the other battles near the borders of England and Scotland.[7] Mr. Crawford makes a valiant attempt to reconcile the two schools by supposing that Arthur was a petty chieftain, "probably in South Wales," who nevertheless fought his battles in Scotland.[8] Another school finds the sites of Arthur's battles in north Wales; in fact, anyone who can find a hill with a name beginning with B-d has as much right as anyone else to claim it as the site of a battle about which nothing is known.

After Nennius, our next so-called authority is the Welsh Annals, which are believed to date from the tenth century. They make no mention of Ambrosius, and transfer to Mount Badon, in a still more miraculous form, Nen-

---

[6] R. E. M. Wheeler: *London and the Saxons*, p. 34.
[7] Elton, op. cit., p. 367; Chambers: *Arthur of Britain*, p. 199.
[8] O. G. S. Crawford, in *Antiquity*, 1935, p. 290.

nius's account of Arthur's miraculous feats at the Battle of Guinnion, the eighth on his list.

Lastly, we come to Geoffrey of Monmouth (c. 1100–54), whose *History of the Kings of Britain* is the real foundation of the belief in Arthur's historicity. The old belief was that Geoffrey was a Welsh monk, who derived his facts from documents or traditions still extant among his countrymen; but this belief is now exploded. It is improbable that Geoffrey was a Welshman, and pretty certain that he used no Welsh sources. "We must then think of Geoffrey as probably rather of Breton than of Welsh blood, as brought up in a Norman environment, on the Welsh marches, but far from Welsh life, and as connected by origin with the political domination of Robert of Gloucester, and by profession with the ecclesiastical circle of Oxford and Lincoln." [9] According to the *Dictionary of National Biography,* his history is compiled from Nennius and a lost book of Breton legends, while the first part of it, according to Chambers,[1] is "obviously a literary exercise on the Virgilian model." This tends to support the view of Dr. Lewis,[2] that Arthur is a combination of Atreus, Thyestes, and other heroes, and that the whole Arthurian cycle was derived originally from classical sources. Chambers also accuses Geoffrey of "modelling Arthur's personality, court and conquests upon those of Charlemagne." [3]

Anyhow, it seems certain that, apart from Nennius, Geoffrey had no British sources whatever, since "the only Welsh treatment of Arthur for which, in its written form, at least, an origin before the late eleventh or early twelfth century can be seriously claimed, consists of obscure allusions in poems difficult to translate." [4] Apart from these and the story of Kulhwch and Olwen, which is believed to date from about 1100, and in which Arthur

[9] E. K. Chambers: *Arthur of Britain,* p. 24.
[1] Ibid., p. 31.
[2] C. B. Lewis, op. cit., pp. 248 ff.
[3] Chambers: *Arthur of Britain,* p. 56.
[4] Ibid., p. 59.

is treated in a highly mythological manner, there appears
to be no Welsh account of Arthur which is not derived
from Geoffrey.

There is not a word in Geoffrey which is more reliable
than his account of Arthur's Continental campaign, of
which Sir John Rhys writes that "it appears on the whole
that Arthur's subjugation of the west of Europe was directly or indirectly founded on the mythic invasion of
Hades by him in the character of a Culture Hero," [5] yet it
is upon Geoffrey that those stories and poems are based
which have given rise to a belief in Arthur's historicity.
It is to these stories and poems that Chambers really refers
when he speaks of "the historical Arthur," [6] and Elton
when he says that "his existence is admitted." [7] We have
seen that there is no evidence which can be admitted as
historical, and even such traditions as exist are purely
mythological.

Let us take a few examples of the latter. There were
three red-tracked ones of Britain, but a greater was Arthur;
for a year no grass or herb grew where one of the three
trod, but for seven years where Arthur trod. There were
three eminent prisoners, but a greater was Arthur, who
was thrice for three nights in magic prisons. He pursued
with his whole army a magic sow from Wales to Cornwall;
he fought with giants and monsters, the latter including
a huge cat. He had a magic sword and various other
articles of magical equipment. He is the wild huntsman,
and as we have seen, the knight who sleeps in a cave. The
ecclesiastical traditions tell us that St. Cadoc agreed to
pay Arthur one hundred red and white cows, but when
the cows reached Arthur they turned into bundles of fern.
Also that Arthur visited St. Padarn and coveted his tunic,
whereupon the saint caused the earth to open and swallow
Arthur and keep him a prisoner till he apologized. This is
the kind of treatment that was meted out to demons, and
it would therefore seem that the early Church regarded
Arthur as a demon. Why it should do so I shall suggest

[5] *Arthurian Legend*, p. 11.
[6] *Arthur of Britain*, p. 207.
[7] Op. cit., p. 363.

presently; here we will merely note that while the traditions associate Arthur, his friends, and his foes with miracles of every description, the one thing that they do not
say is that he fought against the Saxons; in fact, the Saxons
play no part whatever in the traditions. If Arthur had been
a real man, who achieved distinction by fighting against
the Saxons, and if the traditions had any historical basis,
some reference to his fights with the Saxons would be
inevitable. It would, however, be difficult to find anything
less suggestive of history than the traditional tales about
Arthur.

Let us next consider Arthur's character as a landed
proprieter. It has been suggested that the parts of Britain
where there are places named after him might indicate
the limits of his kingdom, and Chambers[8] has compiled a
list of such places. They fall into five groups: (1) Cornwall, Devon, and Somerset; (2) the borders of England
and south Wales; (3) north Wales; (4) a large area, including the north of England and the lowlands of Scotland
as far north as Kincardine; (5) Brittany. It is absurd to
suppose that there was in the sixth century a king whose
kingdom embraced the whole of this area, and it is interesting to note that it corresponds pretty closely with the
area of Brythonic place-names, with the curious exception
of central and west Wales. It is further to be noted that
no real man has ever been commemorated in this way.
Places are, of course, often called after people, but only
if they have been built or inhabited by them. It is very
rare to find a natural feature called after a real person,
yet Arthur's property consists almost entirely of hills,
rocks, and caves, where, as Chambers says,[9] he has to take
his turn as godfather with the giants, the Devil, and Robin
Hood.

He is also connected with Roman sites, and on this
Professor Gruffydd observes: "Archæologists still hope to
find Arthur's Round Table at Cærlleon on Usk; they have
not yet realized that the old caers of the Romans were to
the Britons, in whose minds these legends grew, the sym-

[8] *Arthur of Britain,* pp. 183 ff.
[9] Ibid., p. 183.

bols of a great past in which they had no part, and it was
the wistful memory of ancient greatness which made them
connect their Arthur, born in evil times of good old
Roman blood, with the relics of that greatness which they
saw about them." [1]

That Arthur was of Roman, or indeed of any human,
blood there is, as we have seen, no evidence that can be
admitted, and scholars, especially Welsh scholars, who
are apt to live in a fictitious past, do not realize that illiterates always live in a very real present. The probability
is that the Welsh of the seventh or eighth centuries, having lost all memory of the Romans, as well as of the art
of building in stone, attributed the Roman walls to supernatural agency. The German peasants, as we saw,[2] attribute
the Roman wall to the Devil, but in Wales the Devil had
not yet dispossessed the old gods of the land.

There has, of course, been a great deal of discussion
as to the meaning of the name "Arthur." The euhemerists
would make it a corruption of the Latin "Artorius"; others
derive it from the Welsh *arth,* "bear," which derives support from the fact that he is or was identified with the
constellation of the Great Bear.[3]

Mr. Briffault would derive it from the Welsh *arrdhu,*
"very black," and concludes that " 'the Black One,' leader
of battles, is identical with 'Bran,' 'the Raven,' the leader
in battle of the Celts in every war which they have fought
throughout the ages." [4] It is possible that Bran is a form of
Brennus, and that the Brennus who is said to have led the
Celtic armies in Italy, Greece, and Asia is equivalent to
the Bran who led Celtic armies in Ireland, and who, according to Welsh tradition, was the son of Llyr, the father
of Caractacus, and the converter of the Britons to Christianity. There seems no doubt that the latter was a god
who was identified with the raven. The connection of
"Arthur" with *arddhu* is improbable, but if his name does

[1] W. J. Gruffydd: *Math vab Mathonwy,* p. 346.
[2] p. 34.
[3] J. H. Parry: *The Cambrian Plutarch,* p. 3.
[4] R. Briffault: *The Mothers,* vol. iii, pp. 432, 433 n.

not mean "black," Arthur has certainly been identified with the raven,[5] and also with the chough.[6]

Real men are not identified with ravens, or with bears, and it is possible that both Bran and Arthur had the form of a raven (or bear) banner, which was borne at the head of the armies. We are told that the Norse had such banners. Asser relates that in 878 the men of Devon gained a victory over the pagans, and captured from them the standard called Raven. "They say that the sisters of Hingwar and Hubba, daughters of Lodobroch, wove that flag and got it ready in one day. They say, moreover, that in every battle, wherever that flag went before them, if they were to gain the victory a live crow would appear flying in the middle of the flag; but if they were doomed to be defeated it would hang down motionless, and this often proved to be so." [7] Sigurd, Earl of Orkney, is said to have had a banner that brought victory to those before whom it was borne, but a speedy death to him who bore it. "It was made in raven's shape; and when the wind blew out the banner, then it was as though the raven spread his wings for flight." [8] I can find no account of the banners of the Celts, but Cuchulainn had a very sacred overmantle of raven's feathers, which was worn by his charioteer.[9]

The view that Arthur was a god, however, does not depend upon his connection with a raven banner; it is really implicit in all that we are told of him. It explains why the early saints are said to have treated him so unceremoniously; it explains why the Breton followers of the Norman kings located his legends in Sicily;[1] above all, it explains the strange company that he keeps. "Arthur has none but mythological relatives," says Mr. Briffault;[2] "his father is

[5] Loc. cit.; J. Rhys: *Celtic Folklore,* vol. ii, p. 611.
[6] R. Hunt: *Popular Romances of the West of England,* p. 309.
[7] J. A. Giles: *Six Old English Chronicles,* p. 62.
[8] *The Orkneyingers' Saga,* tr. Dasent, p. 15.
[9] J. Dunn: *The Tain,* p. 187.
[1] Chambers: *Arthur of Britain,* p. 221.
[2] Loc. cit.

the dragon Uther, his sister the goddess Anu, his wife the
'White Lady,' his mistress or sister Morgana, the fairy."
"The Knights of the Round Table," says Elton,[3] "Sir Kaye
and Tristram and bold Sir Bedivere, betray their divine
origin by the attributes which they retain as heroes of
romance." Of Kei we are told, in *Kulhwch and Olwen,*
that among other faculties "he could breathe nine nights
and nine days under water," and that, when it pleased
him, "he became as tall as the loftiest tree in the forest."
In such company a real man would be like Gulliver in
Brobdingnag.

Sir John Rhys[4] supposes that there were two Arthurs, a
mythical and a historic, but whereas he has a great deal
to say about the former, he merely mentions the latter.
Some recent writers have been less cautious; according to
Mr. Crawford, as we have seen, Arthur was a "petty
chieftain," while Mr. Hodgkin[5] describes him as "the harassed leader of a rough war-band." Such statements may
sound reasonable enough, but they are really euhemerism
run to seed. There is some excuse for believing that Robin
Hood was a real outlaw, the boldest and most famous of
his age, but none for supposing that he was one of a
thousand ruffians whose name some accident preserved;
there is some excuse for believing that Sigurd was a great
national hero, but none for supposing that he was an insignificant adventurer; in the same way there is some
excuse for believing that Arthur was the greatest warrior
and leader that Britain ever produced, but none whatever
for supposing that he was a "petty chieftain." Let us turn
back to Nennius: "Arthur fought with the kings of Britain,
but he himself was the war-leader. . . . Nobody laid them
[*sc.* the nine hundred and sixty men] low except he himself alone, and in all wars he came out victorious." Can
it be seriously supposed that this is a historical reference
to "the harassed leader of a rough war-band"? It is, so it
seems to me, quite clearly part of a hymn to a god of war.

[3] Op. cit., p. 248.
[4] *Arthurian Legend,* p. 8.
[5] R. H. Hodgkin: *History of the Anglo-Saxons,* vol. i, p. 182.

CHAPTER VII

HENGIST AND HORSA

The unfortunate results of belief in the historicity of tradition, or what passes as such, are nowhere more apparent than in relation to the settlement of the Anglo-Saxons in England. What are supposed to be the traditions of this settlement are embodied in the *Ecclesiastical History of Beda* and in the *Anglo-Saxon Chronicle*. The former was written between the years 704 and 734,[1] while the earlier part of the *Chronicle* was compiled under the supervision of King Alfred during the last quarter of the ninth century. At this time, so its translator tells us, "the Teutonic settlers of Britain had no notion of giving an account of themselves. Angles, Saxons, and Jutes seem to have forgotten their old traditions by the ninth century." [2]

The *Chronicle* draws largely upon *Beda,* and it is improbable that it was based on any older or better sources. As for *Beda,* it is considered almost sacrilegious to doubt him, and even Mr. Leeds, who will be quoted at some length in this chapter, hesitates to question his accuracy.[3] Yet it is difficult to understand why a monk of Durham, who never left his monastery, should be regarded as an unquestionable authority for events that happened several hundred miles away and two or three centuries before his time, nor why incorrectness in the narration of events of which he could have had no personal knowledge should be considered as reflecting upon his character. Those who place implicit reliance upon his story of Hengist and Horsa have not, it seems to me, considered what his pur-

[1] J. Stevenson: *Beda,* p. iv.
[2] E. E. C. Gomme: *The Anglo-Saxon Chronicle,* p. vii.
[3] E. T. Leeds: *The Archaeology of the Anglo-Saxon Settlements,* p. 84.

pose was, what his authorities were, nor even what he actually says.

"The scope of the *Ecclesiastical History of the English Nation*," says its editor,[4] "is sufficiently indicated by its title. After some observations upon the position, inhabitants, and natural productions of Britain, the author gives a rapid sketch of its history from the earliest period until the arrival of Augustine in A.D. 597, at which era, in his opinion, the ecclesiastical history of our nation had its commencement. . . . This is the period at which Beda ceases to speak of himself as a compiler, and assumes the character of a historian." He deals at some length, and not always accurately, with the Romans in Britain, but skims over the fifth and sixth centuries, and only mentions the pagan Saxons three times. The first mention is the story of Hengist and Horsa; the second is the account of Ambrosius, quoted from Gildas, and the third, placed out of its order, is the story of the "Halleluja Victory" from the legendary *Life of St. German*. The setting of this story suggests that in its original form it was the account, not of a temporal victory over the barbarians, but of a spiritual victory over the demons of heresy.

It is a remarkable fact, though it seems to have been little remarked, that Beda makes no mention of the settlement of his own ancestors in his own country of Northumbria.[5] From this we may conclude that the subject had no interest for him, for though the facts were probably lost, we may be sure that the Northumbrian Angles had some traditions or myths which he could have accepted as history, just as he accepted the miracles of St. German as history.

It is quite clear, in fact, that he had no interest in pagans or paganism at all. His introductory chapters are drawn from classical or ecclesiastical sources, and such facts as he mentions merely form a framework for accounts of conversions, persecutions, and martyrdoms; of the miracles of saints; and of the victories of the faithful

[4] J. Stevenson, op. cit., p. xxii.
[5] It is remarked by Professor Chadwick: *Origin of the English Nation*, p. 35.

over heretics and infidels. To this the sole exception is the story of Hengist and Horsa, and this is less of an exception than it might seem, since the outline of it is derived from Gildas, and several passages are quoted verbatim. Gildas tells us how "at that time all the members of the assembly, along with the proud tyrant, are blinded; such is the protection that they find for their country . . . that these wild Saxons of accursed name, hated by God and Men, should be admitted into the island, like wolves into folds, in order to repel the northern nations." He goes on to tell, with many wails and Biblical quotations, how "a brood of whelps from the lair of the savage lioness" came in three ships, "fixed their dreadful talons in the eastern part of the island," and completely devastated the whole country.[6] He makes no mention of Vortigern,[7] of the Jutes, or of Hengist and Horsa.

From this account Beda omits the rude remarks about the Saxons, and to it he makes a number of additions. Thus he says that those who came over in the three ships, having gained a victory over the northerners, were followed by a greater number from "their own country. . . . Which, being added to the former, made up an invincible army." He goes on to tell us that "those who came over were of the three most powerful nations of Germany, that is, of the Saxons, the Angles, and the Jutes." [8] He seems to imply that the original fleet of three ships was composed of one shipload each of the Saxons, Angles, and Jutes; at any rate he is quite clear that the three nations were combined in one army, and goes on to say that the two first commanders are said to have been Hengist and Horsa, the latter of whom was killed in battle by the Britons, and buried in the eastern parts of Kent, "where

---

[6] H. Williams: *Gildas,* pp. 53–5.

[7] In some versions the words "proud tyrant" are followed by the name Uortigern or Gurthigern, but the editor gives good reason to believe that these names are interpolated (p. 52 n.). The accusation of incest brought by later writers against Vortigern is probably derived from a similar charge brought by Gildas against his contemporary Vortipor, a King of West Wales (p. 73).

[8] *Beda,* ch. 15.

a monument, bearing his name, is still in existence." He then traces their pedigree to Woden, "from whose stock the royal race of many provinces deduce their original."

Let us leave Beda and Kent for the moment and see what the *Chronicle* has to say of the Saxon conquest of Hampshire and Sussex.

Of the former we have a most confused account. In one version the first to land, at Cerdices-ora, were Cerdic and Cynric, with five ships, who defeated the Britons with great slaughter; in another, the first to land, also at Cerdices-ora, were Stuf and Wihtgar, with three ships, who also defeated the Britons. In one version Cerdic and Cynric succeed Stuf and Wihtgar in the Kingdom of the West Saxons, and defeat the Britons at Cerdicesford; in another they conquer the Isle of Wight with great slaughter, and hand it over to their nephews Stuf and Wihtgar. There is also Port, who lands with two ships and two sons at Portsmouth, and "slew a young British man of high nobility."

Of Sussex we are told that Aelle landed with three sons and three ships, defeated the Britons, and later that he and one of his sons massacred the people of Andredesces-ter. After this we hear no more of Sussex, but are told of an Aelle of Northumbria, whose pedigree is given back to Woden, though the Sussex Aelle is given no pedigree.

And now for the facts, so far as we have them. They are derived in part from archæology, and in part from a study of village organization and the laws and customs of land tenure and inheritance. These combine to show that the so-called Jutes were not Jutes but Franks, and that they came, not from Denmark, but from the Middle Rhine; that their area of settlement was south and east of a line running up the Thames to the neighbourhood of Maidenhead, and thence down to Southampton Water; and that they had been established in this area for some considerable time before the Saxons came upon the scene. Later on, the Saxons, who had entered England via the Wash, pushed down into the Thames Valley and gradually conquered the Franks, except those of the Kingdom of Kent. The latter, though they retained their independence, gradually adopted the language, and to some extent the culture, of the Saxons. According to Beda, the Isle of Wight and the mainland opposite were still inhabited by Jutes—that is, Franks—in his own day, though according to the *Chronicle* these districts had been conquered and settled by the West Saxons two centuries earlier.

Both the existing land customs in what was once the Frankish area,[9] and the objects found in graves, show that the culture of the Franks was very different from that of the Saxons. Wheel-made bottle vases are one of its distinctive features. These are found in large numbers in the Frankish cemeteries of the area between Coblenz and Düsseldorf, and also in the "Jutish" area of England, whereas "throughout the whole stretch of country between Denmark and Holland native wheel-made pottery of this type is *never* found. . . . On the one hand it is incredible that had the Jutes come from Jutland, no wheel-made pottery should have been found there, and on the other hand that the Danish types should never have been found in Kent."[1]

Let us now return to the West Saxons. According to the *Chronicle*, the landings that I have mentioned took place during the period 495–514, and during the next few years they conquered the whole of Hampshire. In 552 they took Salisbury, and in 568–71 pushed north into the Thames Valley and drove the Kentishmen from Wimbledon, and the Britons from Bedford, and Eynsham **near** Oxford. Six years later they gained a great victory over three kings of the Britons at Dyrham, in Gloucestershire, and took Gloucester, Cirencester, and Bath.

Archæology shows that this story is pure fiction. The facts seem to be that no Saxon ever landed on the south coast; that no Saxon entered Hampshire until well on in the seventh century; but that, on the other hand, Saxons were well established in Gloucestershire by the middle of the sixth century.

The Saxons, like the Franks, were in pagan times in the habit of burying quantities of weapons, ornaments, and

[9] For which see J. E. A. Jolliffe: *The Jutes.*
[1] E. T. Leeds, op. cit., p. 133.

utensils with the dead, and since a very large number of these graves has been found, the area of pagan Saxondom can be determined pretty accurately, and the graves dated approximately by a comparative study of their contents. If then Hampshire had been closely settled by the West Saxons from the close of the fifth century, as the *Chronicle* tells us that it was, it is inconceivable that some graves of pagan Saxons should not have been found in the county, yet "in the whole of Hampshire, outside the Jutish district, not a single cemetery is known. . . . If the traditions are to be credited with the minutest particle of truth, nothing is more certain than that the invaders who entered Britain from the South did not reach the Thames Valley before the middle of the sixth century, by which time there are excellent reasons for concluding that settlements had been established there, dating at least fifty years earlier." [2] The cemetery at Fairford, eight miles from Cirencester, is a very large one, and many objects found in it can be dated not later than the middle of the sixth century, so that "the whole account of the campaign must be regarded with the gravest suspicion." [3]

Mr. Leeds has more recently resurveyed the evidence concerning the Saxon occupation of Wessex, and concludes that "the archæologist is bound once for all to discard the entries in the *Chronicle* as worthless. . . . The archæological evidence can only be interpreted to mean that the Saxons entered Hampshire and Wiltshire at an advanced date in the period of the settlement, and that too from the north." [4]

Such evidence as we have, then, shows, or seems to show, that the accounts given by Beda and by the *Anglo-Saxon Chronicle* of events in England during the fifth and sixth centuries are not merely unreliable, but quite untrue. The chief reason, I believe, why scholars accept fiction as fact, is that by accepting it as fact they are absolved from the necessity of explaining it, whereas fictions need to be explained. In this case what we have to explain is:

[2] Ibid., pp. 51–2.
[3] Ibid., p. 61.
[4] *Antiquaries' Journal,* 1933, pp. 248–9.

1. Why the only secular story that Beda introduces into his ecclesiastical history should be a fiction from Kent.

2. Why the first invaders of Kent should be represented as Jutish leaders of an Anglo-Saxon army, when they were really Franks operating quite indipendently of the Anglo-Saxons.

3. Why the Saxon conquerors of Wessex and Sussex should be represented as entering by sea from the south, when they really entered by land from the north.

Beda tells us that his principal assistant in his work was Albinus, who was abbot of Canterbury, and that through him he obtained an account of all that had been transacted in the church of Canterbury. "Bede's correspondents, the educated clergy in Kent, were presumably in contact with traditions about the early history of their people," says Mr. Hodgkin,[5] but whatever applies to them should apply to Beda himself, and he quite clearly was not in touch with traditions about the early history of his people. Moreover, he was an Englishman, whereas Albinus was a foreigner. Why should the latter take an interest in one particular aspect of pagan Saxondom?

This brings us to question number two, and the answer I suggest is that the story was a piece of propaganda. Part of it was unquestionably derived from Gildas, and part very likely from myth, but no combination of Gildas and myth could give such a series of categorical falsehoods. The aim of the Kentish ecclesiastics was to make Canterbury the religious capital of England. They had Augustine to support their claim, and Gildas could easily be made to follow suit. What simpler than to place all the incidents of early Anglo-Saxon history in Kent, and make their King's ancestor the commander-in-chief of all the Anglo-Saxons? That they did so is, of course, merely a conjecture, but it seems to explain the facts, and pious frauds of this (and every other conceivable) type were a commonplace of medieval ecclesiasticism. The story no doubt grew with

[5] Op. cit., vol. i, p. 95.

time, since the *Chronicle* knows more about Hengist and
Horsa than Beda did, but the "local traditions," upon
which Gomme, as we saw,[6] relies, seem not to be older
than the eighteenth century. Horsa's memorial, if it ever
existed, was unknown in Alfred's time, since Beda's mention of it is omitted from the translation of his history
which was then made. "Its site was fixed at Horsted, near
Aylesford, after many conjectures by the antiquaries,
chiefly it would seem because the great cromlech in that
neighbourhood had already been allotted to Prince Cati-
gern. The ruins of another Stone-Age tumulus were found
at a little distance . . . and it was supposed that the
chieftain might have been carried up from the battlefield
two miles away to lie near his enemy's tomb. When certain antiquaries visited the place in 1763 the villagers
showed them a heap of flints which had all the appearance
of being refuse stones thrown up by the farmer, and this
has since that time been accepted as the site of the ancient
monument. One point being fixed, it became easy to identify the rest; and hence the apparent certainty with which
localities have been settled for almost all the events in the
legend of Hengist and Horsa." [7]

If ecclesiastics invented this legend, it is most unlikely
that they invented the names, which seem to mean "the
Stallion" and "the Mare." Perhaps they were deities worshipped in the form of horses, or borne at the head of the
armies in the form of horsehead standards.

Our third question was why the Saxons should have
been represented as entering southern England from the
sea, when they really entered it from the Thames Valley.
When we examine the *Chronicle* stories of the landings,
which I have sketched above, we find that they all bear
a suspicious resemblance to the legend of Hengist and
Horsa. The story told, with slight variations in each case,
is how two heroes, descendants of Woden, land from three
ships. They gain a minor victory near the shore, and then,
after pushing farther inland, a complete victory, which
results in their becoming kings of the land. One of the

[6] *Supra,* p. 37.
[7] C. Elton, op. cit., p. 379.

heroes dies, and is buried in a city that bears his name; the other becomes the founder of a dynasty.

There seem to be two possible ways of explaining this story; one is that it is a genuine myth, the common property of all the tribes, and the other that it is the Hengist legend adapted to the circumstances of other kingdoms. In either case we should have to suppose that there was a "Jutish" kingdom on the mainland, as well as in the Isle of Wight, but that is quite likely. The latter explanation is rendered the more probable by the fact that several of the names are clearly fictitious. Thus the name "Port" is derived from the Latin name of Portsmouth, Portus Magnus, while "Wihtgar" is from Wihtgarasburg, "Wight-dwellers'-town," now Carisbrooke. Cerdic, also, is only mentioned in connection with Cerdices-ora, Cerdicesford, and Cerdiceslea, and Cerdic is a Celtic name.[8] We have seen that natural features are seldom called after real men; perhaps the West Saxons traced their royal line back to the oldest Celtic king they could hear of, and Cerdic descendant of Brand is Caradoc (Caractacus) son of Bran; perhaps Cerdic was a Celtic deity after whom some places were named; in any case, there is no reason to suppose Cerdic more historical than Port or Wihtgar. There can be little doubt that these legends were composed by ecclesiastics in imitation of, and perhaps in opposition to, the legend of Hengist. The editor of the *Chronicle* suggests Winchester as the place where it is most likely to have been compiled,[9] and the compiler probably found these legends at the head of the annals of each monastery and, supposing them to be records of fact, tried to combine them into a narrative, but with singular lack of success.

We may throw over the alleged early history of Wessex with the more confidence since we know that the later history is quite unreliable. Cadwaladr, King of the Welsh, is said to have resigned his kingdom, made a pilgrimage to Rome, and died there in 688, "but great obscurity seems to hang over the accounts of this performance; and

[8] C. W. Oman: *England before the Norman Conquest,* p. 224.
[9] E. E. C. Gomme, op. cit., p. viii.

as this, and other actions in the life of that Prince, are related in almost the same words of his contemporary Cædwalla, King of the West Saxons, who died in Rome in that year, there is reason to believe that the monkish historians have confounded the one with the other." [1] Yet the fictions, the miracles, and the blunders of these old monks are allowed, not merely to occupy chapters and even volumes of so-called history, but to oppose a serious obstacle to the progress of scientific archæology.

[1] R. Rees: *The Welsh Saints,* p. 65.

CHAPTER VIII

CUCHULAINN

The tendency of the Greeks in classical times was all towards rationalization. As a result of this, the supernatural beings, whatever one chooses to call them, who had played their parts in early religion, came to be divided into two separate, though never entirely separate, classes. There might be some doubt whether Heracles or Asclepios was a god or a hero, but throughout classical times it was sought increasingly to draw a clear distinction between heroes, who never performed miracles, and gods, who never did anything else.

This attempt by the Greek philosophers to construct a clear-cut theology out of a large number of religious rites, in which both names and theories were little regarded, has led many scholars to misunderstand completely the character of early Greek religion, and of early religion generally. On the assumption that the ideas of a god or of a hero are primitive, they have argued either that the gods were heroes who had been promoted, or that the heroes were gods who had become "faded," or even that the two sets of beings had no connection at all. They then discuss whether the rites performed at various sacred spots should be described as the "tendance" of heroes or the worship of gods, failing to realize that these rites came down from pre-literate times, and that illiterates are no more capable of theology than they are of history. Theology involves definitions, comparisons, classifications, and distinctions, and can therefore develop only in the minds of people who are working over written material, and then only if circumstances permit. In Ireland, unlike Greece, they did not permit. In pagan Ireland there was no writing, and therefore no theology, so that no attempt was made to distinguish between gods and heroes. Then came Christianity, and what had been the recognized religion became the unrecognized religion, and has largely remained so until today. The cloak of pseudo-historicity thrown by the Church over certain of the figures of mythology has deceived some scholars brought up on the classics, but in the traditions gods and heroes have remained undifferentiated.

Mr. Nutt says that in the tenth century the process of transforming "the inmates of the ancient Irish Olympus into historic kings and warriors had already begun," [1] but it was never completed. The miracles were never rationalized, nor were the characters represented as living the lives of human beings. "I found it impossible to arrange the stories in a coherent form," says Lady Gregory,[2] "so long as I considered them a part of history. I tried to work on the foundation of the Annalists, and fit the Fianna into a definite historical epoch, but the whole story seemed trivial and incoherent until I began to think of them as almost contemporaneous with the Battle of Magh Tuireadh, which even the Annalists put back into mythical ages. In this I have only followed some of the story-tellers, who have made the mother of Lugh of the Long Hand the grandmother of Finn. . . . It seems to me that one cannot choose any definite period either from the vast living mass of folk-lore or from the written text, and that there is as good evidence of Finn being of the blood of the gods as of his being, as some of the people tell me, 'the son of an O'Shaughnessy, who lived at Kiltartan Cross,'" This clearly indicates the datelessness which characterizes the genuine traditional narrative.

It would require a volume even to summarize the stories of the Irish traditional heroes, so I shall let the story of perhaps the most famous one, Cuchulainn, do duty for the remainder.

It is difficult to get the incidents of Cuchulainn's career into any sort of order, but the following is an approximation. His conception and birth are attended by various miracles, after which we next hear of him at the age of

[1] A. Nutt: *The Voyage of Bran,* vol. i, p. 189.
[2] *Gods and Fighting Men,* p. 467.

five, when he makes a long journey alone to the court of his uncle, King Conchobar of Ulster. He forthwith defeats at all forms of sport and military exercises the hundred and fifty members of the King's boy corps, and knocks them over, fifty at a time.

His next feat is to destroy with his hands alone a very large and fierce dog; when he finds that it is the watch-dog of Culann the smith, he offers to take its place, and though his real name is Setanta, he is known henceforth as Cuchulainn, "the dog of Culann."

When not yet seven, he demands arms of Conchobar, and smashes all that are offered him till he obtains Conchobar's own. With these, and with the aid of two supernatural horses that he captures, he makes a raid over the border, kills three of the fiercest champions of Ireland, and returns with their heads and other trophies. One of these champions the "little lad" kills by striking him on the forehead with an iron ball, after which he cuts off his head.[3]

Later on he woos Emer, who will not accept him unless he can perform a number of feats, which include the killing of twenty-seven men at one blow. He eventually achieves these and marries her, having in the meantime married Uatach; had a son, Connla, by Aoife; and lived for some time with the goddess Fand, wife of Manannan mac Lir.

The rest of his story is taken up principally with the "Cattle-spoil of Cooley." Queen Maeve or Medb of Connaught wishes for the "Brown Bull of Cooley," and in order to obtain it invades Ulster with all the warriors of the rest of Ireland. The men of Ulster suffer from a peculiar disability which puts them all temporarily out of action, and meanwhile Cuchulainn defends Ulster single-handed, killing a number of champions in single combat, and the rank and file of the enemy at a steady rate of one hundred a day. Eventually the Ulstermen come up; they are attacked and slaughtered in large numbers, but Cuchulainn single-handed restores the battle, and the invaders are routed. After an interlude in the form of a bull-fight

[3] J. Dunn, op. cit., p. 71.

the Irish again invade Ulster, and after a number of miraculous events Cuchulainn is killed with his own spear.

What are we to make of this story? The views that have been put forward fall, for the most part, into three types. We will let Sir William Ridgeway stand for the first type, that of those who believe that you can reduce any legend to history by making your own selection from its incidents. He proves the historicity of Cuchulainn in a very simple way: "Though his exploits are often supernatural, there is no more reason for regarding him as a god than there is for so treating Achilles, Ajax, or Roland." [4] He believes, in fact, like other euhemerists, that a lay figure propped up with other dummies is really standing by itself. He also asserts that the heroes "appear in settings shown by irrefragable historical and archæological evidence to be that of the age in which they are severally said to have lived." [5] There is, however, no historical evidence at all, and the archæological evidence, so far as it suggests anything definite, suggests the period, about the sixth century, when the stories were first written down. Cuchulainn had seven pupils in each eye, seven fingers on each hand, and seven toes on each foot; and he performed some of his most remarkable feats when he was seven years old. The belief that such a monster can be reduced to the status of a human being by the simple process of subtracting his superfluous pupils and digits, and adding an equivalent number to his years, is gradually falling into discredit among mythologists.

A second view of the Cuchulainn stories is that they are sun myths;[6] I shall later try to show that there is no such thing.

The third view is that the stories are a magnificent example of what the Irish imagination can do when it really gets going. I shall deal later with the part played by imagination in the formation of myth, but I would here point out that there seems not to be a single incident in, or feature of, the stories of Cuchulainn or any other Irish

---

[4] *Early Age of Greece,* vol. ii, p. 548.
[5] Ibid., p. 609.
[6] E. Hull: *The Cuchullin Saga,* p. lxviii.

hero which is not found elsewhere. Cuchulainn is in several versions said to be the son or reincarnation of Lugh,
and Lugh is recognized as identical with the Welsh Lleu,
and the Gaulish deity Lug, from whom Lugdunum, the
modern Lyon, derives its name. Cuchulainn himself is
probably a variant of Gawaine, since the latter's name also
means "smith" and they have parallel adventures. The
story of Cuchulainn and the Terrible, for example, corresponds with that of Gawaine and the Green Knight; in
each case the stranger challenges the hero to behead him
and then submit to being beheaded himself. The stranger
is beheaded, and goes off carrying his head; returning at
the appointed time, he causes the hero to kneel down, but
instead of beheading him, merely gives him a light blow.[7]
There are differences which suggest that both were derived
from a common source rather than that one was derived
from the other; the same applies to the David and Goliath
story that I mentioned above.

These resemblances have, of course, been noticed by
many writers; I will quote Wood-Martin[8] on some of
them. "There is a great similarity between the Persian
story of Rustam and the bardic tale of Conloch:[9] an Irish
chief and King Midas were both afflicted with ass's ears;
a king of Macedon and also a king of Erin effected the
destruction of their enemies by apparelling a number of
young men to represent women. Thersites and Conan were
both bald, were great boasters, and great cowards; Balor
and Perseus in some respects resemble each other; in both
stories the precautions taken are almost identical—precautions which were defeated by supernatural means—and in
both instances the decree of destiny is fulfilled by the
murder of the grandfather, while the peculiar property of
Balor's eyes has its parallel in classic myth. The infant
Heracles strangles a serpent while yet in his cradle; the
great Irish hero Cuchullin when a child strangles a huge
watch-dog, the terror of the country-side. The Greek

[7] E. Hull, op. cit., p. xxvi.
[8] W. G. Wood-Martin: *Pagan Ireland*, p. 30.
[9] Or Connla; it is rare to find two writers spelling the same
Irish name in the same way.

Adonis and the brave and gay Diarmuid O'Duibhne are each killed by a boar." The important part played by boars in the stories suggests that they are not of native origin, since, according to the same author,[1] no remains of wild pig have been found in Ireland, though the domestic pig seems to have been introduced at an early period. However this may be, the stories are known to have existed in Greece a thousand years before they are known to have existed in Ireland, so that, to those whose belief in coincidence is not unlimited, the probability of their Irish origin is remote. It may be added that Sir John Rhys[2] devotes two chapters to the tracing of parallels between the adventures of Heracles, Cuchulainn, and the Welsh Peredur.

Some of the chief incidents in Cuchulainn's career are, as we have seen, connected with the Tain Bo Cuailgne, or Cattle Spoil of Cooley, which is in great part the elaborated account of a bull-fight. There were sacred bull-fights in ancient Crete, as there are in modern Spain, and since domestic cattle did not originate in Ireland, it is unlikely that the myths and ritual connected with them originated in Ireland either.

According to some accounts, his boyhood feats took place when he was seven, the Cattle Spoil when he was seventeen, and his death when he was twenty-seven. These figures have obviously no relation to any real dates, since according to other accounts he fought with and killed his own son before the Cattle Spoil,[3] and sound like the reminiscence of a ten-year ritual cycle. Such a cycle, I shall later suggest, is to be found in the Tale of Troy, in which the Rape of Helen, the beginning of the siege, and the fall of Troy take place at intervals of about nine years, with complete blanks between them.

We have still to decide who or what Cuchulainn was. Some of those who disbelieve all the stories are nevertheless inclined to suppose that he was a real person. Mr.

[1] Op. cit., p. 13.
[2] *Arthurian Legend,* pp. 184 ff.
[3] J. Dunn, op. cit., p. 263.

Nutt, for example,[4] holds that while ninety-nine one-hun-
dredths of what was ascribed to him bore no relation to
historic fact, yet it was possible that such a man did actually exist about the date traditionally assigned to him.
Yet, as we saw in Chapter I, tradition never has assigned
and never could assign a date to anything, and we have
no more reason to believe in the historicity of Cuchulainn
than in that of Cyclops, or Cerberus, or any other being
with an abnormal number of features.

Was he then a god? This depends on what we mean by
a god. If by a god is understood a being in the sky, then,
though he can receive prayer and sacrifice, no stories can
be told about him. To become the hero of a story he must
come to earth in some form. What was Cuchulainn's
form? Let us allow Miss Hull to tell us. "On the morrow
Cuchullin came to view the host; also to exhibit himself
in his form of beauty to the wives and womankind and
girls and lasses, to the poets and professors of the men of
Erin. . . . Three sets of hair he had; next to the skin of
his head, brown; in the middle, crimson; that which covered him on the out-side formed as it were a diadem of
gold. . . . About his neck were a hundred linklets of red
gold that flashed again, with pendants hanging from them.
His headgear was adorned with a hundred mixed car-
buncles, strung. On either cheek four moles he had: a
yellow, a green, a blue, a red. In either eye seven pupils,
as it were seven sparkling gems. Either foot of the twain
was garnished with seven toes; both this and that hand
with as many fingers; each one of which was endowed
with clutch of hawk's talon, with grip of hedgehog's claw."
There follows a long description of his gorgeous clothing,
after which we are told that he had "a trusty special
shield, in hue dark crimson, and in its circumference
armed with a pure white silver rim. At his left side a
long and golden-hilted sword. Beside him in the chariot, a
lengthy spear. . . . In one hand he carried nine heads,
nine also in the other; the which in token of valour and
skill in arms he held at arm's-length, and in sight of all

[4] Op. cit., p. 200.

the army shook." [5]

To some people this may seem to be a highly poetical description of an ideal hero, but to me it seems to be a perfectly matter-of-fact description of a very sacred and very monstrous idol, and of a rite in which this idol was the principal figure. What appears to have happened is that in the first place eighteen captives were sacrificed before Cuchulainn; this was no doubt to represent his victorious combats, and also to endow him with life and strength. The great idol was then adorned with all its finery and placed in its chariot, and the captives' heads were hung nine from each arm. Thus equipped, Cuchulainn went in state all round among the people, conferring valour and victory upon the men, fertility upon the women, and prosperity upon all.

Rites of this type are widespread. Probably the best-known is that of Juggernaut, in which a car containing an image of Vishnu is dragged round a prescribed route, conferring good fortune on all who see it. In ancient Babylon, at the New Year festival, the image of Marduk was carried in procession, and Dr. Oesterley believes that in Jerusalem before the Exile there was, at the Feast of Tabernacles, "a great procession with Jahweh in his chariot." [6]

Such rites were common in northern Europe. The image of the god Frey seems to have taken an annual tour round Sweden, conferring fertility wherever it went. It was accompanied by a priestess called "Frey's wife." [7] In Germany the goddess Ertha was periodically taken round in a car drawn by heifers; "it is a season of rejoicing, and festivity reigns wherever she deigns to go and be received." [8] In the fourth century of our era the mighty Mother was still worshipped at Autun, and her image was borne in procession on a car, in order to ensure the

---

[5] E. Hull, op. cit., pp. 178–9; cf. J. Dunn, op. cit., pp. 195–6.
[6] *Myth and Ritual,* ed. S. H. Hooke, p. 136.
[7] B. S. Phillpotts: *The Elder Edda,* p. 119.
[8] Tacitus: *Germania,* xl.

fertility of the fields and vineyards,[9] while to this day "in Catholic countries the statue of the local saint is commonly carried round the village, either annually on his feast-day or in times of exceptional trouble."[1] Anyone who believes that these saints were real people will find reason to modify his opinion in Professor Saintyves's *Les Saints Successeurs des Dieux*.

I conclude:

1. That there is no historical evidence for Cuchulainn's existence.

2. That none of his activities, as narrated in the stories, suggest those of a real human being.

3. That all or most of the incidents of his career find parallels in the careers of other mythical heroes.

4. That the description of him given above is obviously not that of a human being.

5. That rites closely resembling that which the passage quoted appears to describe are known to have been performed in France, Germany, and Sweden; that such rites are at any rate very likely to have been performed in Ireland; and that the central figures in such rites are not real people but images of gods.

[9] Cited by C. B. Lewis in *Folk-Lore*, vol. xlvi, p. 74.
[1] E. K. Chambers: *The Mediæval Stage*, vol. i, p. 119.

CHAPTER IX

THE TALE OF TROY

We saw in the last chapter that Sir William Ridgeway compared Cuchulainn to Achilles and Ajax; in this chapter it will be our task to show that Achilles and Ajax are really as unhistorical as Cuchulainn. This may seem to be a rash undertaking, since dozens of scholars have written books about Homer, and almost all of them have assumed, as a matter of course, that the *Iliad* has a historical basis. It is to be noted, however, in the first place, that with the great majority of these scholars the historical aspect of the *Iliad* has been merely incidental to other aspects in which they were more deeply interested, those of poetry, prosody, and linguistics on the one hand, and the religion and politics of the fifth century B.C. on the other. Classical scholars are, in the second place, for the most part completely ignorant of and indifferent to comparative mythology and ritual, and therefore regard incidents to which parallels can be found in every continent as individual or even unique. Thirdly, of course, these scholars have been brought up in the superstition that tradition is history.

It is (fortunately for me, since my knowledge of Greek is extremely limited) unnecessary for my purpose that I should enter into the most trampled part of the arena of Homeric controversy. I shall not attempt to assign an author or a date to the poems, nor to decide in what dialect they were originally composed. My task will be to give adequate reasons for believing that they have no historical basis, and of these reasons the most convincing will, I hope, be that which shows that the assumption of their historicity results in a *reductio ad absurdum*.

Let us assume, then, that, miracles apart, the *Iliad,* the *Odyssey,* and the cyclic poems are statements of historical fact and that the incidents which they describe centre in a siege of Troy which took place about 1190 B.C. What do we then get? We get a history of Greece beginning, very shakily, about 1250 B.C., blossoming out into a good deal of detail about 1200 B.C., giving us the fullest and most intimate particulars for a period of about twenty years, and a certain number of facts for the next fifty, and then fading out completely for about four centuries. We are told that about 1000 B.C. "the whole of Greece except Athens was under Dorian rule and rapidly relapsed into barbarism; neither tradition nor archæology gives us a glimpse of what was taking place." [1] We are to believe that the most important events of Greek history, the conquests of the Ionians and Achæans and the settlement of Asia Minor, were completely forgotten, while the Dorian conquest was preserved merely in some vague anecdotes of some alleged sons of Heracles. On the other hand an earlier event, the siege of Troy, which, since it had no permanent results, was obviously less important, was remembered in every detail.

The absurdity of this assumption will be more apparent if we transfer the situation to English history. Let us equate Agamemnon with Alfred, and the Dorian Conquest with the Norman Conquest; what do we then get? We should find English history beginning very shakily about A.D. 800; we should then have the fullest details about King Alfred and his Danish opponents, and know exactly what they ate, drank, wore, and said to their wives; what blows were struck in their battles and who were killed. Then we should get a rapidly decreasing body of fact till well before the Norman Conquest, of which we should have nothing but some vague stories of some sons of Rollo, and after that nothing more till about 1400, when we should get the faint beginnings of a history which would burst out into full vigour under the Tudors. I do not suggest, of course, that the circumstances of England were exactly the same as those of Greece, but are there any conceivable circumstances in which the English could have remembered every detail about Alfred, and com-

[1] Peake and Fleure: *The Horse and the Sword,* p. 78.

pletely forgotten Richard I, Edward I, and the Black
Prince? Of course there are not, and there are no conceivable circumstances in which the Greeks could have
remembered Agamemnon, if he had been a real man and
not a god, and completely forgotten those that came after
him. "*Vixere fortes ante Agamemnona,*" says the poet, but
I would rather say: "*Vixere fortes* post *Agamemnona,*"
and that they would have eclipsed his fame had he really
lived. For what is he alleged to have been? The leader of
an army that took one city. The successive waves of
Greek-speaking invaders who swept over Greece, Crete,
the Islands, and the Asiatic coast, and even, if the inscriptions are rightly interpreted, ravaged as far as Palestine
and Egypt, must have had many abler leaders, men whose
names tradition would have preserved, if tradition *ever*
preserved the names of historical persons.

Dr. Leaf [2] attempted to solve this difficulty by a method
of his own. He supposed that the Greeks of the thirteenth
century B.C. were great traders; that their most important
trade was carried on with the Black Sea ports through the
Dardanelles; that the King of Troy, by levying exorbitant
tolls on vessels passing through the Dardanelles, rendered
this trade unprofitable; and that so serious were the consequences of this interference with the sacred principles of
free trade that all the Greeks were impelled, for the only
time in their history, to unite for the purpose of destroy-
ing this enemy of their commerce, and to persist in this
purpose, regardless of cost, until they had succeeded.

It says a great deal for the credulity of scholars that
this theory has been so widely accepted, since not the
smallest scrap of evidence can be adduced in its support.
No ancient author knows of any reason for the siege of
Troy except the rape of Helen, and there is nowhere, even
in the myths in which Dr. Leaf believed so firmly when
it suited him, the slightest suggestion of trade with the
Black Sea, or tolls, or anything of the kind. The only
mythical voyage to the Black Sea was that of the *Argo*,
and in that there is no mention of Troy; nor is the voyage

[2] W. Leaf: *Troy*, and *Homer and History*.

of the *Argo* mentioned in the *Iliad,* though it is supposed to have occurred recently enough before the siege of Troy for Nestor to have taken part in both enterprises.

"The tale of the Argo," Dr. Leaf assures us,[3] "rested on sailors' stories mingled with fantastic mythology. The tale of Troy must from the first have been limited by a tradition of actual facts. My conclusion is that there existed a real record of real events, and that out of this the *Iliad* grew." He does not explain why people should mingle fantastic mythology with sailors' stories, nor how either could arise in connection with places which were, on his own theory, familiar to every Greek trader. Nor is it clear what he means when he says that the tale of Troy must from the first have been limited by a tradition of actual facts, since elsewhere he tells us that "the larger part of the incidents we shall of course dismiss as mere invention." [4]

Dr. Leaf's method is one which has been widely adopted by classical scholars. The process seems to be as follows: The scholar soaks himself in Homeric literature, and in nothing else, until all the incidents that seem to him realistic assume prominence, while those which seem improbable fade into the background; and eventually there arises in his mind a tale of Troy which is for him real and true, although it is entirely subjective. He then goes again through the literature and divides all the statements that he finds in it into two classes; those which fit in with his version become the genuine, original tradition, while those which do not are dismissed as embellishments or interpolations.

Thus Professor Halliday, speaking of the voyage of the *Argo,* asserts that "there is not a great deal of history left when the trimmings are shorn off, but on the other hand, what there is is important. Jason's voyage to the Black Sea was a real event, which helped to make history." [5]

[3] *Troy,* p. 328.
[4] *Homer and History,* p. 28.
[5] W. R. Halliday: *Indo-European Folk-tales and Greek Legends,* p. 64.

Yet "there is no history, I fear, to be got out of the legend of Perseus." [6] And Mr. Burn assures us that "though the legends contain a core of historic truth . . . the poets considered themselves justified in drawing freely upon their imagination." [7]

Since the methods adopted by these and other scholars for extracting "history" from the legends are purely subjective, it is not surprising that no two of them agree as to what is history and what is not. We are to disbelieve most of what Homer wrote; we are to disbelieve a good deal of what Herodotus and Thucydides believed; yet unless we believe faithfully that ten, twenty, or thirty per cent of the tale of Troy is true, we are excommunicate from the fellowship of scholars.

Why? Because it was, in common with many other myths, fables, and fallacies, accepted as fact in less critical times, and because it has an emotional appeal; most people obtain a thrill from stories of adventure and bloodshed, and the thrill is intensified if they can persuade themselves that the stories are true. Besides this, there are many students who pursue their researches with the same mental attitude as that of the reader of detective stories; all the clues are within the covers of the book itself and can be followed up successfully by anyone who has sufficient application and ingenuity.

In both cases the test is verisimilitude, or what seems to be such. Any scene or incident which presents to the reader a convincing picture of prehistoric Greece, as he supposes it to have been, is evidence, if not proof, that such scene or incident is historically true. But, of course, such evidence is no evidence at all. Any competent novelist, if he would allow himself to be coached by a classical scholar, could write a novel of ancient Greece which would be far freer from inconsistencies, anachronisms, and absurdities than Homer is, and which would sound far more convincing to a modern European. Yet it might not contain a single word of historical fact.

Our scholars have, with rare exceptions, fallen into two

[6] Ibid., p. 126.
[7] A. R. Burn, op. cit., p. 18.

serious errors of method. In the first place they have failed
to realize that a literary work, be it the *Iliad* or any other,
must be considered as a whole. We may conclude that it
is fact, or myth, or fiction, or fiction founded on fact, but
we are not entitled to divide it up into bits and to assume
that some of these bits are fact and some fiction, according to the theories we have formed from a study of the
work itself. We may say, for example, that Shakespeare's
King John is a work of fiction founded on fact, but we
are not entitled to decide, from internal evidence alone,
how much is fiction and how much fact. We can only
achieve this by comparing the play with contemporary
records. Such a comparison may be valuable, though not
for historical purposes; as an aid to the study of English
history the play is worthless. The same applies to Homer;
we have, in the *Iliad* and the *Odyssey,* works which obviously contain a great deal that is not historical fact. Even
if we knew, which we certainly do not, that the poems
were founded on fact, we should not be entitled to say
that any one incident which they mentioned was historical,
unless we had confirmation from a reliable source, and if
we had such confirmation we should not, from the historical point of view, have any need of the poems. If for *King
John* we substitute *King Lear* we shall have a truer comparison, since we have no corroboration for King Lear,
and therefore do not regard him as historical.

The other error of method into which Homeric scholars
have fallen is that of discussing the problems raised as if
they were quite unconnected with any other problems. All
are really general problems, problems of tradition, of
mythology, of poetry, particularly the origin of epic
poetry, and of religion, particularly that of the active
interference of gods in human affairs. Nobody is qualified
to make any pronouncement on any of these problems,
as they propound themselves in the *Iliad* or any other
poetical work, unless he has studied them as general questions. Those who have discussed these questions, however,
are almost without exception men brought up in the
classical tradition, so that every discussion begins, instead
of ending, with the Tale of Troy.

The assumption that the Tale of Troy is true has prevented recognition of the fact that there is no single incident in any epic poem for which there is historical confirmation. It is true, as we have seen, that the names of historical persons sometimes appear in myth, but that does not prove the historicity of the myth. The story of the burnt cakes is not proved to be true by the fact that Alfred is a historical person; in fact, its sole claim to historicity, which is, as we have seen, a false one, lies in the fact that Alfred was a historical person. But the heroes of the *Iliad* are not historical persons; we know Alfred from contemporary sources, but we know Achilles only from sources comparable to the story of Alfred and the cakes. I shall later try to demonstrate the mythical character of the Homeric heroes, but shall now show how myth becomes history in the hands of Homeric scholars.

The theory they have put forward is that in the eleventh century B.C. the Dorians, a large and powerful Greek-speaking tribe of Nordic origin, invaded Greece, conquered most of it, and made the most far-reaching changes in its culture. "The Dorian invasion, which is passed over by Homer," says Professor Nilsson,[8] "resulted in the *débâcle* of the older civilization." This theory seems to be based first on the fact that the Greece of Homer differs in almost every possible respect from the Greece of history; and secondly, on the assertion of Herodotus and other classical writers that at a period which can be reckoned at about eighty years after the siege of Troy, the Peloponnesus was conquered by a tribe called the Dorians under the leadership of the sons of Heracles, from whom the Spartan kings claimed descent. The Greece of Homer, however, is in all probability a purely mythical country, and as for the Dorians, according to Herodotus,[9] they were a small tribe of northern Greece, and the sons of Heracles are always represented as *returning* from exile. There is nothing whatever in these stories to suggest the catastrophic invasion of an alien race, yet according to

[8] M. P. Nilsson: *Homer and Mycenae,* p. 239.
[9] I, 56.

Professor Rose[1] they represent "the mythological form of the Dorian invasion, by which the Achaian civilization was brought to an end." We are to understand, it seems, that a complete travesty of the facts can be sufficiently explained by labelling it "mythological."

There are, however, no facts to travesty. There is no reason to believe that the Dorians represent a later invasion. It is easy to contrast Sparta with Athens, but the Spartans were not typical Dorians, nor the Athenians typical non-Dorians, and the social system of Sparta, far from being north European, finds its closest parallels among the Masai and other tribes of east Africa. The Dorian dialect, which is all that distinguishes the Dorians as a whole from other Greeks, is emphatically the dialect not of northern but of southern Greece. The leading heroes of the *Iliad* were said to have come from Dorian lands, and the centres of the worship of Menelaus, of Helen, and of Zeus-Agamemnon were in Sparta itself.

Mr. T. W. Allen[2] asks us to believe that "there is hardly any limit to the accuracy of Greek historical memory"; then how came it that the Dorians of Crete and Argolis had forgotten their own history, but clearly remembered the history of those whom they had conquered and dispossessed? The story of the Dorian Conquest was invented by the scholars to justify them in believing in the historicity of Homer, and this although the story receives confirmation neither from Homer nor from any other classical source.

Mr. Allen speaks elsewhere[3] of "Homer, in his historical capacity, as annalist of the Trojan war," but whatever Homer may have been, he certainly was not an annalist. An annalist is a man who records, year by year, the principal events of the year, and Homer, of course, attempted nothing of the kind. The belief that epic poetry is an early method of keeping historical records, though not peculiar to Mr. Allen, is carried by him to unusual

[1] H. J. Rose: *A Handbook of Greek Mythology*, p. 267.
[2] *Homer—The Origin and Transmissions*, p. 82.
[3] Ibid., p. 135.

lengths. He tells us that "in the heroic age they liked to be told the news, and failing that would put up with ancient history. At the moment of the Odyssey the subjects asked for and listened to were the last great events of contemporary history, the siege of Troy and the return of the Greek sovereigns. The audience could ask the bard to begin the tale at any moment; the whole series was in bardic memory." [4] It is incredible that people ever existed who could say: "You don't know what won the Derby? Oh well, tell us a bit about the Norman Conquest!" and on any theory it seems inconceivable that the Homeric poems were composed soon enough after the event for their contents to come as news to the Greeks.

Professor Nilsson also holds that "epic poetry always deals with historical persons and events, and it may be inferred that its origin is to be found in the praise of living men and the description of contemporary events." [5] The examples which he gives, however, suggest nothing of the kind, and his opinion may be contrasted with that of Professor Gilbert Murray,[6] who asks: "Why do the Homeric poems all refer not to any warfare that was going on at the time of their composition, but to warfare of forgotten people under forgotten conditions in the past? The fact is certain. What shall one say of this? Merely that there is no cause for surprise. It seems to be the normal instinct of a poet, at least of an epic poet. The earliest version of the *Song of Roland* which we possess was written by an Anglo-Norman scribe some thirty years after the conquest of England. If the Normans of that age wanted an epic sung to them, surely a good subject lay ready to hand. Yet as a matter of fact their great epic is all about Roland, a not very important chieftain dead three hundred years before, not about William the Conqueror. The fugitive Britons of Wales made no epic to tell of their conquest by the Saxons; they turned to a dim-shining Arthur belonging to the vaguest past. Neither

[4] Ibid., p. 144.
[5] Op. cit., p. 239.
[6] *The Rise of the Greek Epic*, pp. 229–30.

did the Saxons who were conquering them make epics about that conquest. They sang how at some time long past a legendary and mythical Beowulf had conquered a monstrous Grendel and Grendel's mother and a dragon."

In the same connection Dr. Leaf remarks: "When they [the Normans] crossed the Channel to invade England, they seem to have lost all sense of their kinship with the Saxons, and it is doubtful if they even knew that their name meant Northmen. The war-song which Taillefer chanted as they marched to battle was not a Viking saga, but the song of Roland." [7] He realized that a people can completely forget their past within a hundred and sixty years, yet it never occurred to him to apply this fact to the study of the tale of Troy, any more than it has occurred to Professor Murray to compare the tale of Troy to the tale of Grendel.

The scholars invite us to suppose that Helen was a myth; that Hector was a poetical invention; that Achilles replaced Diomedes as principal hero; that Menestheus was put in to please the Athenians; and that Odysseus does not really belong to the story at all; but we must still, if we wish to be saved, believe that an army of sub-kings and feudal nobles, with their levies, under the command of Agamemnon, High King of Greece, spent ten years in besieging Troy, and eventually took and destroyed it.

Yet even when stripped to these bare bones, the story is full of glaring improbabilities. In the first place we know that it was a matter of the greatest difficulty to keep a feudal army in the field for ten weeks, let alone ten years. We are told that King Alfred's levies, which were besieging the Danish King, abandoned the siege and went home because "they had stayed their term of service and consumed their provisions." [8] The English armies in France were always on a mercenary basis, since the feudal levies refused to follow the king oversea. Froissart tells us that in 1341 the Scotch army insisted, in defiance of the King's wishes, on returning home with its plunder after twelve

[7] *Homer and History*, p. 46.
[8] *Anglo-Saxon Chronicle*, sub. A.D. 894.

days in England.[9] Agamemnon and his army are very different; they "live in huts on the beach, year out, year in, supporting themselves by plunder and decimated by pestilences." [1] And why? The recapture of Helen is the only motive alleged by the Greeks of historical times. To modern scholars, however, such a reason seems inadequate for a ten years' war, so other reasons have been invented. One, as we saw, is the stoppage of the Black Sea trade route, yet this is more obviously absurd, since if there was a trade route there must have been trading ships. The mouth of the Scamander, on Dr. Leaf's hypothesis, was a necessary port of call, and once the straits had been opened we should expect it to be thronged with ships laden with merchandise, at least for half the year, and to find the Greek camp abundantly supplied, and well up in the latest news from Greece. The hundred and fifty miles from Eubœa to Troy can have been nothing to people who were accustomed to sailing to Colchis, eight hundred miles farther on. And why could not the kings and chiefs go home for the winter, as our own officers did as late as Marlborough's day? The answer is that while the siege is mythical, Dr. Leaf's ships and trade are simply fabulous.

Professor Nilsson rejects Dr. Leaf's theory and supposes that the siege was the result of an expedition seeking booty,[2] but is it credible that a rich and powerful monarch, High King of all Greece, should abandon his kingdom and his family and live for ten years in squalor on a beach a few days' sail from home, merely in the hope of sharing in the spoil of one city? Only to those who will clutch at any straw which they think may rescue them from the cold, clear water of critical investigation.

[9] *Chronicles,* tr. T. Johnes, vol. i, p. 101; the fact may be untrue, but the practice is well attested.
[1] G. Murray, op. cit., p. 67.
[2] Op. cit., p. 113.

CHAPTER X

TRADITIONS OF OTHER LANDS

Of Roman tradition little need be said, since Professor
Rose has shown that the stories of Æneas, of Romulus,
and of Tarquin, and many others which our grandfathers
accepted as history, are really late literary productions,
the materials for which were derived or imitated from
Greek sources.[1] His conclusion seems to be that none of
the material which is embodied in the *Æneid* has any basis
in historical fact, and that the tale of how Æneas founded
Rome, though the fiction of a Greek writer, "soon won
credence at Rome, where it seems to have been an article
of faith, at least for diplomatic purposes, by the end of
the First Punic War."[2] If one epic poem can be based
on totally unhistorical materials, which have been developed for the purposes of political or religious propaganda,
so may others, yet it never occurs to Professor Rose to
consider whether similar processes may not have been
at the root of the *Iliad,* nor to ask how it was that the
Greeks had such an enormous corpus of "historical" tradition, whereas the Romans, at least in early historical times,
had none. Nor does he attempt to explain why, if the
Roman "traditions" consist so largely of easily swallowed
fictions, the Greek "traditions" must be accepted as sober
fact. The only reason seems to be that we know a great
deal more about the genesis of the Roman "traditions"
than about that of the Greek "traditions."

The Greeks and Romans were, after all, closely akin,
probably in race and certainly in language and in their
social system. Why, then, were their traditions or their
attitudes to tradition, when we first meet them, so radically

[1] H. J. Rose, op. cit., ch. xi.
[2] Ibid., p. 307.

different? Professor A. C. Pearson[3] supposes that the
Romans borrowed from the Greeks because "they had no
heroic past of their own." But what is the heroic age of
Greece, in the form in which it emerges from the rationalizations of our scholars, but an age of "heroes" who
murder their nearest relatives and massacre everyone else?
Why should we suppose that the prehistoric Romans
were less prone to murder and massacre than their historical descendants? Is there nothing in the stories of the
Punic Wars which would afford material for the plots
of epics and dramas? Of course there is plenty, but it
could not be used because the basis of epics and dramas
was not historical but religious, and just as the prehistoric
Greeks got their religion, and with it their drama, from
the East, so the historical Romans got their religion from
Greece. The traditions, the poetry, the drama, the politics,
and the religion of Greece were linked together in a complex in which genuine history played no part, in the first
place because there was no genuine history, and in the
second because there was no part for it to play; in Rome
the process was much the same except that such genuine
history as there was was deliberately jettisoned to make
room for the politico-religious pseudo-history of the *Æneid*.

We find a similar phenomenon in the Balkans. The
Serbian epic on the Battle of Kosovo has been represented
as a wonderful example of folk-memory, but according to
Dr. Gaster[4] it has little historical foundation, and what
there is is derived from written accounts that are themselves grossly inaccurate. It would seem to be no more than
a modern piece of politico-religious propaganda.

The Russian epic poems called "*byliny*" have been supposed to have a historical basis, but their heroes all end by
becoming saints or monks, and the probability is that
these poems were compiled by monks with the object of
claiming for their monasteries the former possession of
religious pre-eminence and the widest territorial rights.[5]

I shall make no attempt to deal in any detail with non-

[3] *Hastings' Encyclopædia,* vol. i, p. 656.
[4] *Folk-Lore,* vol. xliv, p. 325.
[5] A. van Gennep, op. cit., p. 179.

European traditions, and for two reasons. The first is that the facts are far less readily accessible, and the second that those who are unconvinced by the preceding chapters would hardly be impressed by a chapter dealing with the traditional heroes of India or China. I have, however, satisfied myself that the same factors have operated to produce pseudo-history in Asia as in Europe.

There remains one group of traditions of which it is impossible to avoid some discussion: namely, the Jewish traditions embodied in the Old Testament. It is a necessary part of the thesis I am putting forward in this book to show that whoever regards the Old Testament as a historical work, in the sense in which we understand history, entirely misunderstands its character.

In their scholarly *Introduction to the Books of the Old Testament,* Drs. Oesterley and Robinson tell us that the accounts of the building of the Temple given in the Books of Ezra and Nehemiah are confused and contradictory, and that whereas it is alleged that Ezra preceded Nehemiah, the only possible conclusion that can be drawn from the evidence of the books themselves is that he really reached Jerusalem some fifty years later, and that the whole series of events is put about fifty years too early. "It will thus be seen," they conclude, that the history of a considerable part of *Ezra-Nehemiah* is unreliable. This is to be accounted for: (*a*) by the fact that our book is a compilation, and the sources have been unskilfully put together; (*b*) because the compiler's knowledge of the period of history dealt with was inadequate owing to the want of *data;* and (*c*) because the compiler had some preconceived ideas with which he coloured the history." [6]

They give the date of the arrival of Ezra as 397 B.C., and of the compilation of the book as about 300 B.C.,[7] and according to the usual views of history and tradition there should have been ample data available. The events described—the return from the captivity, the building of the Temple, the expulsion of the foreign women, etc.—were

[6] *An Introduction to the Books of the Old Testament,* p. 124.
[7] Ibid., p. 126.

events that must have been known to the whole Jewish community, and must have created the most profound impression upon them. If historical events were ever preserved by "race-memory," here is a case in which they could not possibly have failed to be preserved; and that these memories, checked with the accurate records and annals which a literate people might be expected to keep, would produce a complete and accurate history seems, according to the theories of the professors,[8] a foregone conclusion. Yet we are told that the official writer, by combining "preconceived ideas" with an "unskillful" handling of "inadequate" data, produced a grossly inaccurate account of events of the highest importance which were less than a century old. And so far was anyone from questioning his narrative that at no very distant date it had come to be universally regarded as verbally inspired by the deity.

What explanation the believers in tradition put forward for these facts I have no idea, but the real explanation is that the compilers of the "historical" books of the Old Testament were not historians writing for students, but theologians writing for the faithful. "Primitive theology," says Dr. Schweitzer,[9] "is simply a theology of the future, with no interest in history," but this is not quite accurate, since to the true whole-time theologian there is no past and no future. Change and decay are apparent and not real, since they are prevented from becoming real by a faithful performance of the ritual. The ritual which now is, is that which was in the beginning, and it is the duty of the theological writer to ensure that it ever shall be. The business of the priests is to perform the ritual with the maximum of regularity and solemnity, but in order that they may be able to carry out successfully their all-important task of renewing the world in the ritual they must have the wholehearted support of the community, and this is to be secured by the establishment of the tradition.

Our professors have judged the compiler of *Ezra-Nehemiah* as a historian, and have convicted him of lack

---

[8] Including Professor Robinson himself, *v. supra,* p. 14.
[9] *The Quest of the Historical Jesus,* p. 342.

of skill, but in my view they have maligned him. The very idea of history was clearly quite foreign to him, and if a critic had attempted to explain to him the principles of historical criticism, he would have failed completely to understand what was meant, and would probably have regarded his critic as afflicted of God. The theory upon which he and his colleagues worked, from the historical point of view a totally false theory, as Professor Hooke and his colleagues have shown,[1] was that every detail of the ritual, as performed in 300 B.C., had been laid down by Moses. Where authority was required for injunctions, these could be put into the mouth of Moses, just as in China "to give these words the requisite authority they are, in accordance with invariable Chinese practice, put into the mouth of an ancient worthy," [2] but there were in existence records with which it was no doubt regarded as dangerous, or at least undesirable, to tamper. Where these records were manifestly irreconcilable with the ritual, it was obvious that they had somehow become corrupted, and it then became the duty of a compiler or editor to make the minimum of amendment necessary to bring the text into a tolerable degree of conformity with the facts, which to the theologian are, it must be repeated, not the facts of history but the facts of ritual. This our compiler achieved so successfully that his results remained uncriticized for over two thousand years.

The historicity of the Old Testament could, of course, be discussed at much greater length, but the foregoing may suffice to show that the historical facts cited, even where great accuracy might be expected, are quite unreliable, and that people who had, within a century, completely forgotten the events connected with the return from the Captivity, are unlikely to have preserved an accurate recollection of events that are alleged to have occurred five hundred or a thousand years before any attempt was made to record them.

[1] Ed. S. H. Hooke: *Myth and Ritual* and *The Labyrinth*.
[2] A. Waley: *The Way and Its Power*, p. 26.

PART TWO

Myth

*

CHAPTER XI

THE GENESIS OF MYTH

We have seen in the preceding chapters that there are no valid grounds for believing in the historicity of tradition, and I have suggested that some distinguished heroes of tradition are really heroes of myth, and that a saga, far from being a record of fact, is really a novel based chiefly upon myth.

Those who have made any study of myths have realized that a myth is not merely an untrue story; they have, however, given very different explanations of myth, explanations which fall into three main classes. What, as I shall try to show, are the wrong explanations are firstly that a myth is a statement of historical fact clothed in more or less obscure language, and secondly that it is a fanciful or speculative explanation of a natural phenomenon. Having dealt with these, I shall show that what a myth really is is a narrative linked with a rite.

Let us begin with the theory of what is known as the "historic myth." This theory is, or seems to be, that people who lived in ages more or less remote from our own felt an urge to transmit to their descendants the facts of their tribal or local history; for some obscure reason, however, they were unable to do this in straightforward language, and therefore had recourse to allegory. These old peoples, it is supposed, carefully transmitted the allegories, or myths, to their descendants, who have continued to repeat them ever since. As the myth-makers omitted to transmit the key, however, the purpose that they had in mind has been frustrated, and the recipients of these myths invariably misunderstood them, either taking them literally or regarding them as a kind of sacred fairy-tale.

It seems to follow from this theory that if our ancestors

had acquired the "historic myth" habit, we should now
have no account of the Norman Conquest except a story
of how a Frenchman married an English heiress against
her will and took possession of her estate, and our only
version of the Hundred Years' War would be a story of
how one of our ancestors kept on jumping over a brook
into his neighbour's garden.

In criticizing this theory, as put forward by Sir William
Ridgeway and others, Mr. Alfred Nutt asked:[1] "Is there
such a thing as an historic myth at all? Do men com-
memorate tribal wanderings, settlements, conquests, sub-
jugations, acquisitions of new forms of culture, or any
of the other incidents in the collective life of a people in
the form of stories about individual men and women? I
do not deny the possibility of their doing so; all I ask for
is evidence of the fact."

I cannot learn that anyone ever gave Mr. Nutt the
evidence for which he asked, no doubt for the very good
reason that there is no such evidence, but the theory is
still widely held. It is a very convenient theory, since any
scholar who has views of his own on the early age of
Greece, or of Tahiti, is able to produce what he can regard
as convincing evidence in their favour by dubbing some
local myth a "historic myth" and placing his own inter-
pretation upon it. Now, to take incidents from myth and
represent them as literal history is bad enough, since, as I
must continue to point out, there is no good reason to
believe that a myth or any other traditional narrative has
ever embodied a historic fact, but to take portions of
myths and to represent them as saying something which
they do not say, and which those who relate them have
never supposed them to say, is infinitely worse. That such
procedure is considered compatible with sound scholarship indicates the gulf which separates scholarship from
science.

Let us start with Professor Gilbert Murray. He tells
us that he strongly suspects the lists of men slain by the
heroes of the *Iliad* to be tribal records condensed and, "of
course," transferred from their original context. He has

[1] *Folk-Lore*, vol. xii, p. 339.

already given us one of these "tribal records." In the
Iliad it is said that Phæstus was slain by Idomeneus, and
fell from his chariot with a crash. On this Professor Murray comments: "Idomeneus is the King of Knossos in
Crete, and Phæstus is only known to history as the next
most important town in the same island. That is to say,
Phæstus *is* the town, or the eponymous hero of the town.
. . . We may well have in this passage a record of a local
battle or conquest in Crete, torn up from its surroundings
and used to fill up some details of slaughter in a great
battle before Troy." Even if we admitted the possibility of
historic myth, it would be difficult to explain why a town
should be represented as falling from a chariot; why an
eponymous hero should be invented for one town but
not for the other; and why the poet should have recourse
to Cretan records to fill in details of a battle before Troy,
since he has imagination enough to enable him to make
"mythological changes and false identifications." Professor
Murray has succumbed to the temptation to treat those
portions of the *Iliad* which fit in with his theories as "real
history," and those which do not as "the emptiest kind
of fiction." [2]

Dr. W. J. Perry tells us[3] that traditions are to be treated
as something ranking as fact, and that if not forced to
support any *a priori* view, but allowed to tell their own
tale in their own time, they frequently serve to throw a
flood of light on dark places. We soon find, however,
that the traditions are not allowed to tell their tale in their
own time, but must tell it in Dr. Perry's. In his view, tales
of gods and culture heroes are reminiscences of real individuals, the first bringers of Egyptian culture to the area
where the tales are told, and when people say that they
were civilized by a man who came from the sky, we must
read instead of "sky" whatever place Dr. Perry supposes
that their culture came from. When a tribe claims that its
culture is due to certain supernatural beings who, among
other feats, told the sun to go down and give them rest,
instead of staying up all the time, we are told that "the

[2] *The Rise of the Greek Epic,* pp. 220–3.
[3] *The Children of the Sun,* p. 104.

claim of the natives that certain beings originated their
civilization is apparently trustworthy." [4] Yet why should
their history be more trustworthy than their astronomy?

Believers in the historic myth are fond of telling us
how easily such myths arise, but never produce any evidence to show that they have so arisen. Thus Mr. M. E.
Lord assures us[5] that "a labyrinthine palace in which
Athenian slaves were killed in a fight with the king's bulls
would easily give rise to the story of the Athenian captives
devoured by a monster half man and half bull." For many
centuries men have been killed every year in the bull-rings
of Spain, yet their death has given rise to no such myth;
this is not surprising, since nobody who had seen a bull
could suppose that fighting bulls have human bodies. The
early Greek vase-painters represent the Minotaur not as a
man-devouring monster but as a helpless-looking creature
being stabbed unresistingly—no doubt a sacrificial victim
wearing a mask.

"Into the ten days' Battle of Dunheath," says Professor R. W. Chambers,[6] "Norse poetry has probably com-
pressed the century-long struggle of Goth and Hun. . . .
For popular tradition will easily turn a desultory conflict
into a single dramatic encounter, but hardly the reverse."
The wars of the Saxons with the Welsh and the Danes
were desultory conflicts, but tradition has not turned them
into a single dramatic encounter, and there seems no reason to believe that what Professor Chambers describes as
easy is in fact possible.

If a process cannot actually be proved to occur, it is
surely the duty of those who postulate it to give some
reason for believing in its occurrence, yet the two examples that I have just quoted, in which scholars describe
as "easy" processes the very possibility of which they have
attempted neither to demonstrate nor to explain, are un-
fortunately typical. It seems to be regarded as the privilege
of a professor of classics or literature to guess the origin of

[4] Ibid., pp. 123–4.
[5] *Classical Journal*, 1923–4, p. 269.
[6] *Widsith*, p. 48.

a particular story and then elevate his guess to the status of a universal rule. What is needed is a comparative study of history and myth, and this, so far as I have been able to carry it, seems to show clearly that the "historic myth" is a fiction.

The same applies to the "nature myth," the theory, that is to say, that myths are fanciful or speculative explanations of natural phenomena. According to Max Müller and his school, all myths are sun myths. "The siege of Troy is but a repetition of the siege of the East by the solar powers that every evening are robbed of their brightest treasures in the West." [7] Alternatively, it is a repetition of the contest between summer and winter, in which summer is defeated every autumn, but revives and becomes victorious every spring.

As a fact, however, there is no contest, either between night and day or between summer and winter, and it never occurs to us to imagine that there is. We say: "It is getting rather dark," and not "Day is giving ground before the blows of Night," and when we feel the first frost it never occurs to us to suggest that the life-blood of summer is oozing away. The latter are the ideas of court poetry, not of everyday life. Mr. Tiddy says that "the people naturally conceive of the Old and New Year as combatants," [8] but the very idea of a New Year is highly artificial. In nature the year has no beginning.

The sun-myth, in its earlier form, is now out of fashion, and has been replaced by a revised version in which myth is represented as "primitive science." The believers in this theory suppose that primitive man was consumed by a thirst for knowledge, and spent much of his time in speculating on the origin of the heavenly bodies, of the seasons, and of life and death. In default of a better explanation, he explained all these phenomena in terms of his own experience, and that is why in the myths the stars and the seasons are represented as human beings.

Thus Andrew Lang thought that "the origin of the

[7] Max Müller: *The Science of Language,* vol. i, p. 515.
[8] R. J. E. Tiddy: *The Mummers' Play,* p. 108.

world and of man is naturally a problem which has excited
the curiosity of the least developed minds," [9] and Sir
Laurence Gomme believed that "everywhere, almost, man
has stood apart for a moment and asked himself the question, Whence am I?" [1]

Professor Halliday similarly supposes that "myths represent the answers given by the human imagination to the
problem of how things came to be. How were Earth and
Sky created or how did evil enter the world?" [2] and Professor H. J. Rose alleges that "in the myth proper, imagination plays freely, poetically also it may be, or grotesquely,
upon some striking phenomenon . . . or the nature and
activities of a superhuman being." [3]

Professor Rose's myth-maker must have been a very
remarkable person. On the one hand, he could not have
been an atheist, for then supernatural beings would have had
no existence for him, and on the other hand he could not
have been a believer, for then the freedom of his imagination
must have been trammelled by the nature of his belief.
This is no quibble; if a man believes in the supernatural,
he must have some beliefs about it, and if he has beliefs
he cannot give free rein to his imagination. All men, both
savage or civilized, are bound to accept, or possibly to
reject, the beliefs of their day; to only the tiniest minority
is it given to go even an inch beyond them. Half a dozen
of the Greek philosophers might qualify as myth-makers
under Professor Rose's definition, and in modern times
perhaps Spinoza and Kant, but did the latter compose
myths? Certainly not, and those philosophers who have
speculated about the origin of evil have not, to my knowledge, produced a rival myth to that of Eve and the Serpent. All these theories are based upon the supposition
that illiterate savages live in a state of highly intellectual
agnosticism, in the luxuriant soil of which, owing to the
lack of scientific cultivation, weeds monstrous or strangely
beautiful are continually springing up.

[9] *Myth, Ritual, and Religion*, vol. i, p. 162.
[1] Op. cit., p. 130.
[2] *Indo-European Folktales and Greek Legend*, p. 5.
[3] *Folk-Lore*, vol. xlvi, p. 11.

This picture is an utterly false one. The savage is interested in nothing which does not impinge upon his
senses, and never has a new idea even about the most
familiar things. In this he is like our own illiterates. At
the elementary schools some knowledge of more remote
subjects is impressed upon them with the aid of books, but
as soon as their school days are over, the majority relapse
into the mental state in which savages remain permanently. It has been held that the curiosity which is dis-
played in some degree by all human beings is evidence of
ability to speculate;[4] is the interest that a herd of cattle
displays in a strange dog evidence of ability to speculate?
Professor Halliday's myth-makers are filled with curiosity
about the origin of the universe and of evil in it, but such
curiosity is not merely unknown among savages, it is
extremely rare among the civilized. How many of us have
tried seriously to understand the theory of relativity or
the doctrine of the Atonement? I wonder whether Professor Halliday can explain why the grass is green, and
whether Professor Rose has reflected imaginatively upon
the causes of volcanic activity. Anyhow, the savage attempts nothing of the kind. In discussing the mythology
of the Bantus, Dr. Lindblom[5] expresses surprise at "their
great lack of feeling that the origin of the most important
phenomena of existence need explanation." We may safely
accept the fact from a most competent observer; his surprise is due to his failure to realize that it is a question
not of feeling but of *thinking*. Thinking, in the sense in
which we use the word when we say that a man is a
"thinker," is a skilled occupation, requiring not merely a
long apprenticeship but a highly specialized set of tools.
Even the simplest speculation about cosmic origins or
moral principles requires a vocabulary of abstract terms,
and such terms are lacking in savage, and even in semi-
civilized languages. In our discussion of the simplest scientific or philosophical questions we use such terms as *cause,
effect, creation, origin, result, nature, reason, idea, image,
theory, problem*—terms which it is difficult to translate

[4] A. Lang, op. cit., vol. i, p. 87.
[5] G. Lindblom: *The Akamba*, p. 252.

into Anglo-Saxon, and impossible to translate into any unwritten language. We can say with confidence that myths
are not the result of speculation, firstly because they are
never expressed in the only forms of language in which
speculation is possible, and secondly because illiterates
never speculate, and the speculations of literate communities lead not to mythology but to philosophy and science.

Professor Malinowski[6] quotes *Notes and Queries in
Anthropology* as saying that "myths are stories which,
however marvellous and improbable to us, are nevertheless related in all good faith, because they are intended, or
believed by the teller, to explain by means of something
concrete and intelligible an abstract idea or such vague and
difficult conceptions as Creation, Death . . . ," and asks:
"Would our Melanesians agree with this opinion? Certainly not. They do not want to 'explain,' to make 'intelligible,' anything which happens in their myths—above all
an abstract idea. Of that there can be found to my knowledge no instance in Melanesia or in any other savage
community. . . . Nor would a Trobriander agree with
the view that 'Creation, Death . . .' are vague and difficult conceptions." He could not possibly do so, since
there is no word for "to create," or even "to make," in
any Melanesian language.[7]

In putting forward a view of myth very different from
that which Professor Malinowski criticizes, I find myself in
the unusual position of being able to quote in its support
a number of distinguished writers, including Professor
Malinowski himself. I shall begin with Professor Hooke,
who defines myth as "the spoken part of a ritual; the story
which the ritual enacts." [8]

"A *mythos* to the Greeks," says Miss Harrison,[9] "was
primarily just a thing spoken, uttered by the *mouth*. Its
antithesis or rather correlative is the thing done, enacted.
. . . The primary meaning of myth in religion is just the
same as in early literature; it is the spoken correlative of

---

[6] In the *Frazer Lectures,* ed. W. R. Dawson, p. 81.
[7] A. M. Hocart: *Kingship,* p. 197.
[8] S. H. Hooke: *Myth and Ritual,* p. 3.
[9] J. E. Harrison: *Themis,* p. 328.

the acted rite. . . . Its object is not at first to give a reason; that notion is part of the old rationalist fallacy which saw in primitive man the leisured and eager inquirer bent on research."

"We shall probably not err," says Sir James Frazer, "in assuming that many myths, which we now know only as myths, had once their counterpart in magic; in other words, that they used to be acted as a means of producing in fact the events which they describe in figurative language. Ceremonies often die out while myths survive, and thus we are left to infer the dead ceremony from the living myth." [1]

Even Professor Rose, whose definition of myth I have criticized above, when dealing with the mythical quarrel of Zeus and Hera and the Platæan rite which "commemorated" it, says that "the legend has pretty certainly grown out of the rite, as usually happens";[2] and Professor A. B. Cook[3] says that "behind the myth [of the Minotaur], as is so often the case, we may detect a ritual performance."

"And not only is the Myth the explanation of the rite," says Professor Thomson,[4] "it is at the same time, in part at least, the explanation of the god. To primitive minds it is a matter of such transcendent importance to get the ritual exactly right (for the slightest deviation from the rules will ruin everything) that the worshippers will not proceed one step without authority. And who is their authority? In normal circumstances the oldest man in the tribe, the worshipper who has been most frequently through this particular ceremony before. And his authority? Well, the oldest tribesman within his memory. And so the tradition goes back and back. . . . But it must end somewhere, and it ends, as a thousand instances show, in an imaginary divine founder of the rite, who becomes the centre of the Myth."

[1] Op. cit., vol. ix, p. 274. It must be admitted that Sir James elsewhere expresses views difficult to reconcile with this.
[2] Op. cit., p. 104.
[3] Op. cit., vol. i, p. 522.
[4] J. A. K. Thomson: *Studies in the Odyssey,* p. 54.

"We must always look for an explanation," says Professor Hocart,[5] "not to the survival, but to the living custom or belief. If we turn to the living myth, that is the myth that is believed in, we find that it has no existence apart from the ritual. The ritual is always derived from someone, and its validity must be established by its derivation. The actors are merely impersonating the supposed inventors of the ritual, and this impersonation has to be expressed in words. Knowledge of the myth is essential to the ritual, because it has to be recited at the ritual."

"Psychologists like Wundt," says Professor Malinowski,[6] "sociologists like Durkheim, Hubert and Mauss, anthropologists like Crawley, classical scholars like Miss Jane Harrison, have all understood the intimate association between myth and ritual, between sacred tradition and the norms of social structure. . . . Myth as it exists in a savage community, that is, in its living primitive form, is not merely a story told but a reality lived. It is not of the nature of fiction, such as we read to-day in a novel, but it is a living reality, believed to have once happened in primeval times, and continuing ever since to influence the world and human destinies. This myth is to the savage what, to a fully believing Christian, is the Biblical story of Creation, of the Fall, of the Redemption." Discussing myths of origin, he says: "We can certainly discard all explanatory as well as all symbolical ex-interpretations of these myths of origin. The personages and beings which we find in them are what they appear to be on the surface, and not symbols of hidden realities. As to any explanatory function of these myths, there is no problem which they cover, no curiosity which they satisfy, no theory which they contain."

The myth, then, has nothing to do with speculations or explanations, any more than it has with historical facts. Strictly speaking, it is nothing but the form of words which is associated with a rite. To give a simple example —when we part from a friend, we shake him by the hand

[5] A. M. Hocart: *The Progress of Man,* p. 223.
[6] Op. cit., pp. 70, 72, 98.

and say "Good-bye." The handshake is the rite; and the expression "good-bye," which is a shortened form of "God be with you," is the myth. By calling upon God to be with our friend, we give strength and validity to the bond which the handshake sets up, and which will draw us together again. In this case, however, the myth has probably been truncated, as it has certainly been contracted. It has now no direct connection with the rite. If, however, when shaking hands on parting, we were in the habit of saying: "King Solomon, when he parted from the Queen of Sheba, shook her by the hand and said: 'God be with you,'" we should give a sacramental character to the rite by attributing its foundation to an ancient and sacred personage; this is what a myth normally does.

The purpose of ritual is to confer benefits on, or avert misfortunes from, those by whom or on whose behalf the ritual is performed, by means of actions and words which from a scientific point of view are entirely ineffective, except in so far as they produce a psychological effect upon the participants themselves. This is, of course, not the view of the ritualists, who usually judge the efficacy of the ritual not by its effect upon themselves, but by its supposed effect upon the forces of nature. Many Africans believe that rain will not fall unless there has been a proper rain-making ceremony; if the rain follows the ceremony, then it is clear that the ceremony has been properly performed, and if rain does not follow, it is equally clear that the ceremony has not been properly performed. Where the ritual can be so easily judged by its apparent results, there is no need of a myth.

Usually, however, the supposed effects of the ritual are far less clearly apparent, so that, if belief in its efficacy is to be maintained, a more complex type of faith is required. This is induced by the myth, which not merely links the ritual of the present with the ritual of the past, but actually identifies the present, in its ritual aspect, with a past conceived solely in terms of ritual—a past, that is to say, in which superhuman figures devote themselves to the performance of acts which are the prototypes of the ritual. The stories of their activities, the myths, then per-

form the dual function of sanctifying and of standardizing
the ritual. This standardization of myth is never complete,
however, before the introduction of writing, when those
myths which are closely associated with rites become
scriptures; other myths become "folklore," as I shall now
try to show.

CHAPTER XII

THE FOLK-TALE

Certain folklorists have divided, or attempted to divide, the traditional prose narrative into three completely distinct classes: the myth, the saga, and the folk-tale or *Märchen*. We saw in the last chapter that the myth is a narrative linked with ritual, and in Chapter V that a saga, though it may sometimes include matter drawn from chronicles or from contemporary history, is a form of novel based chiefly upon myth. Let us now see what the folk-tale really is.

Spence, in his definition of a folk-tale, says that it may be of mythical origin,[1] and Andrew Lang, in the course of a few pages, describes the story of a Jason as a myth, a legend, and a saga, and refer to its parallels as fairy-tales and as popular tales,[2] but other writers, as I said just now, have attempted to draw a hard-and-fast line between the folk-tale or *Märchen* and other types of traditional narrative, and have supposed that the former is a type of fiction, composed by and for the folk—that is to say, the illiterate.

Thus MacCulloch says that all over the world simple stories were invented, and that "as time went on, and man's inventive and imaginative faculties developed, these simple stories . . . became incidents in longer tales. New episodes were invented; the growth of custom and belief would furnish ever new material." [3]

Hartland tells us that in the *Märchen* or fairy-tale "the reins are thrown upon the neck of the imagination," and of uncivilized man that "his imagination predominates

[1] L. Spence: *An Introduction to Mythology*, p. 12.
[2] *Custom and Myth*, pp. 94, 99.
[3] J. A. MacCulloch: *The Childhood of Fiction*, p. 457.

over his reason and his hypotheses about the origin of
things take the shape of tales originating in unbounded
draughts upon his own emotions." [4]

Krappe assures us that "it is certainly excusable to take
the common-sense view and to regard the fairy-tale as a
definite type of popular fiction, primarily designed to
please and to entertain," [5] and Professor H. J. Rose defines
a *Märchen* as "primitive fiction told merely to amuse or
interest the audience and without ulterior purpose. It follows certain well-worn lines, as popular imagination is
very limited."

These views are, I think, demonstrably incorrect. The
facts are:

    1. No popular story-teller has ever been known
to invent anything.

    2. Not only are the incidents in folk-tales the same
all over the world, but in areas of the same language
they are commonly narrated in the same actual
words.

    3. Folk-tales deal as a rule with subjects of which
the folk can have no knowledge.

    4. The exercise of the imagination consists not in
creating something out of nothing, but in the trans-
mutation of matter already present in the mind.

I shall deal with these seriatim, and shall begin by
quoting Hartland against himself. He expatiates upon the
imagination of uncivilized man, but is nevertheless at pains
to show that the popular story-teller never displays any
imagination whatever. He tells us that "the dislike of
voluntary change forbids amendment of formularies
which have long ceased to be understood. . . . It is by
no means an uncommon thing for the rustic story-teller to
be unable to explain . . . episodes in any other way than
Uncle Remus—'She wuz in de tale, en de tale I give you
like hit were gun to me.'" He cites Dr. Steere as saying
that the Swahili story-tellers scarcely understood the sung
parts of their tales, and Dr. Rink as saying of the Eskimo

[4] E. S. Hartland: *The Science of Fairy Tales*, pp. 23, 33.
[5] A. H. Krappe: *The Science of Folklore*, p. 11.

that "the art requires the ancient tales to be related as nearly as possible in the words of the original version." He also tells us that "in these [Campbell's] tales words were often used which had dropped out of ordinary parlance, giving proof of careful adherence to the ancient forms. . . . To sum up," he concludes, "it would appear that national differences in the manner of story-telling are for the most part superficial. Whether told by men to men in the bazaar or coffee-house of the East, or by old men or women to children in the sacred recesses of the European home, or by men to a mixed assembly during the endless nights of the Arctic Circle, or in the huts of the tropical forest, and notwithstanding the license often taken by the professional reciter, the endeavour to render to the audience just what the speaker has himself received from his predecessors is paramount." [6]

"As a rule," says Professor Halliday,[7] "the pride of the professional is rather in the preservation of the old tale; both he and his hearers put a high premium on conservatism." According to Sir John Rhys, the Welsh story-tellers were not inventors but merely editors, and their stories echoes of ancient myths,[8] and we are told that the Irish story-teller "never chose his own words—he always had the story by heart, and recited the words from memory." [9]

The rustic or savage story-teller may seem to be improvising his stories, just as to one who visits a theatre for the first time the funny man may seem to be improvising his jokes. Investigation, however, shows that in illiterate communities not merely do the people as a whole not invent stories, but they do not even tell stories. The telling of stories may only be done by recognized story-tellers, and not only is it incumbent on these to tell the stories in the traditional manner and with the traditional words, but among many tribes they may tell only the particular stories that they have a recognized right to tell.

These being the facts, we are faced with two possible

[6] Op. cit., pp. 6, 18–21.
[7] Op. cit., p. 23.
[8] *Studies in the Arthurian Legend*, p. 175.
[9] P. W. Joyce: *Old Celtic Romances*, p. ix.

explanations. We must conclude either that savages once possessed a faculty of imagination and invention which has unaccountably disappeared, or that the attribution of imagination and inventiveness to savages is erroneous.

We now come to the second point, which is that the same tales are told in many parts of the world. Professor Rose explains this, as we saw, by the limitations of the popular imagination, but while this might conceivably explain the similarity in the incidents, it cannot possibly explain the similarity in the wording and the names. We find, for example, that the fairy-tales of England and France contain not merely the same incidents, but the same or equivalent names. How does Professor Rose account for this? Does he really believe that an English rustic, trying to think of a name for a man who murders his wives, is restricted by his imagination to "Bluebeard," and that a French rustic is similarly restricted to "*Barbe-bleue*"? Or that an Englishman and a Frenchman, devising a name for a girl who meets a wolf, have no possible alternatives to "Little Red Riding Hood" and "*Le Petit Chaperon rouge*"? Unless we form so extravagant a hypothesis, we must conclude that one set of tales is a translation. The argument could be carried much farther, but the above seems enough to show that the fairy-tales of one country are not of popular origin, and this being so, we have no reason to assume that the fairy-tales of another country are of popular origin.

Like the fairy-tale, the folk-play is alleged to be of popular origin. The fact that all over England and a great part of Europe the incidents of the folk-play are very similar might again be accounted for by the limitations of the popular imagination, but what are we to say when we find the couplet:

> "*Here comes I, old Beelzebub,*
> *Over my shoulder I carry my club,*"

with trifling variations in the folk-plays of Lincolnshire, Gloucestershire, Sussex, Cornwall, and other English counties, and of Belfast? [1] Are we to suppose that these

[1] R. J. E. Tiddy, op. cit.

words spring inevitably to the lips of a rustic playwright?

It should be quite clear that to say that a story, song, or play is of popular origin means nothing unless we assume that it actually originated with the people among whom it is now found, or their ancestors. If we find reason to believe that a folk-story has been borrowed, even from the next village, its popular origin becomes suspect, for if one community borrows instead of inventing, another may well do the same, and if one item of what passes as folklore is borrowed, it is at least possible that all is borrowed.

It is, of course, difficult to prove that no folk-tales are of popular origin, but a study not merely of the wording and names, but of the incidents in detail, may be sufficient to show that their popular origin is at least highly improbable. It is often alleged, for example, that the Celtic peasantry are highly imaginative people, and that their imagination expresses itself in fairy-tales, but a detailed comparison of the fairy-tales of Brittany with those of Italy led Coote to the conclusion that none of the Breton tales could be of Celtic origin.[2]

Let us take a story that is found all over the world, the details of which, though they cannot of course prove that it has been diffused from a common source, at any rate strongly suggest it. The story has been discussed by Andrew Lang[3] and by Professor Saintyves,[4] and in its simplest form goes as follows: A youth somehow finds his way to the house of a giant or ogre, who lives in a remote part of the world or in the sky. The ogre has a beautiful daughter, and she and the youth fall in love. The ogre finds the youth and sets him a succession of impossible tasks, such as emptying a large lake with a bucket or cleaning an Augean stable, but the ogre's daughter has magic at her disposal, by means of which the youth is enabled to perform the tasks, to the ogre's intense annoyance. The youth and the girl then decide to elope; the ogre pursues them, but he is delayed by magic obstacles that the girl

[2] H. C. Coote, in *Folk-Lore,* vol. i, p. 212.
[3] *Custom and Myth,* pp. 87 ff.
[4] *Les Contes de Perrault,* p. 272.

places in his path until a river is reached which allows the
lovers to cross, but drowns the ogre.

"The Greeks have the tale," Lang tells us, "the people
of Madagascar have it, the Lowland Scotch, the Celts, the
Russians, the Italians, the Algonquins, the Finns, and the
Samoans have it . . . while many scattered incidents
occur in even more widely severed races, such as Zulus,
Bushmen, Japanese, Eskimo, Samoyeds." Other versions
have come to light since he wrote, and, as he points out,[5]
it is not merely the main features that are the same in the
most remote parts of the world, but even the details. In
many of the versions, for example, the girl throws her
comb to the ground, whereupon it turns into a forest or
thicket, which delays the ogre's pursuit. We may conclude
with Dr. Krappe[6] that "it is unthinkable that a tale with a
plot as complicated . . . should have arisen independently."

There are other tales with a plot as complicated and
a distribution as wide as that just cited. Lang discusses
another of them, that of which the story of Jason is the
type; "we must suppose," he says,[7] "either that all wits
jumped and invented the same romantic series of situations
by accident, or that all men spread from one centre, where
the story was known, or that the story, once invented,
has drifted all round the world." He inclined, as might be
expected, to the last explanation, and we must again insist
that if· one story which a savage tells is derived from an
alien source, it is possible, and even probable, that the
other stories which he tells have a similar origin.

Having seen that the manner in which folk-tales are
told, and the manner in which they are distributed, render
it at least highly improbable that they are of popular
origin, we have next to consider their matter. If folk-tales
were really composed by the folk, we should expect them
to deal with subjects with which the folk are familiar—
matters of village courtship and marriage, of quarrels and
revenges, of seed-time and harvest, of plenty and dearth,

[5] Op. cit., p. 92.
[6] Op. cit., p. 8.
[7] Op. cit., p. 101.

of hunting and fishing—in short, of such materials as were used by Mary Webb in *Precious Bane,* or Pearl Buck in *The Good Earth*—but we should be disappointed. These stories are novels written by and for highly sophisticated people, and the material of folk-tales is of a very different character. It is very seldom that peasants appear in the tales at all. The *dramatis personæ,* when they are not supernatural beings, are kings, queens, princes, and princesses, or other potentates, with their ministers and attendants. The scenes are laid, not in the farmyard or the harvest field, but in palaces, castles, and courts; the plots are concerned not with rural life, but with heroic feats of arms and the succession to kingdoms; and the accessories consist largely of magic jewels, helmets of invisibility, and other objects quite outside the range of a peasant's ideas.

Even when the characters are supposed to be peasants, the situations and incidents are quite unreal. Take, for example, the story of Red Riding Hood: bedridden old women do not really live alone in the heart of wolf-haunted forests; wolves cannot really gobble people up without leaving a trace, and girls do not really mistake wolves, however conversational, for their grandparents. The story was obviously composed neither by nor for people who really lived in danger of wolves, and the father is represented as a wood-cutter merely in order that he may be at hand with a weapon at the proper moment.

In many stories in which the hero ends by ascending the throne and reigning as if to the manner born, he is represented as starting life as a pauper, but this is done, as I shall try to show later, to explain the fact that in the typical myth the hero has to pass through a period of adversity. It is usually found that, though ostensibly the son of a peasant, he is really a prince who in early infancy was either stolen by an enemy or hidden from a tyrant by his friends.

It seems to be supposed, though I have nowhere seen this clearly stated, that the peasant and the savage, though they are great hands at making up stories, are nevertheless incapable of making up the simplest story of the doings of ordinary human beings, and are therefore obliged to have recourse to ogres, fairies, talking animals, and people endowed with supernatural powers, to which conceptions they are led by some mysterious but universal force. It has been suggested that this force operates by means of dreams and hallucinations, but those who make this suggestion fail to realize that dreams and hallucinations cannot put new ideas into the mind.

This brings me to my next point, that concerning the widespread superstition that the imagination is capable of making something out of nothing, or, in other words, that there can come out of a man's mind ideas, whether of fact or fiction, which bear no relation to anything that has gone into it. Most theories of the origin of folklore, though they do not state this definitely, nevertheless imply that savages and rustics possess such powers of the imagination as in reality the most brilliant literary genius has never possessed.

An architect cannot design a new type of house unless he has in his mind or on his desk recollections or records of a large number of existing houses, unless he understands thoroughly the purpose of the different parts of a house, and the means of making access from one to another, and unless he has a thorough knowledge of the materials out of which houses are constructed, and of the means employed for putting them together. In exactly the same way, nobody can hope to be a successful poet or composer of stories unless he has familiarized himself with a large number of poems or stories of different types, both in their general outlines and in the details of their construction; and the better the writers whose works he studies, the better are his own writings likely to be. This simple fact is, of course, the basis of all literary education. In addition, our budding author must, if he is to produce anything possessing the least degree of originality, observe and read a good deal, and thus acquire a large fund of ideas. By drawing upon these he will be able to vary the form and content of his writings; this is the most that he will be able to do, since imagination at its highest is no more than the combination of two or more old ideas

to form a new idea. The "wild fancy" of the savage, of
which we hear so much, could rise to no greater heights
than that of imagining an orgy of meat and beer lasting
two or three days instead of one, and to suppose the unlettered rustic capable of composing the story of Cinderella is as absurd as to suppose him capable of designing
the palace in which she left her slipper.

The belief that folk-tales are the product of "popular
imagination" is due to a confused use of the word *imagination*. Anyone who has seen elephants, or pictures of
elephants, can "imagine" an elephant; that is to say, he
can form a mental picture of an elephant, which will be
more or less accurate according as his memory is more or
less retentive, but which will add nothing to his or anyone else's ideas on the subject of elephants, or on any
other subject. Compare with this the picture of a pterodactyl as imagined by a scientist. Out of some bones and
other fossil remains, together with a wide knowledge of
the appearance and anatomy of birds and of reptiles, he
"imagines" a picture of a pterodactyl which definitely adds
to the stock of human ideas. Imagination of the first type
could not invent a folk-tale, since it can invent nothing,
and even the second type, the infinitely rarer creative
imagination, could invent a folk-tale only if the elements
out of which it was to be composed were present in its
possessor's mind.

In his masterly work *The Road to Xanadu*, Professor
Lowes has taken a portion of Coleridge's *Ancient Mariner*
and has traced every idea, and almost every phrase, in it
to something that Coleridge can be shown to have read.
Professor Lowes says that the poem is a work of pure
imagination, but that "a work of pure imagination is not
something fabricated by a *tour de force* from nothing, and
suspended, without anchorage in fact, in the impalpable
ether of a visionary world. No conception could run more
sharply counter to the truth." [8] He later speaks of "a
strange but widely prevalent idea" that "the shaping spirit
of imagination sits aloof, like God as he is commonly

[8] *The Road to Xanadu*, p. 241.

conceived, creating in some thaumaturgic fashion out of nothing its visionary world. That and that only is deemed to be 'originality'—that, and not the imperial moulding of old matter into imperishably new forms." [9]

It is very few writers, however, who have even devised new forms; literary conventions are universal, especially poetic conventions. These conventions apply just as strictly to ballads and other forms of what are known as "folk-poetry" as they do to literary products. When, for example, Countess Cesaresco describes how "a herdsman or tiller of the soil strings together a few verses embodying some simple thought which came into his head whilst he looked at the green fields or the blue skies," and how "one or two friends get them by heart," [1] she forgets not only that such a process has never actually been known to occur, but that bucolic poetry is perhaps the most sophisticated form of poetry, and that its successful composers, from Theocritus to Wordsworth, have been men of the highest education.

Even so great a poet as Theocritus is less original than is commonly supposed. Speaking of his *Festival of Adonis,* perhaps the most admired of his idylls, Dr. Tyrrell says that he himself had always regarded it as a triumphantly successful piece of character-painting. "But I own," he continues, "that I was grieved to find what seems to me clear evidence that such scenes, in which women inveigh against their absent spouses, were part of the stock in trade of the mimographer, and were constantly reproduced. So also the reviling of servants by their mistresses, which also appears in this idyll. I am sure that Theocritus has handled these scenes with an art altogether transcending that of his rivals, but I had thought that they were the fruits of his own genius and invention." [2] Far from ploughing a lonely furrow, Theocritus was, in fact, rather

[9] Op. cit., p. 428.
[1] Countess Martinengo-Cesaresco: *The Study of Folk-Songs,* p. 59.
[2] *The Idylls of Theocritus,* tr. Calverley, ed. R. Y. Tyrrell, p. xvi.

the winner of a ploughing competition, and if the greatness of a great poet consists merely in improving upon the
efforts of his predecessors or rivals, how can it be supposed that an unlettered rustic could invent themes and
metres for himself?

Hundreds of English poets have dealt on conventional
lines with mountains, primroses, and love's young dream,
and the range of non-European poets is even more
limited. "Everybody knows," says Bain,[3] "that classical
Sanscrit authors have no originality. They do but rhetori-
cally reset and embellish notorious themes; such originality
as they possess lying not in their subject but in its treatment." In China, so Mr. Waley tells us, "innumerable
poems record 'Reflections on visiting a ruin,' or on the
'Site of an old city.' The details are ingeniously varied,
but the sentiments are in each case identical." Innumerable Arabic poems are supposed to be written on the deserted camp site of the loved one's tribe; at first the
hearer is apt to take for an expression of genuine emotion
what he later learns to recognize as an exhibition of
virtuosity.

It is the same with stories; every literary community
has certain types of story outside which none but exceptional geniuses can venture. As for the folk, they may
make minor alterations, mostly for the worse, in existing
poems, stories, or plays, but they never compose them for
themselves.

This fact, like negatives in general, is difficult to prove.
We may note that though the French Canadians have
been in Canada for over three centuries, the songs that
they sing are those which they brought from France. The
editors of a collection of these songs "sought in vain for
evidences of song-creation among the Canadian population." [4] There seems to be nothing in the *Uncle Remus*
stories, except the language, which the Negroes did not
bring from Africa. The English folk-play, which I discussed a few pages back, is not merely much the same,

[3] F. W. Bain: *A Digit of the Moon,* p. x.
[4] *Folk-Lore,* vol. xxxvii, p. 102.

both in incidents and in language, all over the country, but some versions embody long quotations from the works of Congreve and Addison.[5] This is a striking illustration of the fact that the literature of the folk is not their own production, but comes down to them from above.

[5] R. J. E. Tiddy, op. cit., pp. 82, 85.

CHAPTER XIII

MYTH AND RITUAL

The position which we have now reached is that the folk-tale is never of popular origin, but is merely one form of the traditional narrative; that the traditional narrative has no basis either in history or in philosophical speculation, but is derived from the myth; and that the myth is a narrative connected with a rite.

The theory that all traditional narratives are myths—that is to say, that they are connected with ritual—may be maintained upon five grounds:

1. That there is no other satisfactory way in which they can be explained. As the whole of this book is intended to establish this proposition, I shall not refer to it in particular here.

2. That these narratives are concerned primarily and chiefly with supernatural beings, kings, and heroes.

3. That miracles play a large part in them.

4. That the same scenes and incidents appear in many parts of the world.

5. That many of these scenes and incidents are explicable in terms of known rituals.

It was once supposed that the idea of a god or of gods was innate, but thinking persons have realized, since the days of Locke, that there are no innate ideas. The idea that it is natural to believe in the supernatural has only to be so stated to show its absurdity. Apart from innate ideas, we have inspiration and revelation, but even if all the claims made for these were admitted, they would still fail to provide an explanation for at least three quarters of the phenomena connected with the belief in super-

natural beings. Nobody, so far as I know, has claimed
that the quarrels of the gods in the *Iliad* were divinely re-
vealed to Homer.

Passing over the kings and heroes for a moment, we
come to the miraculous elements in our narratives. It may
be said that miracles never happen, but that does not explain the important fact, which is that they are believed
to happen. Further than that, an occurrence is never considered miraculous unless it is believed to be due to the
action either of a supernatural being or of a human being
endowed with supernatural power, and unless it is believed
to have a significant effect upon the fortunes of human
beings. An earthquake is in itself not a miracle; it becomes
a miracle when it destroys the ungodly, or when the godly
have a narrow escape. In religious literature it is used
interchangeably with the word *sign,* and we often hear of
"signs and wonders." Now, a sign is essentially a prepara-
tory act, a minor wonder performed as a preliminary to a
major wonder. In my view, this sign is the ritual act. It
seems to me, that is to say, that when an African rain-
maker pours beer upon the sacred rain-stones with the
appropriate ceremonies, he is making a sign or signal to
the rain to fall.

We find here all the characteristics of a miracle; firstly,
it is performed by a person believed to be endowed with
super-human power; secondly, the end proposed is recognized as a proper one for super-human action; and,
thirdly, the ritual is the recognized means of bringing
about such action.

When we use the expression "to perform a miracle,"
we normally confuse the action of the miracle-worker with
the supposed result of that action. We are apt to think of
the miracle-worker as performing some quite impossible
action, such as turning a person into a pig. If we study
the narratives, however, we shall see that what he really
does is some quite simple action. The conjurer, the sham
miracle-worker, pretends to perform his feats by waving a
wand and saying: "Hey, presto!" but this is all that the
real miracle-worker, the ritualist, does, as a study of the
stories will show. The miracle takes place not as a direct

result of the miracle-worker's act, but as the result of a ceremony in which the miracle-worker's act is the culminating rite.

If we take the story of Cinderella and examine its miracles, we find exactly the same features present as in the rain-making rite mentioned above. In the first place the miracle-worker is a being endowed with supernatural power, the fairy godmother; secondly, the object—that is, the provision of suitable equipment for one who is herself to be a queen, a person endowed with supernatural power—is a proper object for supernatural intervention; thirdly, the fairy godmother is not supposed to be able to make something out of nothing, but must go through the proper ritual. What the beer and the sacred stones are to the rain-maker, the magic wand and the pumpkin are to her. She is, in fact, a ritual personage using ritual objects to perform ritual acts. In the same way we find that the hero, whether of myth, saga, or fairy-tale, cannot injure the monster without the magic weapons; and that nobody else can use the magic weapons to injure the monster. Against the hero with the magic weapons the monster is powerless; he falls at the first blow. That is because the hero is a ritual personage using ritual weapons to deliver a ritual blow. The machinery of the traditional miracle, far from suggesting that it is either the product of an unfettered imagination or the embellished version of a historical incident, bears witness to its ritual origin.

It is not merely myths and fairy-tales that contain these reminiscences of ritual, but the sagas, romances, and even novels which are based upon them, not to mention their verse forms, the epic, the ballad, and even the nursery rhyme. It is proper to use these terms as long as they are understood to refer to the form of the stories, and not their contents, but if people claim, as certain folklorists do, that they can tell from the form of a story whether it originated in fact, fiction, or philosophical speculation, then they have left the realm of science, if they ever were in it, for that of prejudice.

The manner in which traditional stories are transformed in romance is well described by Professor Kittredge, who shows how "supernatural creatures of the most various kinds exchange rôles with bewildering nonchalance, or are reduced to the status of robbers, knights, ladies, or other classes of ordinary mortals. The other World may appear as an island, or a castle, or a cave, or an orchard, or a fair meadow, or even the Christian hell." [1] He later tells us that the substitution of enchanted for supernatural beings is due to rationalization; "it brings the supernatural personages down to the level of humanity, and makes them thoroughly reasonable and natural creatures. . . . The process, then, is of the same kind as that by which gods became heroes, or by which animal spouses became, not real animals, but men transformed for the time into brute shape. As time goes on, however, the very idea of enchantment may itself come to seem unreasonable, and therefore an attempt is sometimes made by the story-teller to represent the strange events as due to natural causes, or to tell them as facts, with no mention of the superhuman. This kind of rationalizing is extremely common in Arthurian romance, and it frequently results in contradiction or sheer incomprehensibility." [2] The same may be said for the rationalizing of our euhemerists.

Professor Gruffydd, dealing with the story of Lleu or Llew, says that the four stages through which it has grown to its present form in the *mabinogi* can be set down as follows:

First stage: Mythology . . . —of Lugh-Lleu as a god we have considerable evidence.

Second stage: Mythology becomes history.

Third stage: Mythological history becomes folklore.

Fourth stage: Folklore is utilized to form literary tales.[3]

It is pretty certain that every old story has passed through a series of vicissitudes, and it is clearly impossi-

---

[1] G. L. Kittredge: *Gawaine and the Green Knight*, p. 77.
[2] Ibid., p. 239.
[3] W. J. Gruffydd: *Math vab Mathonwy*, p. 81; the examples which he cites are very interesting, but too long to quote.

ble to reconstruct the original form by the aid of taste alone. We can, however, say with some confidence that where we have two or more versions of the same story, the older is likely to be nearer to the mythical—that is, the ritual—type. This applies not merely to stories, but also to folk-songs and folk-customs. Dr. C. B. Lewis, after making a study of the nursery rhyme: "Where are you going to, my pretty maid?" and then of the folk-customs connected with May-day, summarizes the question as follows:

"The conclusion, then, is the same as the one we reached with regard to our nursery rhyme: the folk has neither part nor lot in the making of folklore. The source of our folksong and folk customs is religion: on the one hand Christian religion; on the other pagan. At what date in history these elements of religion turned, the one into folksong, the other into folklore, it is difficult to affirm, and indeed it is a different date in each case; but one may perhaps venture to say that it was then the religious origin of the themes in question was finally forgotten. From that moment on, the theme of our song and the details of our customs changed more rapidly than before, were even simplified or whittled down by this or that trait falling into oblivion, until they now appear as pearls of such pure loveliness that only the folk, it is thought, in a far-distant past could have conceived them. Thus folklore and folk-song, at least in the cases we have considered, turn out to be the last stage of all in an age-long evolution, and not by any means the first beginnings." [4]

This age-long evolution probably began, like most of the earlier elements of our culture, in the valleys of the Nile, the Euphrates, or the Indus. Dr. Lewis traces the songs and customs with which he deals back to south-western Asia, the culture of which was largely influenced by that of the great agricultural civilizations. In these countries the livelihood of the people depended upon the river flood, and we have good reason to believe that from very early times they were ruled, or perhaps rather reigned over, by kings whose principal duty it was to ensure by

[4] *Folk-Lore,* vol. xlvi, p. 74.

means of ritual that the floods should be punctual and adequate. The flood myths probably originated as descriptions of this ritual. But the functions of the kings were by no means limited to the production of floods; they had also to ensure the fertility of women and animals, success in war, hunting, and fishing, freedom from disease—in fact, the general prosperity of the community. This duty they discharged by means of a complex ritual, in which they pretended to destroy the old world and create a new one; the descriptions of this ritual are the creation myths, in which the flood myths are included.[5] It is obvious that the kings could not be uniformly successful, and that people would remember years in which the crops or the hunting had been better than last year or the year before. Even among ourselves vague memories of certain facts combined with misconceptions of others readily coalesce into a belief in "good old days," in which things in general were much better than they are now. Such "good old days" among ourselves are often associated with "Good Queen Bess" or "Good King Charles," but in a community without records that very small modicum of fact which among most English people passes for the history of these monarchs would be completely lost, and the Golden Age might be believed to be much more recent and much more golden.

And what do we mean when we say that Charles was a good king? We certainly do not mean that he was a good man; a good king is one whose subjects prosper, whether he is himself virtuous and kindly or not. This applies much more fully in the case of a king whose duties are purely ritual. Just as the good rain-maker is the one who induces good rain, so the good king is the king who induces good crops, good hunting, and so on. The ideal is one, not of supreme moral perfection, but of supreme functional efficiency. Vague memories of especially good kings may lead to the belief in the supremely good king. This king becomes the originator of the ritual, but not in a historical sense, because, it must be repeated, the idea

---

[5] For these see A. M. Hocart: *Kingship,* ch. xvi, and my *Jocasta's Crime,* pp. 141 ff.

of history is meaningless to the ritualist. History is what happens once, but things that happen once only are nothing to the ritualist, who is concerned only with things that are done again and again. Myth is ritual projected back into the past, not a historical past of time, but a ritual past of eternity. It is a description of what should be done by a king (priest, chief, or magician) in order to secure and maintain the prosperity of his people, told in the form of a narrative of what a hero—that is, an ideal king, etc. —once did. And not only a hero, but a heroine, for in ritual the queen is as important, or nearly as important, as the king, and a queen can ensure prosperity and also victory, though she may never go near a battle. Myths are concerned almost entirely with gods and heroes, or goddesses and heroines, because they are accounts of royal ritual.

It may be urged that if all myths are derived from the royal ritual of the Nile-Indus region, then all myths should be alike. In fact, many myths are extremely widespread; this fact has been generally realized, except by exponents of the "Aryan" theory, but has been attributed to the alleged similar working of the human mind. This theory breaks down, however, when it is realized that however widespread certain features of myth and ritual may be, other myths and rites have a distribution comparable, let us say, to that of the Moslem religion. Nobody asserts that, because we find in Java and in Nigeria men who marry four wives and pray five times a day, the human mind works naturally in the direction of four wives and five daily prayers. No belief or practice can be claimed as natural unless it is universal, and even the most widespread myths and rites are not that.

The myth varies with the ritual, and both, especially among the illiterate, tend to reflect political and economic conditions. A ritual developed among a people who both kept cattle and cultivated the soil might spread on the one hand to pastoral nomads, and on the other to cultivators who kept no cattle. One part of the ritual would then die out, and as it would, of course, not be the same part, it might come to be supposed that the two rituals were quite

independent. The beliefs that the sun drives in a chariot
and that the moon sails in a boat are both derived from
ritual, and tend to die out among people who have no
chariots or no boats, though they usually leave traces.

But the political environment is, perhaps, more important than the economic in the development or retention
of myth and ritual. The original ritual, so far as can be
judged from the general pattern, was based on the existence of a king who was killed and replaced annually. A
hundred myths describe his death and the installation of
his successor. Such a system suggests a centralized kingdom with not more than a trinity of gods, gods who represent the old king, the new king, and the queen. Extended
polytheism might be due to the rise of empires, in which
the god of the capital reigns over the gods of the other
cities, or to the existence of loose confederations, such as
that of Greece, in which Zeus is supposed to reign rather
uncertainly over a large number of other deities, just as
Agamemnon is supposed to reign rather uncertainly over
a large number of other kings and chiefs.

Thus myth and ritual, though probably derived, like
logarithms, from a common source, are, so long as they
are alive, and especially so long as they remain unwritten,
continually subject to changes induced by local conditions.
That they have remained in general so similar is evidence,
not of the similar working of the human mind, but of that
inertia which is in general its most salient characteristic.

CHAPTER XIV

MYTH AND RITUAL (*Continued*)

The theory put forward in the last chapter is part of the general theory of the diffusion of culture, over which there has been so much discussion. The protagonists have been on the one hand those who refuse to admit the possibility of diffusion, except where, as in the case of the diffusion of the Christian religion, it cannot be denied, and on the other those who have maintained that all culture was diffused in the same manner, and from the same centre.

"It would be wrong," says Sir E. A. Wallis Budge,[1] "to say that the Egyptians borrowed from the Sumerians or the Sumerians from the Egyptians, but it may be submitted that the litterati of both peoples borrowed their theological systems from some common but exceedingly ancient source." He has told us that "the similarity between the two Companies of gods is too close to be accidental," but we are bound to agree with him that the present state of our knowledge does not enable us to point to any one definite source. That there are many more similarities in the religious systems of Egypt, Mesopotamia, and Palestine, especially in connection with the divine kingship, has been shown by Professor Hooke and his colleagues in *Myth and Ritual* and *The Labyrinth*, in which a dozen learned writers show that the religious systems of those countries "possessed certain fundamental characteristics in common. They were essentially ritual religions aiming at securing the well-being of the community by the due performance of ritual actions. Each of these religions had certain rituals of central importance, and in each the central figure was the king, in whose person the fortune of the state was, so to speak, incarnate.

[1] *From Fetish to God in Ancient Egypt*, p. 155.

In each religion these rituals presented the same general pattern.

"This pattern consisted of a dramatic ritual representing the death and resurrection of the king, who was also the god, performed by priests and members of the royal family. It comprised a sacred combat, in which was enacted the victory of the god over his enemies, a triumphal procession in which the neighbouring gods took part, an enthronement, a ceremony by which the destinies of the state for the coming year were determined, and a sacred marriage.

"Together with the ritual and as an essential part of it there was always found, in some form or other, the recitation of the story whose outlines were enacted in the ritual. This was the myth, and its repetition had equal potency with the performance of the ritual. In the beginning the thing said and the thing done were inseparably united, although in the course of time they were divorced and gave rise to widely differing literary, artistic, and religious forms." [2]

I have quoted this passage here in order again to emphasize the close connection which exists between myth and ritual, and I shall now attempt to show that the myths of other countries, especially of Greece, are inexplicable except in terms of ritual, that many of them are actual descriptions of such a ritual as Professor Hooke describes, and that the accounts of the heroes are really accounts of the rites which the divine king had to perform. But whereas the existing accounts of the ritual of Egypt and Mesopotamia provide only for a pretence of killing the king, the traditions of Greece and less civilized countries point to a ritual in which the king was actually killed, either annually, at the end of some longer term, or when his strength fails, as in some parts of the world he still is.[3]

While the separation of Greek myth from Greek ritual may be due in part to the ancient philosophers, who composed allegories which, though in myth form, had no con-

[2] S. H. Hooke in *The Labyrinth,* p. v.
[3] J. G. Frazer, op. cit., vol. iv, pp. 104, etc.; C. G. Seligman: *Egypt and Negro Africa,* pp. 21 ff.

nection with ritual, it is due chiefly to modern classical scholars, who have failed to realize the close connection between Greek poetry and Greek religion, and to note that the Greek descriptive writers, such as Herodotus and Pausanias, never cite a myth except with reference to some rite or some sacred site. The completely fallacious ideas of myth which scholars derived from their purely literary studies of Homer have been extended over the world; scholars naturally "approached the myths of Egypt, Babylonia, and India in the spirit they had imbibed from their classical studies. They picked out the myths from the texts in which they were embedded, arranged them into neat systems of mythology after the fashion of Hellenistic mythologists, and threw the rest of the texts on the rubbish heap." [4]

Leaving them to be rescued by other hands, I shall now examine some of the myths of Greece, and shall begin with perhaps the best-known, that of Helen.

The story of Helen is as follows: she is the daughter of Zeus and Leda, or of Oceanus and Tethya, or of Tyndareus, or of Nemesis. She is the sister of Castor and Polydeuces, the Heavenly Twins, and is hatched from a swan's egg. She is born in various places. As a girl she is carried off by Theseus, but is rescued by her brothers while Theseus is on a visit to the underworld. On her return to Sparta she is wooed by all the great chiefs of Greece, and chooses Menelaus, in favour of whom her father or stepfather Tyndareus resigns his throne. By Menelaus she has a daughter, Hermione, who is old enough to be betrothed before the Trojan War. Helen elopes with Paris and goes with him to Troy, though in some accounts it is only her phantom that goes to Troy, while she herself remains in Egypt. After the ten years' siege and the death of Paris, she marries Deiphobus, who is killed by Menelaus. After many adventures she returns with Menelaus to Sparta, where they reign splendidly and uneventfully. Of her end there are various accounts. In one version she and Menelaus are transported alive to the Elysian Fields; in another she is expelled by her stepson

[4] A. M. Hocart in *The Labyrinth,* p. 264.

and flees to Rhodes, where she is put to death; a third
makes her end her days as the wife of Achilles.[5]

Many attempts have, of course, been made to euhe-
merize the story. Dr. Leaf says that Helen is "more than
half mythical," [6] by which he means that he can believe
that whatever suits his theories is historically true, and
treat the rest as fanciful additions. Dr. Farnell,[7] with the
incurable romanticism of most classical scholars, finds no
difficulty in believing that "a love episode should be the
cause of a great war," and speaks of lovers running away
together as if the elopement of a queen was an everyday
occurrence. I can, however, find in history no instance in
which a queen has eloped with a foreign prince, or anyone else. He fails to notice that she was carried off at least
four times, by Hermes and by a robber as well as by
Theseus and Paris.[8] The only queens who elope are the
queens of myth, such as Etain, wife of Eochaidh, King of
Ireland, and Guinevere, wife of King Arthur. The latter,
like Helen, is said to have been carried off at least four
times.[9]

There can be no reasonable doubt that this story, with
all its miracles, improbabilities, and inconsistencies, is a
myth; that is to say, it is a story which in its earlier forms
described, and in its later forms tries to combine and explain, the various features and incidents in the worship of
Helen, as it was carried on in different parts of Greece.

Perhaps the most important centre of her worship was
at Sparta. There she had a great festival at which the
maidens rode to her temple in chariots, and wore lotus
flowers in her honor. Herodotus[1] tells us how an ugly and
deformed little girl was taken to the temple of Helen by
her nurse, who stood before the image and entreated the
goddess to free the child from its deformity. A woman
appeared, stroked the child, and said that she should sur-

[5] Smith: *Classical Dictionary;* H. J. Rose, op. cit.; G. Murray,
op. cit., p. 205.
[6] *Troy,* p. 329.
[7] *Greek Hero Cults,* p. 325.
[8] G. Murray, op. cit., p. 206.
[9] E. K. Chambers: *Arthur of Britain,* p. 213.
[1] Ch. vi, p. 61.

pass all the women of Sparta in beauty, which duly came to pass.

At Rhodes she was worshipped as Helen of the Tree, and a story was told of how she had been captured by the women of Rhodes and hanged from a tree.

In Egypt, according to Herodotus,[2] she was worshipped as the foreign Aphrodite, and a story was told of how she had been taken from Paris by an Egyptian king and later handed back to Menelaus.

At Therapnæ she had a temple, where her grave was shown, and in many places trees and wells were sacred to her. She caused the appearance of light round ships (St. Elmo's fire), and was identified with a star. She also seems to have been the moon, since there are grounds for equating Helene with Selene. Further than that, it is probably from her, rather than from the insignificant Hellen, that the Hellenes get their name.

Those who think that a woman could arrive at such a pitch of glory merely because she was exceptionally beautiful and fascinating should reflect upon Cleopatra, the most beautiful and fascinating woman in history. No miracles were performed on her behalf, no temples were erected in her honour, and she owes her fame chiefly to her suicide.

It was not merely Helen, however, and other Greek heroes and heroines of the Tale of Troy who were worshipped as gods or goddesses in Greece, but the Trojan heroes and heroines as well. Hector was worshipped at Thebes, a striking fact to which we shall return later, and Kassandra, the Trojan prophetess, was worshipped at the Spartan cities of Leuctra, Amyclæ, and Therapnæ, as well as in Apulia.[3] Dr. Farnell accounts for these and many other facts connected with the worship of the Homeric heroes by supposing that the Greeks derived a large part of their religion from the *Iliad,* and cites as a parallel the development of Christian saint-worship under the influence of the sacred books.[4] But his whole case for the historicity

[2] Ch. ii, p. 112.
[3] L. R. Farnell, op. cit., pp. 410–11.
[4] L. R. Farnell, op. cit., p. 340.

of Homer is based on the assumption that the *Iliad* started
as the purely secular account of a purely secular war. I
know of no reason for supposing that anyone has ever
derived his religion from a military chronicle, however
skilfully versified.

In order to explain these facts, and the facts of Greek
mythology in general, we shall have to get far from the
romantic rationalizations of Dr. Farnell and his school,
into the atmosphere of ritual. I shall try to convey an idea
of what this atmosphere really is by quoting Professor
Gronbech, who by his exposition of the Norse myths gives
us perhaps as good an idea as possible of what the Homeric poems originally were.

"The poet," he says, "gives his narrative in the past
form as if it were something over and done with. . . .
But the literary form which the myths acquired in the
hands of the poets during the Viking Age and later obscures the actual meaning that was plain to the listeners,
when the legends were recited at the feast, and illustrated,
or rather supplemented, by rites and ceremonial observ-
ances. . . . The legends will not tell us what happened in
some year or other according to chronology; in our crav-
ing for a kernel of historical truth in the myths, we
naïvely insinuate that the myth-makers ought to think in
a system unknown to them for the benefit of our annalistic
studies. . . . Time is, in our experience, a stream of
events descending from the unknown mists of beginning
and running in a continuous flow down the future into the
unknown; to the men of the classical ages the actual life
is the result of a recurrent beginning and has its source in
the religious feast. The festival consists of a creation or
new birth outside time, eternal it might be called if the
word were not as misleading as all others and as inadequate to describe an experience of a totally alien character. When the priest or chieftain ploughs the ritual furrow,
when the first seed is sown while the story of the origin
of corn is recited, when the warriors act the war game,
they make history, do the real work, fight the real battle,
and when the men sally forth with the plough or the seed

or the weapons, they are only realizing what was created in the ritual act.

"Ceremonial forms are the stream of life itself, not narrowing banks against which life grinds its passage. They are solemn because they are necessary. . . . To go with the sun, to grow and let grow with the moon, to carry out the ritual whereby kinship, whether with men or with nature, is strengthened and renewed, whereby the sun is held to its course and earth and heaven preserve their youth and strength, to effect honour and luck, to give the child its name-gift, to drink the cup of brotherhood—this is to live. It is forms which divide the living from the dead.

"Not only the future needed creation, the past too had to be renewed in the *blot* [sacrifice] to retain its reality. The eternity of life lay not in the fact that it had once begun, but solely in the fact that it was constantly being begun, so that the blotman's sacrifice points back as well as forward. In order to do justice to the meaning of the *blot* we must say that it not only condenses and renews the past, but in true earnest creates it over and over again. . . . Now we shall be able to look for the gods where they are really to be found. They are present as power in the events and power in the sacrificers. . . . The reciter and the ritual agent is no less the subject of the poem than the original hero himself, and no less responsible for the happy issue of his enterprise. . . .

"In the history of the sacrificial hall, the individual warrior is sunk in the god, or, which is the same thing, in the ideal personification of the clan, the hero. This form of history causes endless confusion among later historians, when they try their best to arrange the mythical traditions into chronological happenings, and the deeds of the clan into annals and lists of kings, and the confusion grows to absurdity when rationalistic logicians strive by the light of sound sense to extricate the kernel of history from the husks of superstition." [5]

[5] W. Gronbech: *The Culture of the Teutons*, vol. i, p. 249; vol. ii, pp. 106–7, 222, 223, 226, 240, 261.

This view was not confined to the Norse, but was, according to Professor Hooke,[6] general in the ancient world. The cyclic movement of the seasons and the heavenly bodies, together with the ritual system associated with them, "inevitably tended to produce a view of Time as a vast circle in which the pattern of the individual life and of the course of history was a recurring cyclic process." This view of time as a ritual circle seems to have been carried over into Christianity, since, according to Professor James,[7] "in the Eucharistic sacrifice the redemptive work of Christ was celebrated, not as a mere commemoration of a historical event, for in the liturgy the past became the present, and the birth at Bethlehem and the death on Calvary were apprehended as ever-present realities independent of time and space."

It is difficult for those who regard rites and ceremonies as desirable but not indispensable aids to the attainment of certain religious or social ends to understand the attitude f those to whom ritual means life, life in the social as well as in the religious sense. Ritual is far more to millions today than history has ever been to anyone. To all savages religion is ritual, and nothing more, and to most members of the higher religions ritual is far more important than either belief or ethics. People become, and remain, members of religious bodies (and social bodies such as the Freemasons) by performing ritual acts and uttering ritual words. As long as there is nothing novel about these acts and words, nobody troubles about their meaning. That is theology, a matter for the priests; and the chief, almost the sole, object of *their* study is to convince themselves that what they do or direct is right; that is to say, that the ritual and myth are in perfect agreement. Belief in the unity of myth and ritual is what we now call Fundamentalism, and a Fundamentalist is a person to whom the historical past is of no importance compared with the ritual past that is described in the myth. Adam really lived because he lives now—in the ritual. Criticism of the

[6] *The Labyrinth*, p. 215.
[7] *Christian Myth and Ritual*, p. 268.

myth implies criticism of the ritual; hence the indignation of the Fundamentalists at anyone who fails to begin his history of the world with the myth of Adam. The ancient Greeks, who were, with the exception of a handful of philosophers, all Fundamentalists, had no cause to complain of their historians, since these all started their works by paying due respect to the myths, particularly the myth of Troy. They then made a big jump; according to the usual theories it was a jump of six or seven centuries, but it was really a jump from pure myth to history, though their history is not free from mythical elements. The reasons for this are firstly that there were no records upon which they could rely, and secondly that their object was not to build up a solid structure of knowledge of the past which should be available for the future, but merely interest and edify their contemporaries.[8]

The object of the poets was different. It was to combine into more or less coherent stories, and to make available for large audiences, the myths that were periodically enacted or otherwise handed on at the myriad temples and shrines of Greece. Professor Nilsson complains of "that disregard for history and geography which is peculiar to epic poetry," [9] but they were not concerned with history at all, and as for geography, it was merely a question of what would pass muster; their audiences would accept Ithaca as a large and fertile island, just as Shakespeare's would accept Bohemia as a country on the sea coast.

As for the temple myths, out of which, in all probability, the epics were composed, even those who believe in the historicity of tradition realize their ritual origin. Thus Professor Halliday says that "the story of Lycaon, connected as it undoubtedly was with some form of human sacrifice which seems to have persisted up to the time of Pausanias, is an hieratic legend connected with the savage ritual of Lycæan Zeus, appears to me almost certain. The story of the serving up of Pelops by Tantalus may also have had a ritual origin and have been in the first

<hr/>

[8] G. G. Murray, op. cit., p. 2.
[9] Op. cit., p. 118.

place connected with some rite of human sacrifice and sacrament." [1]

Professor Cook refers the legend of Ixion, who was bound to a wheel, to a ritual in which a man was bound to a wheel and sacrificed in the character of the sun-god, and the legend of Triptolemus, who was borne over the earth in a winged chariot, from which he introduced the blessings of corn, to a rite at Eleusis; "the *protégé* of the goddess, mounting his winged seat, was swung aloft by means of a *géranos* or scenic crane." [2] And Professor Hooke[3] says that "both the Minotaur and Perseus myths involve an underlying pattern of human sacrifice, and take us back to a stage when myth and ritual were united."

In spite of his views on Lycaon and the Lycæan Zeus, Professor Halliday assures us that "we may assume with some certainty that a person about whom a legend was told was not a fictitious character, but a real person who once existed." [4] This is a striking example of the self-contradictions into which those who seek to establish the historicity of tradition inevitably fall. These contradictions can be resolved only by supposing that the Greeks were meticulous antiquaries who preserved through the centuries the facts of their history with the most scrupulous accuracy, and at the same time that they were people of the wildest imagination, who invented the most ridiculous stories about their ancestors, and believed in them as soon as they had invented them. And through all this haze of pseudo-history and pseudo-fiction we can see, not clearly, yet clearly enough, the Greeks for what they really were: a highly religious people, for whom the past existed, as for the vast majority of the human race it still exists, solely in the ritual. In the light of this fact, for I venture to assert categorically that it is a fact, let us return to the Tale of Troy.

[1] Op. cit., p. 103.
[2] Op. cit., vol. i, pp. 211, 218.
[3] In *Myth and Ritual*, p 6.
[4] Op. cit., p. 61.

CHAPTER XV

MYTH AND RITUAL:
THE TALE OF TROY

The scientific, as contrasted with the literary, study of the Homeric poems has hardly yet begun, and cannot take us very far until a sufficient number of students has realized that the poems have no historical foundation, but that as documents illustrating the development of religious ideas and beliefs they are of the highest importance. It is impossible for one who, like myself, is neither a Greek nor a German scholar (for there is much untranslated matter on this subject in German) to do more than try to point out the direction that in my belief these studies will take.

We must first try to form a picture of Greece as it really was about 700 B.C. It was in some respects analogous to England in A.D. 600; that is to say, it was occupied by tribes of barbarians who had blotted out an ancient civilization and were themselves beginning to be civilized through alien influence. Of the Greeks, as of the Saxons, we know nothing from historical, and little from archæological, sources of the origin and history of these tribes, but of the Greeks we know much less than we do of the Saxons, for the period of darkness is much longer, and we have nothing to correspond with the late classical literature. There is this other difference: that whereas the Saxons never progressed very far along the path of civilization, a very small proportion of the Greeks rapidly reached a pitch of intellectual eminence which has rarely been rivalled. That this progress was extremely rapid, and that it was based upon alien elements, are shown not merely by the known facts of contemporary and earlier Asiatic culture, but by the manners and customs of the generality of the Greeks, which up to the end of the classical period were still almost incredibly barbarous.

About 700 B.C., then, when we first begin to know something of the Greeks, we find a small educated class making, under the most favourable social and political conditions, the most phenomenal progress from a foundation of thought and knowledge which was entirely non-Greek, and a vast majority of illiterates, who knew nothing, and could know nothing, of their past history, but who were largely absorbed in their religion. This religion, though one in origin, and generally similar in ritual, had retained or acquired varying features in the more or less isolated cities, islands, and rural valleys; it consisted in the sacrificial worship of "heroes" at local shrines, combined with group meetings at highly sacred sites for the periodical performance of more important or more generalized rites. There were in historical times a number of these group meetings, at Delphi, at Olympia, at Delos, at Dodona, at Mycale, and elsewhere, the rites at which, especially the games and contests, suggest developments or survivals from a different state of society, a state in which the kingship played a highly important part. The type of kingship suggested by these rites, and by the survivals of the kingship in historical Greece, such as that of the archon at Athens, who was called the "king," and the extremely limited monarchy at Sparta, is a kingship of a purely ritual character. There is a great deal to suggest that the winners at the games were the successors of kings who became kings as the result of success in a ritual contest, and that in prehistoric Greece—that is, Greece before about 700 B.C.—kings were purely ritual figures, regarded as the personification of Zeus, and liable to be sacrificed at the end of a fixed period, which Sir James Frazer finds grounds for believing to have been eight years.[1] This aspect of the kingship, as I hope to show, is implicit in Homer and the rest of the myths, but taken as historical documents, they give a very different picture.

The kings of Homer, taken literally, are not in the

[1] Op. cit., vol. iv, pp. 58, 87; also vol. ii, p. 177.

Greek sense kings at all, but tyrants who gain their thrones by successful adventure and whose powers are limited only by their capacity for exercising them. Now, the ritual kingship as we find it in the fifth century B.C. is merely a survival represented by a number of rites and institutions, all of them more or less in a state of decay. If Homer wrote history, we must then suppose that after his time the type of kingship which was familiar to him disappeared and was succeeded by a very different type, which had time to rise, thrive, and decay before the fifth century; and that the Greeks of the latter period had forgotten almost everything about the later type of kingship, but had preserved a vivid recollection of the earlier.

All the difficulties, including those set out in Chapter IX, disappear when we realize that the Homeric poems, or rather the songs and stories out of which they were composed, are myths—that is, ritual narratives, connected with one or more of the group meetings mentioned above —and that the ritual performed at these meetings was very similar to, if not identical with, the ritual pattern described by Professor Hooke.[2] It may be remembered that the principal features of this ritual are the death and resurrection of the king, a sacred combat, a triumphal procession and enthronement, and a sacred marriage; and the difference I suggested was that in Greece the actual killing of the king survived longer than in the more civilized countries to the south and east. However this may be, there is, as we have seen, evidence that the kingship in prehistoric Greece was a temporary office, and that the kings were either actually killed or else reinstated after a pretended death, at the end of eight years. Now, in Greek the eight-year period was called a nine-year period, since both the first and last years were included,[3] and we find that in the Tale of Troy all the important incidents take place in the first and tenth years of the siege, and that in the mythological cycles, especially those of Troy and Thebes, all the important events are represented as taking place at inter-

[2] *Supra,* p. 150.
[3] J. G. Frazer, op. cit., vol. iv, p. 59 n.

vals of about ten years. But if the ritual king's reign is eight years, his ritual life is longer, since, as we shall see later, the most important events in it take place before he is actually installed. This may explain the discrepancy between the eight- and the nine- or ten-year periods, since, as we must always bear in mind, these periods are ritual— that is to say, recurrent and not historical.

The question now arises whether these rites were actually performed at Troy and at Thebes, and the probability on the whole seems to be that they were, and that the two rituals were identical. There are many resemblances between the stories of Troy and Thebes. Both were built where a cow lay down. Both were unsuccessfully attacked, but ten years later stormed and razed to the ground. According to Hesiod, all the heroes of Greece were killed at one or the other. The Greek fleet that is to attack Troy meets at Aulis, a place most inconvenient for this purpose, but most convenient for an attack on Thebes, of which it is the port. Hector is a leading hero of both cities. Whether these and other resemblances are due to the partial combination of two different stories or the splitting up of what was one original story is not certain, but the latter seems more probable when we realize how easily mythical incidents can be located at actual places, and also transferred from one place to another. There is no difficulty about this, for, as we have seen in the stories of Robin Hood and other heroes, the place where the ritual is performed becomes the place where the incidents of the myth originally occurred.

We find a good example of this in Java. The war of the *Pandawa*, which forms the subject of the great Indian epic, the *Mahabharata,* is also the subject of the most popular Javanese poem, and the war is believed by the Javanese to have taken place in Java; "not only the countries mentioned in that war, but the dwelling-places and temples of the different heroes who distinguished themselves in it, are at the present day pointed out in Java." [4] The ritualistic attitude towards the past which could transfer all the sites and incidents of a mythical war from India

[4] T. S. Raffles: *History of Java,* vol. ii, p. 76.

to Java could transfer all the sites and incidents of a mythical war from Asia to Troy or Thebes.

What probably happened was that when the later forms of this kingship ritual were introduced into Greece, they were at first associated by the small independent tribes with the myths of their own gods or heroes, and that later attempts were made to combine these myths into one story. This seems to have happened in Palestine, where the origin of circumcision ritual was attributed to three different heroes, Abraham, Moses, and Joshua.[5]

The principal attempt to combine the myths of Greece into one story was, of course, made by Homer. And who was Homer? Homer, so Professor J. A. K. Thomson tells us, was the title given to the victor in the conquest of minstrelsy held at the festival of Apollo at Delos. He was the eponymous hero of the hymn-singers and sacred dancers, and was originally identical with the Delian Apollo.[6] "The hymn," Professor Thomson continues,[7] "has given birth to the heroic epos. For these 'men and women' are the old local Daimones—Achilles, Helen, and the rest. Their legends have combined to form one great legend recited at the Delian festival in honour of Apollo the Father god of all the Ionians. . . . The hymn gradually added to itself more and more of the inherited or borrowed legends of the Ionian race until it grew into the proportions of all 'Homer.' And as Homer was the traditional author of the original hymn, so he remained the traditional author of all the rest."

Yet although the Homeric poems are concerned almost entirely with the doings of gods and worshipped heroes, and although in classical times the poems were, as Professor Thomson shows, sacred poems recited at sacred festivals, yet most classical scholars are so obsessed by their literary aspect that they become quite incapable of realizing their religious character. Thus Professor Nilsson holds that "the return and vengeance of Odysseus is not

[5] E. O. James in *Myth and Ritual*, p. 152. A similar phenomenon in America is described by Professor R. H. Lowie in the *American Anthropologist*, vol. 16, p. 107.

[6] *Studies in the Odyssey*, pp. 205, 207, 224.

[7] Ibid., p. 229.

an heroic legend but a novel," [8] and even Professor Gilbert
Murray regards the poems as "elaborate works of fiction." [9]
As usual, these writers hover precariously between the
fact theory and the fiction theory, but can they really believe that people compose fictitious tales about the gods
they worship, and recite these tales at sacred festivals?

Mr. Burn[1] says that "Andromache is almost certainly
a creation of the poet's brain. Her and her husband's function in the poem is simply to supply a foil to the other
characters." But again let us turn to Java, and there we
find in the sacred epic, which is of Hindu origin, a general
similarity to the Tale of Troy, and parallels to many of
its characters and incidents. In particular the account of
the parting of Salia from his wife Satia Wati and his
subsequent death bears a striking resemblance to the account of Hector's parting from Andromache and his subsequent death.[2]

That the hero king, at the conclusion of his tenure of
office, normally goes out of the city to be killed we shall
see in the next chapter; it may well be that a ceremonial
parting from his consort formed part of the ritual in
Greece and Java as it did in Mexico, where the man who
took the part of the "god of gods" bade farewell to his
consorts at a fixed spot before ascending the pyramid at
the top of which he was to meet his doom.[3] Here again
we must emphasize that what has to be explained is not
the fact that a man should bid farewell to his wife before
going to his death, but that such an incident should form
part of a sacred poem. The idea that the subject-matter
of hymns is drawn from domestic scenes, real or fictitious,
is erroneous.

Let us now try to get a more general idea of the ritual
of which this scene formed a part. Mr. W. F. J. Knight[4]

[8] Op. cit., p. 137.
[9] Op. cit., p. 231.
[1] Op. cit., p. 18.
[2] R. S. Raffles, op. cit., vol. i, p. 510. The parallel is mine.
[3] J. G. Frazer, op. cit., vol. ix, p. 279.
[4] In *Folk-Lore,* vol. xlvi, p. 106.

notes that the name of Troy is widely associated with mazes or labyrinths, and that various incidents in the *Iliad* correspond with known features of a once widespread maze ritual, and says that "the goddess or one of the heroines of Troy corresponds to the maiden who stays in the nucleus of a maze during a maze ritual, or to the princess who is united to a hero in northern myths after he has penetrated to the heart of a mountain, sometimes by the aid of a magic horse." He goes on to show that ring magic and armed dances are connected both with fertility and with military defence. The wooden horse is then a ritual beast akin to Pegasus and Sigurd's horse Grani, and is not, as has been absurdly supposed, a genuine military stratagem.

The *Iliad* is, then, on Mr. Knight's showing, an account of a ritual that includes a sacred combat and a sacred marriage. But there is much more in the Homeric poems than this. Professor Hocart gives a list of twenty-six features that characterize the ceremonies attendant on the installation of kings in all parts of the world. I believe that all of these are to be found in the Homeric poems, but the search would occupy a large volume, and I shall be content to touch on two which he includes in his list and one which he does not. He begins his list with "(A) The theory is "that the King (1) dies; (2) is reborn, (3) as a god." [5] In Fiji during a chief's installation the same ceremonies are observed as at his death, and after his installation he is nursed as a new-born babe for four days. In ancient India, according to the scriptures, the officiating priest invested the new king with garments called "the caul of sovereignty" and "the womb of sovereignty," and "thereby caused him to be born." In Egypt the Pharaoh is shown on monuments being suckled by the wife of the principal god. [6] In these cases the ceremonies of death and resurrection and rebirth are symbolized, but at Umundri, in Nigeria, the rite is performed more literally. There,

---

[5] *Kingship*, p. 70.
[6] Ibid., pp. 74, 77, 84.

according to Mr. Jeffreys,[7] the officiating priest says to
the candidate for the kingship: "You are about to enter the
grave; rise up again with a vivid and shining body." The
candidate is then prepared for burial in the usual way, and
buried in a grave dug outside his own house. His wives
wail and the usual mourning ceremonies are performed. At
sunset he is dug up, washed, and whitened all over with
clay, and thus fulfils the prayer that he should rise with
a white and shining body. Henceforth he is regarded as a
god. We can now understand why heroes visit the underworld, the dwelling-place of the dead. They do so in order
that they may return from the dead as gods. Odysseus,
therefore, visits the dead as part of his progress to the
divine kingship, and Heracles, Theseus, Orpheus, and
Dionysos do the same. I may add that according to Mr.
Knight[8] "the Latin word *inire,* the origin of our word
'initiation,' has been thought with reason to have been
directly used for ritual entry into the earth, as in sacrificial
burials."

After the king has been installed, he makes a tour of
his dominions, always starting from the east and following
the course of the sun, and at each of the four quarters
receiving the homage of vassals. According to the Buddhist
scriptures, a king, when he has performed this rite, becomes a "wheel monarch." [9] In the other rituals discussed
by Professor Hocart the rite has become a mere procession
round the city, like our Lord Mayor's Show, which, of
course, follows his installation. It would seem, however,
that Dhu'l Qarnein, the Two-horned One of the Qurân,
was also a "wheel-monarch," [1] as was Dermot, King of
Ireland, who "on his regal circuit travelled right-handed
round Ireland," and after visiting the four provinces re-
turned to Tara.[2] These were inland kings, but the king of
the Ægean must have made his progress by sea, and the

---

[7] M. D. W. Jeffreys, in a paper read to the International
Congress of Anthropology, 1934.

[8] Loc. cit., p. 107.

[9] A. M. Hocart, *Kingship,* p. 23.

[1] Qurân, sura xviii, 83 ff.

[2] S. H. O'Grady: *Silva Gadelica,* p. 86.

Odyssey, though it has had other ritual features incorporated in it, would seem to be in the main an account of such a progress. The story of Sinbad the Sailor perhaps embodies a similar myth, the ritual aspect of which seems to have found its last expression in the voyages of the Areoi, the guilds of sacred actors of Polynesia.

One of the most important duties of the divine king is to rekindle the sacred fire. This rite is still performed annually at Jerusalem, though not by the normal method, which is to rotate a pointed piece of hard wood in a hole made in a piece of soft wood. In this form the rite is almost world-wide. Professor A. B. Cook[3] adduces much evidence to suggest that the story of how Odysseus plunged his heated bar into the Cyclops' eye is derived from a fire-making rite, and that his title of "Ithakos," which has led to the belief that he came from the island of Ithaka, may be equivalent to "Ithax," which is an alternative name for Prometheus, and means "the fiery one." Just as "Odysseus" is the king's cult title in his character of the wolf-god,[4] so may "Ithakos" be his cult title in his capacity as kindler of the sacred fire.

It would be possible, and indeed easy, to find parallels in myth and ritual for every incident in the Odyssey, but those given should be enough to convince any person of open mind that there is a great deal more in it than meets the eye. No argument can make any impression on the minds of the orthodox scholars, who refuse to look outside the text and are content to believe that Odysseus was a real man, whose exploits gave rise to his fame, and whose fame stimulated a blind man to invent his exploits.

There is one phenomenon that actually connects "the holy town of Ilium," which, though a foreign town, was loved by Zeus, the god of the Greeks, "above all cities and all nations of the earth," [5] but which he nevertheless allowed to be destroyed, with the historic city near the entrance to the Hellespont—the affair of the Locrian maidens.

[3] Op. cit., vol. i, p. 327.
[4] J. A. K. Thomson, op. cit., p. 16.
[5] *Iliad*, vi, p. 448.

Every year, from prehistoric times down to 200 B.C., and probably later, the Locrians, a people whose chief town was Opous, about twenty miles north of Thebes, sent a tribute of two noble maidens to Troy, or Ilium as it was then known. The citizens of Ilium met them and attempted to kill them, but usually without success, since they were guarded by a body of their fellow country-men, who smuggled them through an underground passage into the Temple of Athena. Once there, they were safe, but lived for a year a despised and degraded life as temple slaves, after which they were replaced, but were con-demned to perpetual celibacy. On the rare occasions when one of the maidens was slain, her slayer received the thanks of the citizens, and her body was destroyed by a particular ritual. The Locrians made frequent attempts to rid them-selves of this burden, but were always threatened by the Delphic oracle with disaster.

The explanation of this remarkable proceeding given in classical times was that it was a punishment imposed upon the Locrians for the conduct of their great cult-hero, Aias Oileus, who at the sack of Troy had violated Kassandra in the Temple of Athena. Dr. Farnell, of course, accepts this story as historically true, and in so doing misses its whole point. "No incident was more likely," he says,[6] "than that a certain Greek leader should have violated the purity of a temple." But the incident, far from being "likely," is represented as unparalleled; that is why, accord-ing to the story, it received a unique punishment. Professor Nilsson also fails to realize that the whole proceeding was unique, since he suggests[7] that Locris was a colony of Troy, and appears to suppose that annual tribute of maidens from a colony to the mother city was normal.

Now we must note in the first place that the whole procedure was sacrificial; the maidens, if not killed, went through a rite of pretence burial, from which they emerged as vestals. This rite has no connection whatever with the alleged crime of Aias, but is connected with another myth, that of the theft of the Palladium by Odysseus and Dio-

[6] Op. cit., p. 301.
[7] *Iliad*, vi, p. 46.

medes, who were said to have entered Troy by the same underground passage.[8] Secondly, it seems that the name "Oileus" is closely connected with "Ilion," [9] so that Aias, whose second name it was, may be suspected of being the eponymous hero of Ilium, while Kassandra, like Athens, was a city-goddess, and may be identical with her. It may be added that Pausanias describes a very similar ritual at Athens.[1]

We know from what Professor Hocart[2] tells us that the installation of a king normally includes a sacred marriage and a human sacrifice, and I suggest that of the two maidens, who were always drawn from the alleged descendants of Aias, one was originally the divine bride and the other the divine victim. Anyhow, we know that Aias had an elaborate cult in Locris, and on the supposition that he was a real man we must conclude that the Locrians, looking back through the long centuries of their history, could find no citizen worthy of honour except a second-rate buccaneer whose infamous conduct had brought upon them eternal injury and disgrace.

Dr. Farnell's belief that personalities can be vividly remembered for eight hundred years or more is astonishing, since he must have realized how little we know, even assuming tradition to be true, of Greek prehistory. Did he really believe that during a period of at least four centuries there was nobody in Greece who possessed a personality? Of course he could not have, but like most classical scholars he had been so thoroughly soaked in the belief that tradition is history that any other view of it was inconceivable. And even those scholars who have realized that tradition in its main features is myth are ready to jump back to pseudo-history on the smallest provocation. Thus Miss Jessie Weston, in her *From Ritual to Romance,* after dealing with a large group of Grail stories, concludes that these stories "repose eventually, not upon a poet's imagination, but upon the ruins of an august and

[8] W. F. J. Knight in *Folk-Lore,* vol. xlvi, p. 101 n.
[9] L. R. Farnell, op. cit., p. 302.
[1] I. xxvii, 3.
[2] Op. cit., p. 71.

ancient ritual, a ritual which once claimed to be the ac-
credited guardian of the deepest secrets of life." [3] Yet she
supposes that certain historical incidents have crept into
these narratives. For example, the story of how King
Amangens outraged one of the Grail maidens and took her
golden Cup from her, in which action he was imitated
by his knights, may be the record "of an outrage offered
by some, probably local, chieftain to a priestess of the
cult." [4] Yet this story is clearly analogous to that of Aias
and Kassandra, which we have just been discussing. And
the story of how Ghaus, a squire of King Arthur, dreams
of taking a golden candlestick from a chapel in the forest,
and of being attacked by an ugly black man, and awakes
to find himself mortally wounded, may have 'made a profound impression on the popular imagination owing to the
youth and possible social position of the victim." [5] Victim
of what? Miss Weston failed to realize that accounts of
isolated outrages do not find their way into ancient and
august rituals, and that successful breaches of taboo, far
from being recorded, are ignored and their very possibility
denied.

Mr. Nutt tells us that "the development of the mythical
literature connected with the Tuatha de Danann may now
be safely sketched. Originally, it doubtless consisted wholly
of chants forming part of the ritual, and of legends ac-
counting for and interpreting ritual acts." [6] Yet even Mr.
Nutt, as we saw,[7] thought that there might be some historical foundation for the Irish myths. How could legends
that account for and interpret ritual acts have a historical
basis?

Hartland, again, realized that "the ceremony at Coventry
is a survival of an annual rite in honour of a heathen goddess, from which men were excluded." [8] The ceremony to

[3] J. Weston: *From Ritual to Romance,* p. 176.
[4] Ibid., p. 163.
[5] Ibid., p. 171.
[6] A. Nutt: *The Voyage of Bran,* vol. ii, p. 194.
[7] *Supra,* p. 95.
[8] Op. cit., p. 92.

which he refers is, of course, that associated with the name of Lady Godiva, and was probably similar to that at Banbury, where a fine lady rode on a white horse. Yet he postulates a different origin for many stories of the same type.

Similarly MacCulloch, who, as we saw,[9] attributes so many traditional tales to imagination, realizes that some myths are connected with ritual. "Some of these," he says of the Algonquin stories,[1] "are myths, and in this group we have those which are recited at the initiation of candidates . . . as well as some which are not now recited, but are believed to have formed part of the sacred ritual long ago. All form part of a mythological cycle dealing with the life of the hero-divinity, Manabush." The Homeric poems are also mythological cycles dealing with the lives of hero-divinities, but nothing arouses the fury of our scholars so much as the suggestion that these cycles are founded upon ritual. It is scarcely an exaggeration to say that in their view the Tale of Troy is a sober record of historic fact, composed entirely of scraps of picturesque fiction.

There is nothing in Homer that we cannot find elsewhere; "in other poems we observe the ancient ritual underlying poetical composition, as the substratum on which the poets have moulded a literary form; when for instance the Eddaic description of Sigurd's dragon-killing and wooing of the sleeping woman in armour culminates in a ritual toast . . . the succession of the scenes is probably governed by the procedure of the feast. . . . Thor's voyage to the giant Geirrod is really a description of the ritual journey of the sacrificer and his assistants to the cattle-fold, and their procedure there." [2]

With this we may compare the opinion of Professor Saintyves, who holds that the magical transformations in Hop-o'-My-Thumb and similar tales are really *étapes coutumières* in the initiation ceremony, and that ogre,

[9] *Supra*, p. 129.
[1] Op. cit., p. 460.
[2] W. Gronbech, op. cit., vol. ii, pp. 229, 274.

giant, devil, dragon, troll, sorcerer, and cannibal are merely
titles for a liturgical personage, the tempter or terrifying
devil of the initiations.[3]

As in the myth, the epic, the saga, and the fairy-tale,
so also in the ballad we find that the basis is ritual. "The
earliest form of the ballad in France seems to have been
a little wooing-dance acted as a sort of May-game and
originating in the ritual wedding. There are great numbers
of such wooing-dances in Sweden and Denmark. . . . A
Danish ballad even remembers the significance of the ritual;
Ridder Stig drinks to his lady-love so that 'field and wood
blossom there at.' " [4]

[3] Op. cit., pp. 275, 303.
[4] B. S. Phillpotts, op. cit., pp. 200, 202.

CHAPTER XVI

THE HERO

In the earlier chapters of this book I took a succession of well-known heroes of tradition, and attempted to show that there is no justification for believing that any of these heroes were real persons, or that any of the stories of their exploits had any historical foundation. In the course of the discussion I had frequent occasion to suggest that these heroes, if they were genuinely heroes of tradition, were originally not men but gods, and that the stories were accounts not of fact but of ritual—that is, myths. As my chief object in those chapters was, however, to show that the heroes had no claim to historicity, I made no attempt to link them, or the beliefs connected with them, to any general ritual scheme. Before so doing, it seemed desirable to demonstrate, both theoretically and by examples, the intimate association of myth with ritual, an association that has been recognized by many leading students of these subjects, and upon which depends the validity of the conclusions I have reached.

Some years ago I had occasion to study the myth of Œdipus, and to try to analyse it,[1] and I was struck by the similarity of many of the incidents in it to incidents in the stories of Theseus and Romulus. I then examined the stories of a number of other traditional heroes of Greece, and found that when these stories were split up into separate incidents, there were certain types of incident which ran through all the stories.

Whether these parallels have any significance, or whether they are merely coincidences, the sort of thing that might happen to or be readily invented about any hero, are ques-

[1] *Vide* my *Jocasta's Crime.*

tions to which we shall come later. My first task is to show
that the parallels exist, and for that purpose it is necessary
to tabulate and number them. What I have done is to take
a dozen heroes whose stories are narrated in sufficient
detail, to tabulate the incidents in their careers, and to
regard as typical such incidents as occur in the majority
of the stories. By tabulating these typical incidents, I have
arrived at what appears to be a pattern, in which I include
all incidents, whether they are miraculous or whether they
seem insignificant, which occur with sufficient regularity.
I have then fitted the pattern back on to my dozen heroes
and, finding that it fits, have extended it to a number of
heroes from outside the classical area, with what have
been to me surprising results.

I should like it to be quite clear that in the potted biographies which follow there is no intention of giving a
complete account of the heroes. Irrelevant incidents and
alternative versions are omitted, and no attempt is made
to distinguish between genuine mythology—that is, mythology connected with ritual—and the imitation mythology
which probably forms a large part of the stories of Arthur
and of Romulus. The wearing of an imitation sword may
be just as significant as the wearing of a real one, and it
is with the uniform of the heroes and not with their out-
fitters that I am at present concerned.

The pattern, then, is as follows:

(1) The hero's mother is a royal virgin;

(2) His father is a king, and

(3) Often a near relative of his mother, but

(4) The circumstances of his conception are unusual, and

(5) He is also reputed to be the son of a god.

(6) At birth an attempt is made, usually by his
father or his maternal grandfather, to kill him, but

(7) He is spirited away, and

(8) Reared by foster-parents in a far country.

(9) We are told nothing of his childhood, but

(10) On reaching manhood he returns or goes to
his future kingdom.

(11) After a victory over the king and/or a giant, dragon, or wild beast,

(12) He marries a princess, often the daughter of his predecessor, and

(13) Becomes king.

(14) For a time he reigns uneventfully, and

(15) Prescribes laws, but

(16) Later he loses favour with the gods and/or his subjects, and

(17) Is driven from the throne and city, after which

(18) He meets with a mysterious death,

(19) Often at the top of a hill.

(20) His children, if any, do not succeed him.

(21) His body is not buried, but nevertheless

(22) He has one or more holy sepulchres.

Let us now apply this pattern to our heroes, and we will start with

ŒDIPUS

His mother, Jocasta, is (1) a princess, and his father is (2) King Laius, who, like her, is (3) of the line of Cadmus. He has sworn to have no connection with her, but (4) does so when drunk, probably (5) in the character of Dionysos. Laius (6) tries to kill Œdipus at birth, but (7) he is spirited away, and (8) reared by the King of Corinth. (9) We hear nothing of his childhood, but (10) on reaching manhood he returns to Thebes, after (11) gaining victories over his father and the Sphinx. He (12) marries Jocasta, and (13) becomes king. For some years he (14) reigns uneventfully, but (16) later comes to be regarded as the cause of a plague, and (17) is deposed and driven into exile. He meets with (18) a mysterious death at (19) a place near Athens called the Steep Pavement. He is succeeded by (20) Creon, through whom he was deposed, and though (21) the place of his burial is uncertain, he has (22) several holy sepulchres.

He does not seem to have been regarded as a legislator; apart from that we may award him full marks.

THESEUS

His mother, Æthra, is (1) a royal virgin, and his father is (2) King Ægeus, who is (4) induced to have intercourse with her by a trick. He is also (5) reputed to be the son of Poseidon. At birth he is hidden from the Pallantidæ, who (6) wish to kill him, and (8) reared by his maternal grandfather. We hear (9) nothing of his childhood, but on reaching manhood he (10) proceeds to Athens, (11) killing monsters on the way. He marries (12) several heiress princesses, but (13) succeeds to the kingdom of his father, whose death he (11) causes. For a time (14) he reigns peacefully, and (15) prescribes laws, but later (16) becomes unpopular, is driven (17) from Athens, and (18) is thrown or falls from (19) a high cliff. His supplanter, Menestheus, is (20) no relation. His burial-place is (21) unknown, but bones supposed to be his are placed in (22) a holy sepulchre at Athens.

He scores twenty.

ROMULUS

His mother, Rhea, is (1) a royal virgin, and his father is (2) King Amulius, who is (3) her uncle, and (4) visits her in armour. He is also (5) reputed to be the son of Mars. At birth (6) his father tries to kill him, but (7) he is wafted away, and (8) reared by foster-parents at a distance. On reaching manhood he (10) returns to his birthplace, and having (11) killed his father and gained a magical victory over his brother, he (12) founds Rome and becomes king. His marriage is uncertain, and he is said to have performed some feats after his accession, but he (15) prescribes laws, and (16) later becomes unpopular. Leaving the city (17) after his deposition has been decided upon, he is (18) carried to the sky in a chariot of fire. His successor is (20) a stranger. His body (21) not having been found, he is (22) worshipped in a temple.

We can give him eighteen points.

HERACLES

His mother, Alcmene, is (1) a royal virgin, and his
father is (2) King Amphitryon, who is (3) her first cousin.
He is reputed to be (5) the son of Zeus, who (4) visited
Alcmene in the guise of Amphitryon. At his birth (6)
Hera tries to kill him. On reaching manhood he (11) performs feats and wins victories, after which he (10)
proceeds to Calydon, where he (12) marries the King's
daughter, and (13) becomes ruler. He remains there (14)
quietly for some years, after which an accidental man-
slaughter compels him (17) to flee from the country. He
disappears (18) from a funeral pyre (19) on the top of
Mount Œta. His sons (20) do not succeed him. His body
(21) is not found, and (22) he is worshipped in temples.

He scores seventeen points.

PERSEUS

His mother, Danaë, is (1) a royal virgin, and his father
is (2) King Proetus, who is (3) her uncle. He is also
reputed to be (5) the son of Zeus, who (4) visited Danaë
in a shower of gold. His mother's father (6) tries to kill
him at birth, but he is (7) wafted away, and (8) reared
by the King of Seriphos. We hear (9) nothing of his
childhood, but on reaching manhood he (11) kills a
dragon and (12) marries a princess. He then (10) returns
to his birthplace, where he (11) kills his father or uncle,
and (13) becomes king. We hear (14) nothing of his
reign, and his end is (18) variously reported, though in
one version he is killed by his successor. His children (20)
do not succeed him. His burial-place is (21) unknown,
but he is (22) worshipped at shrines.

He scores eighteen points.

JASON

His mother, Alcimede, is (1) a princess, and his father
is (2) King Æson. His uncle, Pelias, (6) tries to kill him
at birth, but (7) he is spirited away, and (8) brought up
at a distance by Cheiron. We hear (9) nothing of his

childhood, but on reaching manhood he wins the Golden
Fleece, and (12) marries a princess, after which he proceeds (10) to his birthplace, causes (11) the death of
Pelias, and (13) becomes king in his stead. He is afterwards (17) driven from throne and city by his uncle's
son, and his end is (18) obscure. His children do not (20)
succeed him. His burial-place is (21) unknown, but he is
(22) worshipped at shrines.

He scores fifteen points.

BELLEROPHON

His mother, Eurymede, is (1) a princess, and his father
is (2) King Glaucus. He is also (5) reputed to be the son
of Poseidon. We hear (9) nothing of his childhood, but
on reaching manhood he (10) travels to his future kingdom, (11) overcomes a monster, (12) marries the King's
daughter, and (13) becomes king. We hear (14) nothing
of his reign, but later he (16) becomes hated by the gods,
and (17) goes into exile. His fate is (18) obscure, though
it includes (19) an attempted ascent to the sky. His children (20) do not succeed him, and his burial-place is (21)
unknown, but he was worshipped (22) at Corinth and in
Lycia.

He scores sixteen points.

PELOPS

His mother, Dione, is (1) a demigoddess, and his father
is (2) King Tantalus, but he is also (5) reputed to be the
son of Poseidon. His father (6) kills him, but the gods
restore him to life. We hear (9) nothing of his childhood,
but on reaching manhood he (10) proceeds to his future
kingdom, (11) defeats and kills the King, (12) marries
his daughter, and (13) becomes king. He (15) regulates
the Olympic games, but otherwise we hear (14) nothing
of his reign, except that he banishes his sons, who (20)
do not succeed him. He has (22) a holy sepulchre at
Olympia.

We can give him at least thirteen points.

ASCLEPIOS

His mother, Coronis, is (1) a royal virgin, and his father is (5) Apollo, who (6) nearly kills him at birth. He is (7) spirited away, and (8) reared by Cheiron at a distance. On reaching manhood he (11) overcomes death, becomes (13) a man of power, and (16) prescribes the laws of medicine. Later he (17) incurs the enmity of Zeus, who (18) destroys him with a flash of lightning. His burial-place is (21) unknown, but (22) he has a number of holy sepulchres.

He scores at least twelve points.

DIONYSOS

His mother, Semele, is (1) a royal virgin, and his father is (5) Zeus, who is (3) Semele's uncle by marriage, and who (4) visits her in a thunderstorm. Hera (6) tries to kill him at birth, but (7) he is miraculously saved, and (8) brought up in a remote spot. We hear (9) nothing of his childhood, but on reaching manhood he (10) travels into Asia, (11) gains victories, and (13) becomes a ruler. For a time he (14) rules prosperously, and (15) prescribes laws of agriculture, etc., but later (17) is carried into exile. He (18) goes down to the dead, but afterwards (19) ascends Olympus. He seems (20) to have no children. He has (21) no burial-place, but (22) numerous shrines and temples.

We can give him nineteen points.

APOLLO

His mother, Leto, is (1) a royal virgin, and his father is (5) Zeus, who is (3) her first cousin. At birth he is (6) in danger from Hera, but (7) his mother escapes with him, and (8) he is reared at Delos. We hear (9) nothing of his childhood, but on reaching manhood he (10) goes to Delphi, where he (11) kills the Python, becomes (13) king, and (15) prescribes the laws of music, etc.

We can take him no further, but he has scored eleven points.

Zeus

His mother, Rhea, is (1) a goddess, and his father is (5) the god Cronos, who is (3) her brother. His father (6) tries to kill him at birth, but (7) he is spirited away, and (8) reared in Crete. We hear (9) nothing of his childhood, but on reaching manhood he (10) sets forth for Olympus, (11) defeats the Titans, (12) marries his sister, and (13) succeeds his father as king. He (14) reigns supreme, and (15) prescribes laws. Nevertheless he has (22) a holy sepulchre in Crete, and (19) hilltops are particularly sacred to him.

He scores fifteen points.

The lives of the Old Testament heroes have been heavily edited, but the same pattern is nevertheless apparent. Let us take three examples:

Joseph

His mother, Rachel, is (1) the daughter of a patriarch, and his father, Jacob, is (2) a patriarch, and (3) her first cousin. His mother conceives him (4) by eating mandrakes. In his childhood his brothers (6) attempt to kill him, but he is (7) saved by a stratagem, and (8) reared in Egypt. On reaching manhood he is (11) the victor in a contest in dream-interpretation and weather-forecasting, is (12) married to a lady of high rank, and (13) becomes ruler of Egypt. He (14) reigns prosperously, and (15) prescribes laws. We hear nothing of his later years, but the mention of a king who "knew not Joseph" suggests that he fell into disfavour.

Anyhow, we can give him twelve points.

Moses

His parents (1 and 2) were of the principal family of the Levites, and (3) near relatives; he is (5) also reputed to be the son of Pharaoh's daughter. Pharaoh (6) attempts to kill him at birth, but (7) he is wafted away, and (8) reared secretly. We are told (9) nothing of his childhood, but on reaching manhood he (11) kills a man, and

(10) goes to Midian, where (12) he marries the ruler's daughter. Returning (10) to Egypt, he (11) gains a series of magical victories over Pharaoh, and (13) becomes a ruler. His rule lasts a long time, and (15) he prescribes laws, but later he (16) loses the favour of Jehovah, is (17) removed from his leadership, and (18) disappears mysteriously from (19) the top of a mountain. His children (20) do not succeed him. His body (21) is not buried, but (22) he has a holy sepulchre near Jerusalem.

He scores twenty points, several of them twice, or, if we include Josephus's account, even three times.

ELIJAH

After (11) a victory in a rain-making contest, he becomes (13) a sort of dictator. A plot is made against him (16), and he flees (17) to Beersheba, after which he (18) disappears in a chariot of fire. He had previously (19) brought down fire from heaven to a mountain-top. His successor, Elisha, is (20) no relation. His body is (21) not buried, but (22) he has a holy sepulchre.

We know nothing of his parentage and birth, but can give him nine points.

We find the same pattern in the life of a Javanese hero.

WATU GUNUNG

His mother, Sinta, appears (1) to be a princess, and his father is (2) a holy man. Since his mother sees his father only in a dream, the circumstances of his conception are (4) unusual. When quite young, he incurs his mother's wrath, and she (6) gives him a wound on the head. He (7) flees into the woods and does not return. We are told (9) nothing of his childhood, except that he is brought up by a holy man in (8) a far country. On reaching manhood he (10) journeys to a kingdom where (11) he kills the King, and (13) becomes king in his stead. After this he (12) marries his own mother and sister, who do not recognize him. For a long time he (14) reigns uneventfully, and has a large family, but eventually his mother recognizes the scar she gave him when a child, and is over-

come with grief. The gods having (16) refused his request
for another wife, he (17) invades heaven, but the gods,
having learned by a stratagem the answer to his riddle and
the secret of his invulnerability, put him to death (19)
there by (18) separating his arms. His sons do not (20)
succeed him, and (21) there is no mention of his burial.

His story, as given by Sir Stamford Raffles,[2] is obviously
incomplete, yet its resemblance to the Œdipus myth is
striking, and we can give the hero eighteen points.

Let us now transport ourselves to the Upper Nile, where
we find that Nyikang, the cult-hero of the Shiluk tribe, is
represented as following a career that affords a number of
resemblances to our pattern.[3]

NYIKANG

His mother, Nyikaia, was apparently (1) a crocodile
princess, and his father was (2) a king. We hear (9)
nothing of his childhood, but when he reaches manhood
his brother (6) tries to kill him. He goes (10) to another
country, and (12) marries a king's daughter. After (11)
a number of victories, actual and magical, he (13) becomes king. For a time he reigns (14) prosperously, and
(15) prescribes laws, but at last the people begin (16) to
complain against him. Distressed at this, he (18) disappears mysteriously. Though (21) not buried, he (22) has
a number of holy sepulchres.

He scores fourteen points.

Let us now come nearer home and consider some of the
heroes of northern Europe:

SIGURD OR SIEGFRIED

His mother, Siglinde, is (1) a princess, and his father
is (2) King Sigmund, who is (3) her brother, and whom
she (4) visits in the guise of another woman. On reaching

[2] *History of Java*, vol. i, pp. 421–4.
[3] *Vide* D. S. Oyler in *Sudan Notes and Records*, vol. i, pp.
107, 283.

manhood he (10) performs a journey, (11) slays a dragon, (12) marries a princess, and (13) becomes a ruler. For a time he (14) prospers, but later (16) there is a plot against him, and he is killed. He is (19) the only man who can pass through a ring of fire to a hilltop.

He scores eleven points.

The next two examples I shall give are Celtic and are interesting as showing how variations of the same theme can exist in the same culture area. The story of Llew Llawgyffes is given by Professor W. J. Gruffydd.[4]

Llew Llawgyffes

His mother, Arianrhod, is (1) a royal virgin, and his father is apparently Gwydion, who is (2) a prince, and (3) her brother. The circumstances of his conception are (4) unusual, since his mother believes herself to be a virgin at the time of his birth. As soon as he is born he is (7) spirited away by his father, and (8) nursed by a foster-mother. When less than two years old he is (9) a "big lad," and (10) returns to the court. With his father's help he (11) wins magical victories, (12) marries a supernatural being, and (13) becomes a ruler. For a time he rules uneventfully, but later (16) loses favour with his wife, who (17) induces him to leave his court. He is (18) speared, but flies off in the form of an eagle, from (19) a curious elevated position. He has (20) no children and (21) no real death or burial.

He scores seventeen points.

Arthur

His mother, Igraine, is (1) a princess, and his father is (2) the Duke of Cornwall. He is, however, (5) reputed to be the son of Uther Pendragon, who (4) visits Igraine in the Duke's likeness. At birth he is apparently in no danger, yet is (7) spirited away and (8) reared in a distant part of the country. We hear (9) nothing of his childhood, but on reaching manhood he (10) travels to Lon-

---

[4] *Math vab Mathonwy*, pp. 17 ff.

don, (11) wins a magical victory, and (13) is chosen
king. After other victories he (12) marries Guinevere,
heiress of the Round Table. After this he (14) reigns
uneventfully, and (15) prescribes the laws of chivalry, but
later there is (16) a successful conspiracy against him,
while (17) he is abroad. He meets with (18) a mysterious
death, and his children do not (20) succeed him. His
body is (21) not buried, but nevertheless he has (22) a
holy sepulchre at Glastonbury.

He scores nineteen points.

Traces of the pattern are also to be found in the story of

ROBIN HOOD

His father is a Saxon yeoman, but he is also (5)
reputed to be the son of a great noble. We (9) hear
nothing of his youth, but on reaching manhood he leads
a life of debauchery until compelled to fly (10) to Sherwood, where he (11) gains victories over the Sheriff of
Nottingham, (12) marries Maid Marian, the Queen of
May, and (13) becomes King of May and ruler of the
forest. For a long time he reigns, and (15) prescribes the
laws of archery, but eventually illness overtakes him, and
he (17) has to leave the forest and meets (18) a mysterious death in (19) an upper room. He (20) has no children. The place of his death and burial are (21) variously
given, but (22) miracles were performed at his tomb at
Kirkley, in Yorkshire.

We can give him thirteen points.

Cuchulainn also scores a good number of points, and
it is interesting to compare these heroes of myth with
Hengist, who makes a journey, wins a victory, and becomes
a king, but otherwise is not alleged to have done anything
which brings him within the pattern. But the story of
Hengist, as I have tried to show, is not myth but pseudo-
history. It may be added that although several of the incidents are such as have happened to many historical
heroes, yet I have not found an undoubtedly historical hero

to whom more than six points can be awarded, or perhaps seven in the case of Alexander the Great. The differences between the hero of myth and the hero of history will emerge from our discussion of the significance of the pattern, which had better be left to another chapter.

CHAPTER XVII

THE HERO (*Continued*)

The fact that the life of a hero of tradition can be divided up into a series of well-marked features and incidents—I have taken twenty-two, but it would be easy to take more—strongly suggests a ritual pattern. I doubt whether even the most fervent euhemerist would maintain that all these resemblances are mere coincidences; and if not, then three possibilities remain. The first is that all, or some, of the heroes were real persons whose stories were altered to make them conform to a ritual pattern; the second is that all, or some, of them were real persons in whose lives ritual played a predominant part; and the third is that they were all purely mythical. A discussion of this question will be attempted in the next chapter; in the present one I shall review the incidents of the hero's career, as they appear in the foregoing stories, and make some suggestions as to their significance.

The first point to be noted is that the incidents fall definitely into three groups: those connected with the hero's birth, those connected with his accession to the throne, and those connected with his death. They thus correspond to the three principal *rites de passage*—that is to say, the rites at birth, at initiation, and at death. I shall have more to say on this when we reach point number nine; let us now start at the beginning.

In connection with the first two points, we note that whenever there are royalties available, the hero is the son of royal parents; that he is nearly always the first child of his mother and, except where his father is a god, of his father, and that with very few exceptions his father does not marry twice. There is, of course, nothing marvellous in all this—some historical heroes have been the eldest child of monogamous royal parents, but I have laid stress upon it because it seems to be typical of the traditional hero, and is definitely not typical of the historical hero.

There is, it is true, a type of folk-tale in which the hero (or heroine), though of obscure origin, obtains a royal spouse and a throne, but this type of tale is probably derived from romances based on the central part of the myth, in which, as we have seen, the hero, though really of royal birth, appears, so to speak, out of the blue. In these tales we are never told of the hero's death, but merely that he "lived happily ever afterwards," which seems to suggest a desire to omit, rather than falsify, the latter part of the myth.

The fact that the hero's parents are often near relatives brings to mind the widespread custom by which kings marry their sisters, with which I have dealt elsewhere.

The circumstances in which our hero is begotten are very puzzling. When, as in the case of Heracles, a god takes the form of the hero's father, we are reminded that the Pharaoh, on particular occasions, approached his queen in the guise of a god.[1] In our stories, however, the circumstances, though almost always unusual, are extremely various, as are the guises in which the god appears. He may take the form of a thunderstorm, a bull, a swan, or a shower of gold. We may suspect, however, that the attribution of divine birth to a hero is not the result of his heroism, but is derived from the ritual union of a princess to her own husband, disguised as a god. It is comparatively easy for a man to disguise himself as a bull or swan, but while the thunderstorm and the shower of gold present greater difficulties and require further investigation, they clearly suggest a ritual rather than a historical origin for the stories.

We now come to the attempt on the hero's life at birth, which happens in almost every case and is one of the most striking features of the pattern. We are all familiar with such rites as that of the Phœnicians, by which the eldest son was burnt as a sacrifice to Moloch; in our stories, it would seem, a pretence is made of sacrificing the child,

[1] J. G. Frazer, op. cit., vol. ii, p. 133.

and sometimes an animal is sacrificed instead. It is often the father who tries to kill the infant hero, and this brings the stories into line with that of Abraham and Isaac. The attempt on the life of Moses, like that of nearly all the other heroes, was made at birth, but the story of Abraham and Isaac suggests that at one period the Hebrews performed this rite at puberty. We may note that while a ram was sacrificed in place of Isaac, Jacob appeared before his father wearing the skin of a kid, and Joseph wore a special garment which was soaked in goat's blood. We may perhaps suppose that a pretence was made of killing the child, which was wrapped in the skin of a sacrificed goat, and soaked in its blood. Such a rite accounts for some of our stories, such as that of Pelops, and also the widespread story of the Faithful Hound. Sometimes, it would seem, the child itself was wounded in the leg; hence perhaps the name "Œdipus," "swell-foot," and the many heroes who are lame, or who have scars on their legs. Many of the infant heroes, however, are set afloat in baskets or boxes, and these stories are found not merely in Greece and western Asia, but as far east as Japan.[2] I shall discuss them no further, except to say that while the story of the attempt on the infant hero's life can be explained as ritual, it is, though not miraculous, absent or at any rate extremely rare in the case of genuinely historical heroes.

Having escaped death, our heroes are all removed to a distance, and are usually brought up by a foreign king, though Jason and Asclepios are brought up by Cheiron. The latter is easy to understand if we suppose that Cheiron was the title given to a prince's official tutor, but nearly all our heroes are brought up by kings. This suggests several possibilities. The first is that it was actually the practice for kings to send their sons to be brought up by other kings, as we read of in the story of Hakon Adalstein's fostri. The second, which I have put forward elsewhere,[3] but which I am by no means confident about, is

<hr />

[2] B. H. Chamberlain: *The Kojiki*, p. 21. Frazer collects a number of these stories: *Folklore in the Old Testament,* vol. ii, pp. 437 ff.
[3] *Jocasta's Crime*, p. 195.

that princes succeeded their fathers-in-law, but became
their sons by formal adoption. This might lead to a belief,
or a pretence, that they were their real sons who had been
removed at birth. The third is the opposite of the second.
It is that it was part of the ritual that the prince, though
a native, should pretend to be a foreigner. The question
needs much more investigation than I have been able to
give it.

We next come to point number nine: that we are told
nothing of the hero's childhood. This may seem unimportant, since there are, of course, many great men of
whose childhood we know nothing. In such cases, however, we equally know nothing of the circumstances of
their birth. We may know the place and date, but that is
all. With our heroes it is quite different; their birth is the
central feature in a series of highly dramatic incidents—
incidents that are related in considerable detail, and such
as seldom, if ever, occur in the lives of real people. The
most exciting things happen to our hero at birth, and the
most exciting things happen to him as soon as he reaches
manhood, but in the meantime nothing happens to him at
all. If, as I suppose, our hero is a figure not of history but
of ritual, this is just what one would expect, since as a
general rule children take no part in ritual between the
rites at birth and those at initiation. The story of the hero
of tradition, if I understand it aright, is the story of his
ritual progress, and it is therefore appropriate that those
parts of his career in which he makes no ritual progress
should be left blank. I would compare the blank that
occurs during childhood with the blank that occurs after
his installation as king has been completed.

The fact that on reaching manhood the hero forthwith
sets out on a journey from the land of his upbringing to
the land where he will reign is, of course, involved in the
problem I have discussed under point number eight—that
is, his being reared in a far country. It is a remarkable
fact, however, that his victories almost always take place
either on the journey or immediately after arrival at his
destination. He makes a definite progress from a far country to the throne, and all his feats and victories are con-

nected with that progress. Another remarkable fact is that
the hero of tradition never wins a battle. It is very rarely
that he is represented as having any companions at all,
and when he has, he never trains them or leads them. The
warrior kings of history, whether civilized or barbarian,
have won their renown as leaders. When we think of them
we think of serried ranks, of the Argyraspides, of the
Tenth Legion, of the Guard which dies but does not sur-
render, and the impis which think it better to go forward
and die than to go back and die. But there is nothing like
that in the stories of the heroes of tradition. Our hero's
followers, if any, are out of the way or killed off when his
crucial fight takes place. All his victories, when they are
actual fights and not magical contests, are single combats
against other kings, or against giants, dragons, or celebrated animals. He never fights with ordinary men, or even
with ordinary animals. And the king whom he fights is the
king whom he will succeed, and who is often his own
father. It is also possible that the monster with which the
hero fights is merely the reigning king in disguise, or, in
other words, that the reigning king had to wear an animal
costume or mask in which to defend his title and his life.
I will return to that later, but will first touch on the magical contest, which seems sometimes to be more important
than the actual fight. Œdipus wins his throne by guessing
a riddle, Theseus his by finding the way out of a maze.
The magical victories of the three Jewish heroes are all
connected with rain-making: Joseph successfully prognosti-
cates the weather; Moses is successful in a series of magical
contests in which rain-making is included; and Elijah
defeats the prophets of Baal in a rain-making contest.
Power over the elements is the most unvarying characteristic of the divine king, and it would seem that sometimes at least the candidate for the throne had to pass in a
rain-making test.[4]

Our hero, then, has to qualify for the throne in two
ways: he must pass a test in some such subject as rain-

[4] Some interesting suggestions on this point are made by Dr.
C. B. Lewis: *Classical Mythology and Arthurian Romance,*
pp. 41–5.

making or riddle-guessing, and he must win a victory over the reigning king. Whether this was a real fight or a mock contest in which the conclusion was foregone we cannot be certain. There have undoubtedly been many cases in which the king was put to death at the end of a fixed term, or when his powers began to wane. There may have been cases in which there was a fair fight with equal weapons between the king and his challenger, but the evidence for them is rather uncertain. What several of the stories suggest is that the old king was ritually killed, and that his successor had to kill an animal—wolf, boar, or snake—into which his spirit was supposed to have entered. I shall refer to this again when we come to point number eighteen.

After passing his tests and winning his victories, the hero marries the daughter, or widow, of his predecessor, and becomes king. It has often been assumed from this that the throne always went in the female line, and that the reigning queen or heiress could confer the title to it upon her husband simply by marrying him; in other words, that any man who managed to marry the queen became king automatically, whatever his antecedents, and that the only way in which any man could lawfully become king was by marrying the queen. Such an assumption is going a great deal beyond the evidence of the stories, which suggest that the new king established his title to the throne by his birth, his upbringing, and his victories. There were, it would seem, recognized qualifications for the kingship, just as there were recognized qualifications for the queenship. We do not know for certain that the new queen was really the old queen's daughter, any more than we know for certain that the new king was really the old king's son. There may have been a ceremony of adoption in both cases, and in many tales of the Cinderella and Catskin types the future queen has to achieve her journey, her tests, and her victory. There is evidence, too, that at Olympia the winner of the girls' race became Hera, just as the winner of the men's race became Zeus.[5]

Anyhow, the fact that our hero marries a princess and

[5] J. G. Frazer: *The Golden Bough,* vol. iv, p. 91.

at the same time ascends the throne is far from proving
that he ascends the throne by virtue of his marriage. It
may merely indicate what we know from other sources
to be a fact: namely, that a *hieros gamos* or sacred marriage normally formed an essential and highly important
feature of the coronation or installation ceremony. I know
of no case, in any age or country, in which a man has
become king simply by marrying the queen; he must first,
so far I can learn, have qualified for the throne, either by
birth or by performing some feat or passing some test, and
our heroes seem all to have qualified in all these ways.
Even in modern Europe marriage never confers the right
to a throne; princes and princesses who marry unqualified
persons, who contract, that is to say, what are called mor-
ganatic marriages, not merely fail to raise their partners to
the throne, but lose their own title to it. It is difficult to
believe that the rules were less strict in ages when the ritual
functions of a king and queen were far more important
than they are today. The chief qualification for the throne
has always been the possession of power, the power that is
conferred by divine descent and the absorption of divine
wisdom, and that is demonstrated by victory over the elements and over man. The conqueror may become king,
since by his conquests he proves his possession of power,
but that it has ever been believed that such power is conferred by a simple marriage ceremony is unproved and
improbable.

Our hero has now become king, and what does he do?
It might be supposed that, having shown himself so brave
and enterprising before coming to the throne, he would
forthwith embark upon a career of conquest; found an
empire and a dynasty; build cities, temples, and palaces;
patronize the arts; possess a large harem; and behave generally as the conquering heroes of history have behaved,
or tried to behave. The hero of tradition, however, in this
as in most other respects, is totally unlike the hero of history. He does none of these things, and his story, from the
time of his accession to the time of his fall, is as a rule a
complete blank. The only memorial of his reign, apart
from the events that begin and end it, is the traditional

code of laws that is often attributed to him. As a fact, however, a code of laws is always the product of hundreds, if
not thousands, of years of gradual evolution, and is never
in any sense the work of one man. One man, a Justinian
or a Napoleon, may cause laws to be codified, or may alter
their incidence, but it has never been suggested that all,
or even any, of the laws in their codes were devised by
these monarchs. It is well known, in fact, that they were
not. On the other hand it has been clearly shown by Sir
James Frazer[6] that the Ten Commandments, in their familiar form, could have had nothing to do with Moses,
since the original Ten Commandments, whoever first composed them, were entirely different. It seems clear, then,
that the attribution of laws to a hero of tradition is merely
a way of saying that they are very old and very sacred.

Our next point is that the hero of tradition, unlike most
heroes of history, normally ends his career by being driven
from his kingdom and put to death in mysterious circumstances. Sigurd is the only one of those whom we have considered of whose death we have a clear and non-miraculous
account; even of Joseph we are told nothing of what happened between his father's death and his own. We may
conclude that deposition and a mysterious death are a
part of the pattern, but a puzzling feature is that there is
nothing to suggest that the hero suffers a defeat. As he has
gained the throne by a victory, one would expect him to
lose it by a defeat, but this he never does.

Œdipus kills his father and marries his mother; one
might expect that one of his sons, or some other prince,
would kill him and marry Jocasta, or, if she were too old,
Antigone, and become king. Creon, however, who succeeds
him, does so by turning the oracle against him, and several
others among our heroes fall out with a god and, of course,
get the worst of it. Others become unpopular with their
subjects. In either case the hero's fall from favour is not
gradual but sudden; at one moment he is apparently in
full favour both with gods and men, and the next he has
no friends, either human or divine.

The hero's death is mysterious, but one thing clear about

[6] *Folklore in the Old Testament,* vol. iii, p. 115.

it is that it never takes place within the city. Usually he is driven out, but sometimes he has left the city on some sacred mission. Then there is the hilltop, which appears in the stories of Œdipus, Theseus, Heracles, Bellerophon, and Moses, and which is suggested in several of the others. Taken in conjunction with the chariot of fire in which Romulus and Elijah disappear, and the lightning flash that kills Asclepios, it seems justifiable to conclude that in the most usual form of the rite the divine king was burned, either alive or dead, on a pyre erected on a hilltop, and that he was believed to ascend to the sky, in some form or other, in the smoke and flame. It is possible that, before being burnt, he was compelled to fight with and be defeated by his successor, but in the majority of stories there is nothing to suggest this.

The fact that the hero is never succeeded by his son—Nyikang seems to be the sole exception—might suggest that the inheritance went in the female line, but then no hero is succeeded by his son-in-law. If the king reigned for eight years only, and married at his coronation, his children could not succeed him, since they would be too young, but they might succeed his successor, and there is some evidence that this is what happened. The succession at Thebes is not easy to make out, but Creon seems to have preceded and succeeded Œdipus, and also to have succeeded his sons. Perseus is said to have killed and succeeded Proetus, and to have been killed and succeeded by the latter's son. Ægisthus kills and succeeds Agamemnon, and eight years later is killed and succeeded by the latter's son Orestes. There were two royal families at Sparta, and it is possible that originally they reigned alternately.

The last point to be considered in the hero's career is that although he is usually supposed to have disappeared, yet nevertheless he has a holy sepulchre, if not several. I have attempted to explain his disappearance by suggesting that he was cremated, but if kings were cremated they could hardly have a sepulchre in the usual sense of the term, since we know that in all forms of religion the essential feature of a sepulchre, or shrine, is that it is supposed to contain the bones, or at any rate some of the bones,

of the holy person to whom it is dedicated. A great deal
has, of course, been written on the customs of the Greeks
with regard to the disposal of the dead, and their beliefs
about the Otherworld, but I am here concerned merely
to consider the rites which are suggested by the hero
stories, and what they suggest to me is that, while ordinary
people were buried, the bodies of kings were burnt, but not
burnt thoroughly, so that the bones were left and could be
buried. I understand that this view was put forward by
Dörpfeld, though on different grounds, some thirty years
ago, but I have not been able to see what he wrote. At
any rate, similar customs are found in many parts of the
world.

In conclusion, I should like to make it quite clear that I
do not claim to have produced final solutions for any of
the problems I have discussed in this chapter. What I
have tried to show is that they are problems of custom and
ritual, and not problems of history.

CHAPTER XVIII

THE HERO (*Continued*)

In the last two chapters I have shown, I hope, in the first place that a definite and highly complex pattern is to be traced in the accounts which we have of traditional heroes from many parts of the world, but especially the eastern Mediterranean, and secondly that all the features of this pattern can be identified as features of known rituals. It remains to consider the general meaning and idea at the back of the "hero," and how far traditional heroes were ever real men. Let us consider the latter point first. In so doing we must ask in each case two questions: whether there is any contemporary record of the hero's existence, and whether he is alleged to have done anything that is *not* mythical. As to the former we cannot, of course, be absolutely certain, but it seems pretty safe to say that, although some of them, such as Arthur and Robin Hood, are alleged to have lived at dates when written records were made, yet of none of them, with the very doubtful exception of Elijah, can it be said that we have contemporary evidence for their existence. The exception of Elijah is doubtful not merely because we do not know when the passages relating to him were written, but because he has perhaps less claim than any of the others to be considered historical, since, apart from his running twenty miles across country, nothing is reported of him which is not miraculous.

And this must be our criterion. When we are certain that nothing about our hero was written down till a century or more after his alleged death, we can conclude unhesitatingly that he is mythical, but when we are not certain we must judge as best we can by the reported incidents of his career. They may, of course, have been rationalized, as

Elijah's have not been, but even when they have been so rationalized we can often recognize them as mythical, since the rationalizers as a rule cannot get away from the pattern, the pattern I dealt with in Chapter XVI.

The fact, however, that our heroes sometimes go beyond this pattern does not indicate that they are historical, since they may merely get into another pattern. The Twelve Labours of Heracles, for example, are outside my pattern, but they are clearly ritual and not historical; similarly the water that allows Moses to cross safely but drowns his pursuer forms part of a widespread myth with which I have already dealt.[1]

It is possible that some of the heroes were real persons, whose actions were recorded, but whose real careers became for some reason swamped by myth. I shall discuss in the next chapter the attribution of mythical features to historical characters, but that is another matter, since in the case of these historical characters it is their historic deeds that are important, and the myths mere excrescence. Alexander's alleged miraculous birth does not affect our view of the Battle of Arbela. But if we subtract the myths from the heroes with whom I have dealt, little or nothing remains. Miracles and mythical incidents are all that we are told of them, or at least all that is of any interest. What would the story of Perseus be without the Gorgon's head, or that of Bellerophon without his winged steed? Very little, and even Moses would be much less interesting without his magic rod. It may be suggested that King Alfred is less interesting without the cakes, but though such foolish stories may amuse the unlettered, they are a nuisance to serious students of the life and times of this great ruler. Would anyone, however, venture to say that the story of Medusa is a nuisance to students of the life and times of Perseus? Of course this story, and the dragon-slaying, make up the life of Perseus; apart from these and his mother's brazen tower there is nothing to distinguish him from a score of heroes. The difference between the story of a historical character and that of a hero of tradition is that in the former case we may find myths or fables loosely

[1] *Supra,* p. 134.

and as a rule unsuitably tacked on to a record of well-attested fact, while in the latter the story consists of some striking miracles against a background of typical myth.

The old-fashioned view—namely, that all these heroes were real men, whose eminence led to their deification or canonization—was put forward by Sir William Ridgeway, who tells us that "dramatizations of his exploits or sufferings, like dances, eulogies, paintings, and statues, is one of the regular methods of propitiating a man of outstanding personality, at every stage from his actual lifetime, after his death when now canonized as hero or saint, and finally when he may even have been promoted to the foremost rank of the great divinities." [2] Here Sir William, as throughout his works, assumes what he professes to prove; he fails to observe the pattern that runs through these hero stories, and finally he controverts himself, since he shows that those who receive cults are, on the assumption that they were real people, persons of quite insignificant personality. Thus he says that "popular deification often arises out of mere pity for those who have suffered tragic fates, such as the boy-bridegroom, Dhola, who died on his wedding-day," [3] and that "if it should turn out that in some, at least, of the rites and shrines of Cybele representations of the body of Attis were exhibited . . . then the evidence will point still more directly to his having once been a youth, whose tragic fate . . . impressed his contemporaries, and led to his worship." [4]

The theory that people are in the habit of making gods out of youths who happen to be killed out hunting or to die on their wedding-day not only is absurd in itself, but is in flagrant contradiction to what he says about outstanding personalities, since if Dhola and Attis had been real persons, they obviously could not have been outstanding personalities.

Sir William Ridgeway and many of those who think like him seem never to have asked themselves why people

[2] W. Ridgeway: *Dramas and Dramatic Dances*, p. 210.
[3] Ibid., p. 208.
[4] Ibid., p. 92.

worship gods. That pity has ever led to worship is both
highly improbable in theory and against all the known
facts. These show that the idea of deity and the idea of
power are and always have been inseparably connected.
The power of the god may be for good or for evil, it may
be general or particular, but power he always has, and it
is this power, and nothing else, that leads to his worship.
All the names and attributes of a god are names and attributes of power. The god may die, since death may be a
promotion to a higher sphere, but he dies of his own
volition. It is in this fact that we must look for an explanation of the phenomenon discussed in the last chapter:
namely, that though the hero gains his throne by a victory,
he never loses it by a defeat. The end of most of the heroes
is, as we have seen, left obscure, but a number of them,
such as Dionysos, Heracles, Moses, Elijah, Nyikang, are
represented as committing suicide, and thereby securing
promotion to divine rank. We have also good reason to
believe that Attis was thought of as a hero who attained
through suicide his promotion to divine rank. We will
return to Attis presently. Here we must note that he was
believed by his worshippers to possess power in the highest
degree, the power of conferring everlasting life. No attempt, so far as I can learn, has been made to explain why
anyone should suppose that a youth of whom nothing was
known but that he met with an accidental death should be
capable of conferring everlasting life.

Egyptologists fall into a similar error when they suppose
Osiris to have been a real man. Dr. Blackman, for example,
thinks that he was an early king who "did much to advance
agriculture and civilization in general among his subjects,
and who met his death at the hands of a rebellious . . .
vassal." [5] But in real life no progressive monarch has been
deified, or even sanctified; any interest in him that may
survive his death is purely historical. Dr. Blackman appears to suppose that the ancient Egyptians, feeling the
need for a supreme deity, hunted about for a suitable man
upon whom to confer this title, and found him in the
shape of a defeated king, or, alternatively, that it was the

[5] In *Myth and Ritual,* p. 38.

defeat and death of Osiris that led the Egyptians to believe in the existence of omnipotent deities.

Euhemeros was, of course, a sceptic, and he was concerned rather to explode religious beliefs than to explain
the nature of religion, but his theory has had very wide
effects, and many people, including those whom I have
quoted, have mistaken for science what was really anti-
religious propaganda. "The gods, according to this theory,"
says Professor Bevan,[6] "were kings and great men of old,
who had come to be worshipped after their death in gratitude for the benefits they had conferred. On this view there
was nothing monstrous in using the same forms to express
gratitude to a living benefactor. In so far as the worship of
living men arose from these conditions, it was a product,
not of superstition, but of rationalism." In Greece, in the
fourth century B.C., there is no doubt that people did say:
"X is a very powerful monarch; let us deify him," and
even: "Y *was* a very fine man; let us deify him," or words
to that effect, but such an attitude is, as Professor Bevan
says, a product of rationalism. It throws no light on the
origin of the belief in gods, nor does it bear any resemblance to the normal attitude of worshippers towards the
deities they worship. These are conceived of as superhuman
beings of unlimited power, and between these beings and
organized bodies of men there exists a continuing relationship of mutual service. With this relationship we are not
here concerned further than to try to ascertain what part
the hero plays in it. To do so we must study certain heroes
from an angle rather different from that adopted in Chapter XVI.

In his *Mexico before Cortez*,[7] Mr. J. E. Thompson tells
us that "there is one man who stands out against this background of confusion, although he, too, emerges a shadowy
figure in floodlights fogged by contradiction. This was
Quetzalcoatl, possibly the last Toltec ruler. Quetzalcoatl,
which means quetzal-bird-serpent, was also the name of an
important Mexican deity, whose name was borne by the
Toltec high priests, who were in turn temporal rulers.

[6] In *Hastings' Encyclopædia*, vol. iv, p. 525.
[7] p. 20.

Great confusion has naturally ensued, for the acts of god and individual are inextricably confused."

We find that Quetzalcoatl was represented as or by:

1. A sky god.
2. The living representative of a line of priestly rulers.
3. An idol, part man and part bird-serpent.
4. Certain animals; to wit, the quetzal-bird and the serpent.
5. An ancient hero.

Let us now transport ourselves to the Upper Nile and return to Nyikang, whose career we have already examined. We find that he is represented as or by:

1. A sky god.
2. The living representative of a line of priestly rulers, the divine king.
3. An idol, "the effigy called Nyikang."
4. Certain animals, particularly a species of white bird.
5. An ancient hero.[8]

Let us now descend the Nile to ancient Egypt. There we find that Horus was represented as or by:

1. A sky god, whose eye was the sun.
2. The living representative of a line of priestly rulers, the Pharaoh.
3. An idol, showing him as a man with a hawk's head.
4. The hawk.
5. An ancient hero.

Moving on into Asia, we find that Attis, whom, as we saw, Ridgeway supposed to have been a youth, was represented as or by:

1. A sky god, responsible for the weather and the crops.

[8] C. G. and B. Z. Seligman: *The Pagan Tribes of the Nilotic Sudan,* pp. 37 and 75 ff.

2. A high priest who regularly bore the name of Attis.

3. An idol made from a pine-tree.

4. A bull.

5. An ancient hero.[9]

The foregoing gods or heroes, whichever one chooses to call them, have all been represented by euhemeristic writers as real men. Now let us consider Dionysos. He was:

1. A sky god, and at his festival at Athens, the great Dionysia, was represented by:

2. His priest,

3. His image, and

4. A bull. He was also

5. An ancient hero.

On this last point we have other evidence than that he scores nineteen points out of twenty-two in my pattern of the traditional hero. He is sometimes actually addressed as a hero in ritual:[1] and at Megara there was a shrine to "Dionysus the Ancestor," [2] which suggests that the Megarians, at any rate, regarded him as a real man. I cannot find, however, that any scholar regards Dionysos as a real man, though the reasons for so doing seem just as good as those for regarding any other prehistoric hero as a real man.

It seems clear, however, that these and other gods, whether they have been supposed to be promoted men or not, have a definite pattern in their attributes and their cult. In the first place they are sky gods, responsible for the weather and the crops; in the second they are incarnate in kings or priests; in the third they are represented by idols and other objects of cult; in the fourth they have an intimate relation with certain species of animals. Finally they are believed to have been heroes who once lived upon earth, and whose careers corresponded more or less com-

[9] Frazer: *Golden Bough,* vol. v, pp. 263 ff.

[1] A. C. Pearson in *Hastings' Encyclopædia,* vol. vi, p. 653.

[2] L. R. Farnell, op. cit., p. 64.

pletely to the pattern we have discussed at length in the last two chapters. To assume that these hero stories were earlier than the rest of their attributes is as purely gratuitous as to assume that the non-miraculous is always earlier than the miraculous, or that the gods in the Homeric poems are late interpolations; such assumptions arise from obsession by euhemeristic theories and not from a study of the facts, since the facts, both of myths and of cult, afford no grounds for supposing that any of the attributes is older than the rest. The conclusion that suggests itself is that the god is the hero as he appears in ritual, and the hero is the god as he appears in myth; in other words, the hero and the god are two different aspects of the same superhuman being. The myth describes the victories that the hero won over the forces inimical to his people, the laws and customs which he instituted for their benefit, and finally the apotheosis that enables him still to be their guardian and guide. When recited in full it embraces all his attributes, as god, as divine man, as idol, and as animal, and thus explains and justifies the whole of the ritual with which he is worshipped.

With a few distinguished exceptions, such as Professor J. A. K. Thomson, scholars have failed to realize this connection between the god and the hero. The reason for this is that they tend to concentrate on a very limited class of phenomena. Brought up on Homer and the Attic dramatists, they pay less attention to what the heroes are actually alleged to have done than to the words that the poets have put into their mouths. On these they base character studies of the heroes, failing to recognize that the words are not those of the heroes but are those of the poets. The fact is, I am afraid, that scholars as a class are romantically rather than scientifically minded. The reading of the *Iliad* or of the *Seven against Thebes* fills them with emotion, but since they are unwilling to admit that it is emotion of similar type to that experienced by the small boy who reads *Treasure Island,* they attempt to conceal it by throwing over it a veil of pseudo-history. This veil takes the form of a fabled Heroic Age, in which, apparently, the principal features of life were dragons, single combats, and elope-ments. In my view it is just as reasonable to suppose that there was once a Comic Age, in which life was made up of back-chat, disguises, and practical jokes, and a Tragic Age, in which people were always murdering their nearest relatives, and true love led to untimely death.

This seems to have been the view of Sir William Ridgeway, who believed not only in a Heroic Age, but in a Comic Age as well. He tells us that "it is in the *kyogen* [Japanese comedy] that we get the true pictures of the social and national life of the Oshikaga period (1338–1597). It was a period of high ideals, with a few great men towering above the rest and bearing witness to the priestly holiness and knightly bravery of an age gone by. These are brought before us in the *no* [tragedy]. But it was also a period of mediocre performances; the country swarmed with contemptible and ignoble lords and knights who disgraced their swords, and priests who disgraced their religion. Mingled with these were dreamy scholars, who were incapable of managing their money matters, and innocent country people who were the sport of every designing rascal." [3] It is astonishing that he should have taken the stock figures of comedy for real people, but not more so than that he and others should have taken the stock figures of myth for real people. All three conceptions, those of the tragic, the heroic, and the comic, are derived from the poets, and the poets were not interested in historical fact. It may be objected that poets nevertheless do sometimes mention historical facts, and that myths are sometimes attached to real historical heroes. We must next consider how this comes about.

[3] W. Ridgeway: *Dramas and Dramatic Dances*, p. 333.

CHAPTER XIX

MYTH AND THE HISTORIC HERO

If I were to find it stated in one account that X had a black beard, and in another account that X always wore a red coat, I might combine these two statements into one and say: "We are told that X had a black beard and always wore a red coat." By so doing I should be following the example of many historians and of all pseudo-historians, and should be making a statement that is inaccurate, misleading, and quite unjustifiable. For we are not, in the example I have given, told that X had a black beard *and* always wore a red coat. The "and" is supplied by me, and I have no right to supply it unless I give my authorities for the two statements, and show that they are of similar origin and equal value. It is possible that one may be historical, derived, that is to say, from contemporary written records, while the other may be based on dramatic or pictorial representation, or some other form of tradition. To combine into a single narrative statements derived from dissimilar sources is to supply false links, and false links are equivalent to false statements. Yet our pseudo-history, and even our history, are full of such false links; the practice has always been to accept as history any tradition that can be fitted in, and the distinction between history and tradition has thereby become blurred to such an extent that its existence is barely recognized. So far has the process gone that we find eminent writers describing as "historical," characters for whose existence there is no historical evidence at all. If, however, we take any really historical person, and make a clear distinction between what history tells us of him and what tradition tells us, we shall find that tradition, far from being supplementary to history, is totally unconnected with it, and that the hero of history and the hero of tradition are really two quite different persons, though they may bear the same name. I shall illustrate this fact by studying in some detail what is told us by history and by tradition of King Henry V.

King Henry V gained a glorious victory at Agincourt, and afterwards captured Paris. He married the French King's daughter, was recognized as his heir, and became ruler of a great part of France. He died in the midst of his victorious career. This career created a great impression upon the people, not because England benefited from his victories, which she did not, but because a king's victories have always been regarded as a proof of divine favour, and a guarantee of national prosperity. The deposition of his son, King Henry VI, was probably due in the main to a belief that the repeated defeats of his forces in France were indications of divine disfavour. At any rate the prolonged misfortunes of his reign afforded a striking contrast to the sensational victories of his father. The latter became an ideal hero, and tradition proceeded, with great promptitude, to provide him with what were regarded as the requisite antecedents. I shall explain later what I mean by this.

Into the accounts of Henry V's youth made famous by Shakespeare it is unnecessary to go in any detail. They tell us that he spent the years preceding his accession in rioting and debauchery in and about London, in company with highwaymen, pickpockets, and other disreputable persons; that he was imprisoned by Chief Justice Gascoigne, whom after his accession he pardoned and continued in office; and that after his accession his conduct changed suddenly and completely. The authorities for these stories are Sir Thomas Elyot's *The Governor* (1531) and Edward Hall's *Union of the Noble and Illustrious Houses of Lancaster and York* (1542). These two highly respectable authors seem to have relied largely on matter already in print, some of it traceable to within fifty years of Henry's death. I know of no argument for the historicity of any traditional narrative which cannot be applied to these stories; their credentials are equal to any, and far better than most—yet there is not a word of truth in any of them.

The facts are these: In 1400, at the age of thirteen, Henry became his father's deputy in Wales, made his headquarters at Chester, and spent the next seven years in almost continuous warfare with Owen Glendower and his allies. In 1407 he led a successful invasion of Scotland. In 1408 he was employed as Warden of the Cinque Ports, and at Calais. In the following year, owing to his father's illness, he became regent, and continued in this capacity till 1412. During this period his character as a ruler was marred only by his religious bigotry, and what seems to be the only authentic anecdote of the time describes the part he played at the burning of John Badby, the Lollard. In 1412 an attempt was made to induce Henry IV, whose ill-health continued to unfit him for his duties, to abdicate, but his refusal to do so, together with differences on foreign policy, led to the withdrawal of the future Henry V from court, probably to Wales, till his father's death a year later. He did not reappoint Sir William Gascoigne as Chief Justice, and there is no foundation for the story that the latter committed him to prison.

These facts are drawn from the *Dictionary of National Biography,* which sums up the account by saying that "his youth was spent on the battlefield and in the council chamber, and the popular tradition (immortalized by Shakespeare) of his riotous and dissolute conduct is not supported by any contemporary authority." According to Sir Charles Oman, "his life was sober and orderly. . . . He was grave and earnest in speech, courteous in all his dealings, and an enemy of flatterers and favourites. His sincere piety bordered on asceticism. . . . His enemies called him hard-hearted and sanctimonious. . . . The legendary tales which speak of him as a debauched and idle youth, who consorted with disreputable favourites, such as Shakespeare's famous Sir John Falstaff, are entirely worthless." [1]

Even had there been no contemporary records of Henry's youth, there are points in the account adopted

[1] C. W. Oman: *A History of England,* pp. 219–220.

by Shakespeare which might lead a sober critic to doubt
its veracity. Many of the episodes are in themselves highly
improbable; it is difficult to imagine who could have transmitted them with knowledge and safety, and they are quite
out of keeping with Henry's activities as king, all of which
suggest a long apprenticeship to war and statecraft. An
idle and dissolute scapegrace transformed in an instant
into the first soldier and statesman of his age would indeed be an astonishing spectacle. Had, however, our critic
ventured to express his doubts, with what scorn would he
not have been assailed by our rationalizing professors!
"Here," they would have said, "is an impudent fellow who
pretends to know more about the fifteenth century than
those who lived in it. The facts which he dares to dispute
were placed on record by educated and responsible persons, the leading historians of their day. Could anything be
more absurd than to suppose that they would circulate dis-
creditable stories about a national hero at a time when the
facts of his career must have been widely known?"

Yet these stories are, as we have seen, quite untrue.
They were written down by men who, if they did not know
that they were untrue, could easily have found out, and
they have been, and still are, accepted by thousands in
preference to the truth.

We cannot, however, suppose that these stories were
pure invention. We have seen that imagination is not the
faculty of making something out of nothing, but that of
using, in a more or less different form, material already
present in the mind. We must conclude, then, that those
who composed the traditional stories about Prince Henry
applied to him, in a more or less modified form, stories
which they had heard in a different but not dissimilar connection. We shall fail to explain the origin of these stories
unless we can trace the materials from which they were
composed.

We have seen that the Falstaff stories, as we may call
them, since it is round Falstaff that they revolve, are not a
supplement to history, nor even a travesty of history. The
Prince Henry of history, who spent his time trying to suppress the Welsh and the Lollards, and the Prince Henry

of the stories, who spends his time roistering with Falstaff, may meet on the field of Shrewsbury, but they are really creatures of quite different worlds, and the world of the latter is the world of myth.

In this world of myth the principal characters are two, a hero and a buffoon, who meet with various adventures together, and live on terms of the greatest familiarity. Whence did the imagination of Shakespeare and his predecessors derive their materials for depicting such characters and incidents? The name of Falstaff may be a corruption of that of Sir John Fastolf, but their careers and characters bear no resemblance. The figure of Falstaff may have resembled that of some sixteenth-century knight, but such knight could obviously not have associated with Prince Henry. What has to be explained is not that there should be supposed to have been a man of that name, figure, and character, but that a man of such characteristics should have been associated, so closely associated, with King Henry V. It is quite clear that Shakespeare and his predecessors regarded Henry as a great hero, and it follows that they regarded association with a man of disreputable character, such as Falstaff was, as being in keeping with the character of a great hero. Elyot and Hall did not need comic relief as an excuse for introducing ribald stories, and the Falstaff incidents in Shakespeare form the principal part of the plays. It seems clear that to Shakespeare's audiences the proper way for a budding hero to behave was to roister with a drunken buffoon.

There is ample evidence that this idea did not arise in the sixteenth century, but is both ancient and widespread. In Greek mythology Dionysos is, as we have seen, the type or youthful hero, and is in the habit of roistering with Silenos, a fat, drunken buffoon. The great traditional hero of the Arab world, Hârûn ar Rashid, roisters with Abu Nuwâs, his drunken jester, and though Hârûn and Abu Nuwâs are historical, the stories told of them are not.[2] In the Indian drama there is a stock comic character called Vidusaka, who acts as a faithful, though ludicrous, companion to the royal hero, and is represented as a hideous

[2] W. H. Ingrams: *Abu Nuwâs, passim.*

dwarf.[3] Professor Ker gives us some examples from medieval literature. Thus in *Garin of Lorraine* we have Galopin,
the reckless humorist. He is ribald and prodigal, yet of
gentle birth, and capable of good service when he can be
got away from the tavern. In *Huon of Bordeaux,* Charlot,
son of Charlemagne, appears as the worthless companion
of traitors and disorderly persons. In the saga of *Burnt
Njal, Kari,* when avenging his father-in-law, is accompanied by one Bjorn, a comic braggart, to whom, as Professor Ker points out, he owes his preservation.[4] Leif the
Lucky, the alleged discoverer of America, is, as we have
seen,[5] accompanied by his father-in-law, who is a figure of
fun, gets drunk, and babbles in a foreign tongue. The same
idea, that of the noble knight with a comic, drunken
squire, appears in Don Quixote.

In the Ampleforth (Yorkshire) folk-play, the clown
says:

*"I was always jovial and always will be, always at one
     time of year,*
*"Since Adam created both oxen and plough, we get plenty
     of store and strong beer."*

He makes a series of quips in verse, after which he and
the King rattle swords together.[6] In the pantomime the
clown is closely associated with the harlequin hero, and at
the circus the clown is privileged to joke at the expense of
the master of the ring.

There can be no doubt that Falstaff falls within the
class of persons who are variously termed fools, clowns,
jesters, buffoons, etc., and we shall be able to explain the
part he plays only if we can explain the origin of this class.
Why did kings and other important people keep a fool or
jester, a licentious character whose sallies were often di-
rected at his master? That they did so purely for fun is a
cheap rationalization; the official position, the recognized

[3] E. Welsford: *The Fool,* p. 62.
[4] W. P. Ker, op. cit., pp. 281, 310, 314.
[5] *Supra,* p. 69.
[6] E. K. Chambers: *The English Folk-play,* p. 140.

costume, the coxcomb and bladder, emblems of fertility, and the immunity from reprisal or punishment, all mark out the fool as a holy man. We learn that in 1317, when King Edward II was keeping Pentecost at Westminster, a woman disguised as a "histrio" rode into the palace and delivered an insulting letter to the King. The doorkeepers, when blamed, said that it was against the royal custom to deny admission to any "minstrel" upon such a solemn occasion.[7] It would seem that on holy days fools were particularly sacred.

The idea of Falstaff as a holy man may seem absurd, and he is, of course, a compound character, but that Shakespeare had at the back of his mind the idea that Falstaff was a holy man is suggested by his death. "Nay, sure, he's not in hell; he's in Arthur's bosom, if ever man went to Arthur's bosom. 'A made a finer end and went away, an it had been any christom child . . . 'a babbled of green fields." [8] It seems clear that Shakespeare intended him to die in the odour of sanctity, and, while it would be dangerous to stress Arthur in this connection, the sanctity seems pagan rather than Christian.

And what did Falstaff do when alive? For the most part he got drunk and then uttered wise saws in a whimsical manner. This suggests that he, or rather his prototype, was a soothsayer or prophet. A soothsayer or prophet is a person who, when in a state of religious ecstasy, usually induced by some intoxicant or narcotic, discloses things that are hidden from the people at large. But that was not his original function, since knowledge of things unseen, even knowledge of the future, was in pre-racing days of little real value. If custom and circumstance mould your life, and you marry, sow, or fight as they dictate, and never otherwise, there is little point in knowing what the result of your actions will be. The original function of the prophet was not to foretell what was going to happen, but to ensure, by the appropriate ceremonies, that what was wanted to happen should happen. The appropriate cere-

[7] E. K. Chambers: *The Mediæval Stage,* vol. i, p. 44.
[8] *King Henry V,* Act ii, Scene iii.

monies included, as in many parts of the world they still
include, the use of intoxicants or narcotics to put the
prophet into a proper condition for prophesying.

The story of Balaam contains no mention of intoxicants, but the scene of his meeting with the angel is laid
in a vineyard, and his first being unable and then able to
see the angel suggests some kind of trance. At any rate we
see clearly the function of a prophet: "Come now therefore, I pray thee," says Balak, "curse me this people . . .
peradventure I shall prevail." [9] Balaam is to perform the
proper ceremonies, which include sacrificing on seven al-
tars, and is then to prophesy the defeat of the Israelites.
This will enable Balak to defeat them, for he knows that
no king can gain a victory unless that victory has been
properly prophesied.

We are told that among the ancient Arabs the menaces
which the poet-seer hurled against the foe were believed to
be inevitably fatal, and that their pronunciation was attended by peculiar ceremonies, such as anointing the hair
on one side of the head, letting the mantle hang down
loosely, and wearing only one sandal. The ancient Irish
poet possessed similar powers. "The Irish *glam dichenn*,
like the Arabic *hija*, was no mere expression of opinion,
but a most potent weapon of war, which might blister an
adversary's face or even cost him his life. Like the Arabic
hija, too, it was at one time accompanied with ritual action; it was uttered 'on one foot, one hand, one eye.' " [1]

It is possible that in very early times every king was his
own prophet; that is to say, it was his duty to intoxicate
himself and then prophesy whatever was required. Traces
of such a custom seem to survive in certain ceremonial
drinks that are drunk by chiefs or priests only. We find,
however, a general tendency for kings to perform their
religious duties by deputy. It would then be necessary for
the king's prophet to accompany him to war, and I suggest that this explains the presence of Falstaff, with a
bottle of sack in his pocket, on the field of Shrewsbury.

It need not be supposed that Shakespeare had all these

[9] Numbers xxii, 6.
[1] E. Welsford, op. cit., pp. 80, 89.

ideas present in his mind, but he was soaked in mythology and folklore, and certainly seems to have had some of them. He associates prophecy with drunkenness and drugs: "Plots have I laid, inductions dangerous, by drunken prophecies," says King Richard III,[2] and Banquo, when the witches have prophesied and disappeared, speaks of eating "the insane root that takes the reason prisoner." [3] This root is no doubt the mandrake or mandragora, which Iago includes among the "drowsy syrups." [4]

When Prince Henry sees Falstaff lying apparently dead, he says: "I could have better spared a better man." [5] He has in this scene the character not of a reprobate but a hero, and it is therefore the hero who cannot spare the drunken buffoon. I may perhaps be thought to lay too much stress on trifles, but such points are trifles only to those who cherish the illusion that poets derive their ideas from their own inner consciousness.

The discussion has been a long one, but it is intended to serve two purposes. The first is to show that the foundations of tradition are totally different from the foundations of history, and that, if our data are at all adequate, we can easily separate the two. The second is to show that when Sir James Frazer speaks of "the miraculous features which gather round the memory of popular heroes, as naturally as moss and lichens gather about stones," [6] he is speaking without the book. The traditions that have gathered about the memory of King Henry V are, as I have tried to show, mythical, but there is nothing miraculous about them. Shakespeare, like all his contemporaries, believed in miracles, and used them in his dramas—for example, in the scene in *Macbeth* from which I have just quoted. He did not, however, use them in connection with Henry V, and the reason is simple: the miraculous features associated with victorious heroes in the myths were dragons, magic swords, and helmets of invisibility, and in the sixteenth

---

[2] Act I, Scene i.
[3] *Macbeth*, Act I, Sc. iii.
[4] *Othello*, Act III.
[5] *King Henry IV*, Pt. I, Act v, Scene iv.
[6] *Folklore in the Old Testament*, vol. iii, p. 97.

century people had ceased to believe in these, though they
still believed in ghosts, witches, and fairies. The association
of myths and miracles with historical characters, far from
being a matter of random accumulation, is, like all the
phenomena of human culture, the result of processes
which can be studied and explained. The subject requires
fuller treatment than I can give it here, but that it is governed by rules I have no doubt, and I suggest the following:

First, the person with whom the myths are to be associated must not be too recent, or the true facts of his career
will be remembered, nor too remote, or he will have been
superseded and forgotten. About fifty years after his death
is a probable time for myths to be first associated with a
historical character, but this period may be extended if his
career has been recorded, and if his fame has not been
eclipsed by a later comer of similar character.

Secondly, he must have been famous or notorious in
certain definite connections, and his exploits or misfortunes must be such as to afford pegs upon which the myths
can be hung.

Thirdly, the miracles that the myths contain will be
attributed to the historical character if, when the myths
are first attached to him, the possibility of such miracles
is still believed in; otherwise they will be omitted.

The first two of these rules follow from the conclusions
reached in previous chapters, and indeed should be fairly
obvious. It should, however, be noted that this association
of myths with historical characters is literary and not
popular. There is no evidence that illiterates ever attach
myths to real persons. The mythical stories told of English kings and queens—Alfred and the cakes, Richard I
and Blondel, Queen Eleanor and Fair Rosamund, Queen
Margaret and the robber, and so on—seem to have been
deliberately composed; a well-known character and an old
story were considered more interesting when combined.
"Even from very early times," says Professor Nicoll,[7]
"there had been a tendency in the morality to substitute

[7] *The Theory of Drama,* p. 164.

for a pure abstraction some typical and well-known royal figure. Bale's *King Johan* is a good example of this."

As regards the third rule, I cannot find that anyone has studied the attribution of miracles to real people. Miracles fall into two classes: those which people believe to be possible in their own times, and those which they believe to have taken place only at certain periods in the past. There is nothing natural in the belief in miracles; people have to be taught to believe in them just as they have to be taught everything that is not patent to the senses. The idea that a stupid and ignorant person will necessarily believe in werewolves or magic swords is quite baseless. A miracle is a phenomenon that can be produced, on the appropriate occasions, by gods and sacred personages, but never by ordinary people. Early man, however, knew nothing of gods or sacred personages. No doubt he was often surprised at occurrences of which he had no experience, but mere surprise does not lead to a belief in miracles; it has first to be combined with certain definite religious beliefs. A miracle, as we have seen, is not any wonder, but a particular type of wonder—that is, a ritual wonder—and it must have needed a long and intensive subjection to ritual influences before people learned to believe that the ritual transformation of a man into a wolf was a real transformation.

The history of the Devil affords an interesting example of this process. Originally, it would seem, he was a ritual character who wore the horns of a bull or goat, probably the divine king in his capacity as the promoter of fertility. Later, apparently, the horns came to stand for the old king, their actual wearer, as opposed to the new king, their future wearer, and so the Horned Man became the antagonist of the Hero. Eventually he stepped out of the ritual into real life, and became, what to millions he still is, a figure far more real than any historical character has ever been to anyone.

The date at which the life of a saint was written can be judged by the part played in it by the Devil. Many of the early saints are purely mythical; their lives are nothing but hero myths with the sacred marriage left out. Later we get lives of saints who were real persons, into which encounters with the Devil and other mythical features have been introduced, but it is quite untrue to say that such incidents gather naturally about them. They have been introduced deliberately in order to make the stories conform to what at the time was regarded as the correct type. But whereas the utmost that can be allowed to a modern saint are limited powers of supernatural healing, encounters with supernatural beings are still tolerated in the lives of ancient saints.

The same tendency is to be seen in Shakespeare. In plays such as *Macbeth* or *The Tempest,* staged in remote regions or long-past ages, the hero's familiar, Hecate, or Ariel, may appear and disappear miraculously, since the audience was prepared to accept miracles under such conditions. But Prince Henry could not convincingly have been given an attendant sprite; Falstaff, though as mythical as Hecate or Ariel, is very much more solid.

I have dealt at length with Prince Henry and Falstaff because the myths are familiar and the facts readily accessible, but a study of any hero to whose name myths have become attached would show the clear-cut line that separates the historical hero from his mythical namesake. "From the researches of J. Bédier upon the epic personages of William of Orange, Girard de Rousillon, Ogier the Dane, Raoul de Cambrai, Roland, and many other worthies, it emerges that they do not correspond in any way with what historical documents teach us of their alleged real prototypes." [8]

"All history," said Dr. Johnson, "so far as it is not supported by contemporary evidence, is romance." [9] This is perfectly true, since romance is often myth in disguise, and if historians, instead of telling us what, in their opinion, is "not improbable," were to bear it in mind and consider carefully the channels by which any alleged fact has been or could be transmitted, we should less often find myth masquerading as history.

[8] A. van Gennep, op. cit., p. 173.
[9] J. Boswell: *A Tour to the Hebrides,* p. 335.

NOTE.—Professor Hocart, though in general agreement with my views, disagreed with my explanation of the clown. "The clown," he said, "is the earth-cousin of the sky-king, and so does everything topsy-turvy."

PART THREE

Drama

*

same applies to the go... ... ... blue-black and half flesh-colour (by which she is easily recognized." [4] She could hardly require recognition except on the stage.

There is a curious incident in the saga of *Burnt Njal* when Njal's sons ask for help at the Thing. According to the story, Skarphedinn is one of the best-known men in Iceland, and has been attending the Thing regularly for forty years, yet four of the chief men in the island use almost exactly the same odd formula in asking who he is. We are told that he "had on a blue kirtle and grey breeks, and black shoes on his feet, coming high up his leg: he

CHAPTER XX

THE BASIS OF DRAMA

✳

In the previous parts of this book I have attempted to show that traditional narratives are never historical; that they are myths, and that a myth is a story told in connection with a rite. In the following chapters I shall attempt to show that it is the dramatic features of ritual which give rise to the myth—that is, to the traditional narrative—and that all, or at any rate most, traditional narratives show, by their form and their content, that they are derived neither from historical fact nor from imaginative fiction, but from acted ritual, that is to say, ritual performed for the benefit of, and in the presence of, a body of worshippers who take either no part in it, or a very small part. Ritual performed in this way may be described as dramatic ritual or ritual drama. There can be little doubt that all drama is derived originally from ritual drama, but before discussing ritual drama let us first decide what we mean by the word "drama."

When we say that an incident is "dramatic," we mean that it resembles the incidents we are accustomed to see represented on the stage, but differs from the normal incidents of life. We imply that what happens in real life is seldom dramatic. I would go further, and say that what happens in real life is never really dramatic, that is to say, that it is never really like what is represented on the stage.

It is often said that the best plays are those which most nearly resemble real life, and to say that scenes or incidents represented on the stage are artificial is generally held to be a severe condemnation. As a fact, however, nothing like real life ever has been, or ever could be, represented on the stage. There are three rules that apply to all dramatic performances. They are:

1. Everything said or done upon the stage must be clearly audible or visible to the audience.

2. Everything said or done upon the stage must be related to the plot or main theme of the drama.

3. The interest of the audience must never be allowed to flag.

When we say that a situation is dramatic we imply that these rules have been observed, but in real life they never are. Nothing has ever happened in real life that, if presented on the stage exactly as it happened, would hold the attention of an audience for half an hour. The difference between a play which is regarded as realistic and one which is not is that while in the latter there is nothing which bears any resemblance to real life, in the former the actors say and do what real people might conceivably say and do, but they say and do in a couple of hours interesting and exciting things which in real life would take weeks or months. All the dull things that happen in between are left out; we spend most of our time in working, eating, sleeping, washing, and dressing and in talking about them when we are not doing them, but the actors in drama seldom do any of these things, or even mention them. The reason for this is that even in the most realistic drama the actors are not really attempting to imitate real life; they are acting a drama, and must conform to the conventions of the drama. Their utterances, their facial expressions, their actions, and their gestures must be highly artificial if they are to be clearly heard and seen from the gallery; even their whispers must be audible to hundreds. When making love or quarrelling, the actors must take care to face, or half face, the audience; on the stage it is quite in order for the whole court to turn their backs upon the king. One glance at the photograph of a dramatic scene is enough to assure us that it is not a scene from real life.

And not only is the manner of the drama totally different from that of real life, but the plots are like nothing that really happens. In a drama the leading characters must be the same throughout, and the incidents must follow one another in a connected sequence; everything must work up to a climax. How different are our own lives as we look back upon them from the life of a hero of drama! In our case everything, or at least everything that might be considered interesting, is completely disconnected. The failure of our first love-affair drove us to thoughts of suicide, but we have now forgotten the girl's married name. The man with whom we had that terrible row—last year we saw a notice of his death in the newspaper, and were mildly interested. The place where we lived and worked for years, and which held everything that made life worth living, is now a memory that grows daily fainter. It is the same with any historical character; he can be brought into drama only by means of a purely fictitious continuity of action. To revert, for example, to the subject of the last chapter, we find that Shakespeare causes the defeat of Scrope's rebellion to be announced to King Henry IV on his deathbed, though it really took place eight years earlier.[1] But the important feature of the scene is the myth of Prince Henry's trying on the crown. We are so much accustomed to getting our history from dramas and romances that we find it difficult to realize that the historical drama is little more than a combination of fiction and pageantry.

The characters of the drama, even when they are given historical names, are not individuals but types. This is essential, in order that their idiosyncrasies, of both appearance and character, may be instantly recognized by the audience. Real people are seldom, if ever, sufficiently distinguished in appearance, and sufficiently consistent in conduct and expression. The arts of caricature and satire consist in giving a quasi-dramatic character to real people by exaggerating their idiosyncrasies.

The point of all this is that when we say that a story is dramatic, we mean that the characterization is well marked, that the dialogue is pertinent, that the interest is sustained, and that everything works up to a climax; we mean, in other words, that it is something very different from a description of scenes from real life.

It is this dramatic quality which is characteristic of the

[1] *King Henry IV,* Pt. II, Act IV, Scene iv.

traditional narrative, whatever form it may take, and which affords us a further proof, or at any rate further evidence, that the traditional narrative is not drawn from real life. The dramatic character of the Tale of Troy is noted even by those who believe it to be based on history. Thus Mr. T. W. Allen, who supposes, though without any evidence to justify the supposition, that a chronicle of the siege of Troy was kept by the bards, considers that "our *Iliad* and *Odyssey* are two episodes as arranged by Homer out of the chronicle . . . they are dramatized." [2] Dr. Pickard-Cambridge, discussing the dithyrambs of Bacchylides, which deal almost entirely with incidents in the Trojan and Theban cycles, observes that "it is noticeable also how large a proportion of the poems is occupied by speeches in the first person; and though these are woven into a narrative, they give the poems a dramatic quality like that which Aristotle finds and praises in Homer." [3]

Modern classical scholars, like Aristotle himself, may profess to be interested in historical fact, but it is really literary form that absorbs them, and that causes them to admire the dramatic. They mistake dramatic truth for historical truth through their familiarity with the former and ignorance of the latter. Historical truth is as a rule brutal, inconsequential, and apparently meaningless. It is therefore apt to be less interesting and far less æsthetically satisfying than dramatic truth. But the great difference between them lies in the fact that whereas historical truth is objective, dramatic truth is subjective; that is to say, it is subject not to conditions imposed by external necessity, but to its own conventions. The villain of the drama meets with "poetic justice," for such is the convention, but the villain of real life too often dies in the odour of sanctity.

Had the Tale of Troy been a true tale—that is to say, the account of historical facts—the siege would have been brought to an end within a few weeks, either by the defection of the Greek army, by an epidemic of dysentery which carried off the leading warriors, or by the storming of Troy,

    [2] T. W. Allen: *Homer—The Origin and Transmission*, p. 169.
    [3] A. W. Pickard-Cambridge: *Dithyramb, Tragedy and Comedy*, p. 45.

in which Helen was murdered for the sake of her ear-rings
by some nameless Greek. It is of such episodes that true
history consists, but from the dramatic point of view they
are untrue, since they further no plot and bring out no
characterization.

We may conclude, then, that the Tale of Troy has a
dramatic and not a historical basis, since it exhibits all
the characteristics of drama—I shall discuss more of them
presently—and none of the characteristics of history. The
same applies to all the traditional tales that we considered
in the earlier chapters. Incidents from the Tale of Troy
were, of course, drama to the Athenians of the fifth century B.C., and many stories from Teutonic or Celtic tradition are drama to us, in the form, for example, of Wagner's
Ring of the Nibelungs, his *Tristan and Isolde*, and Bough-
ton's *The Immortal Hour*. And these stories are readily
transformed, in my view retransformed, not only into
drama, but into that form of sung drama which we call
opera, which requires its plot to be simple and dramatic
even more than does the spoken drama, and is therefore even farther from real life.

Shakespeare's so-called "histories" are not really historical. When we examine them, we find that the dramatic effect is produced by the introduction either of
fictitious characters, or of incidents and dialogues for
which there is no historical warrant. Even then the dramatic effects are far less successful than in such plays as
Hamlet and *Othello*, in which the dramatist is completely
untrammelled by considerations of historicity.

Of the sagas, Professor Ker notes that the best passages
are the most dramatic;[4] in other words, those passages
which give the greatest satisfaction to the reader are those
farthest removed from real life. Olrik says of *Loki's Wrang-
ling* (*Lokasenna*) in the *Elder Edda* that it is "a short—we
may say a dramatic—poem," and notes that the dialogue
form affords "a possibility of imparting more tension to
the action than is possible in the ordinary heroic lay."[5]

Dialogue is the essence of drama, and wherever we find

[4] W. P. Ker: *Epic and Romance*, p. 202.
[5] Op. cit., p. 155.

dialogue we may suspect a dramatic origin. It is hardly an exaggeration to say that there is no such thing as a recorded dialogue between historical persons. The nearest approaches to it are perhaps to be found in Boswell's conversations with Dr. Johnson and Lord Stanhope's conversations with the Duke of Wellington; the latter, though the author tells us that he always made a record the same day, or at latest the next, are little more than scraps and paraphrases, and although Boswell was "very assiduous in recording" Dr. Johnson's conversation, not much more can be said of that; from neither would it be possible to produce anything resembling those dramatic dialogues which figure so prominently in traditional narratives, and are so often accepted as historical.

One of the largest of recent biographies is Mr. Winston Churchill's *Marlborough;* the correspondence is voluminous, but anyone who wished to learn how the Duke expressed himself in conversation would be disappointed. Nor do we find any conversation in the writings of the great diarists; Pepys and Evelyn often report the gist of conversations, but never the words. Snatches of conversation are occasionally reported in the abundant political and diplomatic correspondence of the sixteenth and seventeenth centuries, but these are intended to emphasize particular points in the case that the writer is trying to make; the edifying repartees that the religious apologists put into the mouths of their martyrs must be regarded with suspicion.

Going farther back, we find a good deal of dialogue in *Froissart,* but Froissart was a romancer as well as a chronicler, and most of his dialogue, with its sententious politeness, suggests the study rather than the camp or the battlefield. He is also most conversational where he is least reliable; in the story of the burghers of Calais, for example, we are given the alleged actual words of the King, the Queen, Sir Walter Manny, and the burgesses, yet the story, though it has been accepted by many historians, is probably fictitious. It is not mentioned by those who wrote nearest to the date, and there are other circumstances which led M. Levesque[6] to regard it as poetic embroidery.

[6] Quoted in T. Johnes: *Froissart's Chronicles,* vol. i, p. 188 n.

It is impossible to go through all the earlier chronicles, but it may be mentioned that there is no dialogue in the *Anglo-Saxon Chronicle*, and the little that is to be found in Henry of Huntingdon is in those of his stories which are the most remote from probability.

The point of the foregoing is not to suggest that no writer ever recorded a remark made by a king or other distinguished person; nothing seems more likely than that this should have been done. The surprising thing is that there is so little to be found which can even be claimed as genuine. If the conversations of eminent persons were really remembered, handed down orally, and eventually recorded, as those maintain who allege the historicity of, for example, the Book of Genesis, the *Iliad*, and the Icelandic sagas, there should then be in existence, in one form or another, a vast literature of the utterances of such persons as King Alfred, William the Conqueror, and Richard I, even if three quarters of what was remembered were never written down, and of what was written down, three quarters were lost. The point is not that what there is is probably mythical, but that there is so little which can even put in a claim to historicity. I doubt very much whether all the words that have been put into the mouths of all the kings of England from the earliest times to the year 1500, if they were put together, would amount to the length of the shortest Icelandic saga, since even in the mythical stories of the kings direct speech plays but a minor part.

In this they differ from the genuinely traditional narrative in all its forms, as well as from the Greek hero-tales and Norse sagas, which, as we have seen, are partly traditional and partly literary. In ballads and fairy-tales the "marked preference for direct speech," which Ridgeway[7] found in the Homeric poems, is equally marked. I have taken a number of ballads at random and found none of which dialogue does not make up at least half. In many the dramatic form is pretty obvious: "It must be noticed that this ballad, with its three persons, and these couplets of question and reply, is really a little drama," says An-

[7] *Dramas and Dramatic Dances,* p. 154.

drew Lang.[8] He is speaking of the French ballad of *Le Roi Renaud,* of which there are variants in Italy and Scotland, but the same applies to ballads generally. The Welsh triad dealing with the meeting of Arthur and Tristram was, according to Sir John Rhys,[9] intended to be sung to music. The three characters, Arthur, Drystan, and Gwalchmai, utter in turn verses of which the first two lines are a kind of refrain, and the third carries on the action of the "little drama." It was, in fact, a kind of cantata.

Many ballads are quasi-historical, and the determined euhemerist could no doubt get history out of them, as he does out of the sagas. The sagas, as we have seen, are novels based on ballads, and the ballads, like the myths, the epics, and the fairy-tales, all, as I shall try to show, originate in the ritual drama.

[8] *Folk-Lore,* vol. i, p. 108.
[9] *The Arthurian Legend,* p. 380.

CHAPTER XXI

THE LANGUAGE OF THE DRAMA

✳

The dialogue, as we have just seen, is an essential feature of the drama, but it is by no means the only form of expression by which the traditional narrative betrays its dramatic origin. In this chapter I shall deal with four others.

We find, in the first place, that the characters, whatever their supposed nationality, all speak the same language.

Secondly, we often have detailed accounts of incidents and conversations which are supposed to have taken place in secret or in solitude.

Thirdly, we find that introductions, prophecies, and boasts are characteristic features.

And fourthly, the characters are often represented as speaking in verse.

On the English stage, of course, all the characters speak English. In the folk-play there is a character who is supposed to be a Turk, but it never occurs to anyone that Turks speak Turkish. In this, as in all other respects, the "folk" follow the example of the educated; we all listen without surprise to Julius Cæsar speaking Elizabethan English, and so soaked are we in the dramatic conventions that many people quote the words of Shakespeare as if they were actually the words of Cæsar. We realize, however, that while Cæsar is a dramatic character who speaks English, he was also a historical character who spoke Latin. Like King Henry V, and every other historical character who has been dramatized, he exists for us as a kind of dual personality, of which one or other aspect is uppermost in our minds, according as they are at the moment more occupied with history or with drama.

But no one, I suppose, has ever imagined Sir Andrew

Aguecheek as an Illyrian or Autolycus as a Czech, or has
wondered whether Hamlet's speeches were originally written in runes; whatever their titular country, period, and
language, their real home is the stage, their period the day
on which they are acted, and their language English. They
are characters in the drama, and apart from it have no
existence.

We find the same phenomenon in the *Iliad*. Hector and
Kassandra are in theory Asiatic foreigners, yet their names
are Greek, their manners and customs are Greek, and
their language is Greek. "But allowance must here be
made," says Dr. Leaf,[1] "for poetic needs; these prescribed
free communication by speech between both parties, and
it is certainly not possible to deduce from this that Acha-
ians and Trojans spoke the same language." Sir Andrew
Aguecheek's use of English does not, of course, prove that
English and Illyrians spoke the same language, but Sir
Andrew's name, his language, and his conversation show
that Shakespeare did not seriously intend to represent him
as a foreigner. Similarly, everything that we are told of
Hector shows quite clearly that the composers of the *Iliad*
did not seriously intend to represent him as a foreigner.
And there was no reason why they should; the Illyrians of
Shakespeare's time *were* foreigners, but the Trojans of
Homer's time, whenever we suppose that to have been,
were Greeks. The Greeks may have known that Troy was
once a non-Greek city, just as Mycenæ was a non-Greek
city, and as we know that London was once a non-English
city. But just as "Londoner" means Englishman to us, so
"Trojan" must have meant Greek to the Greeks of the
seventh or sixth century B.C. An allied Greek army might
attack Troy, just as an allied Greek army might attack
Thebes, but this would not make the Trojans any more
than the Thebans foreigners. This attitude may have
changed when Troy, and all Asiatic Greece, had become
part of the Persian Empire, and considerable alterations
may have been made in the text of Homer after this date,
but the main lines of the story were undoubtedly laid

[1] *Troy*, p. 343.

down before, at a time when the idea of a war on equal terms between Greeks and barbarians, or Europeans and Asiatics, must have been inconceivable. It was based on a dramatic ritual in which the hero's antagonist was just as much a Greek as the hero himself.

After the Potiphar's-wife incident in the myth of Bellerophon, Proetus sends Bellerophon off to Lycia with a letter to the King, his father-in-law, asking the latter to have him murdered. This form of letter was perhaps as well known in classical Greece as in India at the much more recent period when the poet tells us that:

I sent my Kitmutgar once with a note unto the beak:—
"Please give the bearer half-a-dozen lashes for his cheek." [2]

It is difficult to believe, however, that at any time at which Belerophon can be supposed to have lived, even if writing was in use, kings would have written to each other in this style, even if they understood each other's language. Ridgeway[3] accepts the story as proof that a letter written in Argolis could be read in Lycia, but it was probably a stage device, capable of being used with great dramatic effect. The myth seems to be a combination of the Potiphar's-wife incident with the David and Uriah story, both of which have a wide range. It is the latter with which we are here concerned; we find a king of Munster sending his son over to Scotland with a request for his immediate decapitation carved upon his shield,[4] and a similar incident occurs in *Hamlet*,[5] where the hero sails for England, accompanied "by letters conjuring to that effect, the present death of Hamlet." David, of course, sends his instructions to Joab to "set Uriah in the forefront of the hottest battle" [6] in writing, but that a letter is not an essential feature of the story appears from the Mexican parallel, in which King Nezahualcoatl, in

[2] Aliph Cheem: *Lays of Ind*, p. 149.
[3] *Early Age of Greece*, vol. i, p. 209.
[4] W. G. Wood-Martin: *Pagan Ireland*, p. 45.
[5] Act II, Scene iii.
[6] 2 Samuel xi, 15.

similar circumstances, gives oral instructions to two chiefs
to bring the destined victim into the thickest of the fight.[7]
Ridgeway himself [8] gives a variant from Burma, in which
the King, having fallen in love with his brother's wife,
sends the brother off to suppress a fictitious rebellion, and
meanwhile forcibly marries the wife.

It is to be noted that in all these stories the protagonist
is a king; with the omnipresence of kings in tradition I
shall deal later; there seems to me to be no doubt that
these stories are from dramas of ritual origin, and it is
absurd to attempt to draw from them conclusions as to
the diffusion of the Greek language. Moreover, as we
have seen, Ridgeway's conclusion is the opposite of Leaf's.

It is remarkable, however, that the unity of language
in tradition has been so little noticed. When the champion
of the Firbolgs meets the champion of the invading Tuatha
de Danaan, the former is agreeably surprised to hear the
latter speak good Irish.[9] It was no doubt the recorder,
mistaking a dramatic incident for history, who was surprised at the invader's linguistic ability. If so, he must have
possessed the rudiments of a critical faculty, a faculty in
which most of his successors have been conspicuously
lacking.

Let us now turn to the second dramatic feature of the
language of tradition, the secret that is public property.
We find in many traditional narratives a detailed account
of incidents and conversations which, even if they had
really taken place, could not possibly have been reported.

Most present-day readers are so much soaked in fiction,
in novels in which the novelist describes at length what
passes through his heroine's mind in the seclusion of her
bedroom, that it seldom occurs to them to ask how deeds
or words performed or spoken in private came, if true, to
be reported, and, if untrue, to be imagined. In the first
case it is always possible, if a speech was made or a conversation took place at a court or in a council chamber,
that someone who was present made notes of what was

[7] W. H. Prescott: *The Conquest of Mexico,* vol. i, p. 168.
[8] *Dramas and Dramatic Dances,* p. 245.
[9] Lady Gregory: *Gods and Fighting Men,* p. 4.

said, but it is very seldom that such a possibility is en-
visaged in a traditional narrative. It is not merely that
there is no one there who can write, but often there is no
possible listener at all. "If this is true, how came it to be
known?" is a question historians might ask much oftener
than they do.

If, on the other hand, what is reported in the traditional
narrative is not true, why was it invented? I am not referring to simple lies, calculated to benefit the speaker or
injure his enemies, but to what is known as fiction. I have
already shown, or tried to show,[1] that fiction is never the
result of pure imagination, but is composed from matter
already present in the composer's mind. What is it, then,
that has suggested to novelists and story-tellers the idea of
describing what passes in the mind of another person? It
is probably the dramatic soliloquy, originally a ritualistic
incantation. And this explanation fits equally well the quasi-
historical conversations that could not possibly have been
reported. They are, in fact, merely variants of the same
dramatic feature. I touched on this question earlier[2] when
discussing King Alfred and the cakes, and I will now give
some examples in which the dramatic form is more evident.

The account of the "Cattle-spoil of Cooley" begins with
a long "pillow-talk" between King Ailill and Queen Medb.[3]
As a prologue to a drama, this conversation is in place;
as an alleged real conversation it seems absurd. It is just
possible, however, that it really took place and was reported; in the next example there is no such possibility.
In another Irish tale the sons of the King of Ulster spy
upon the sons of the King of Iruath. We are told exactly
what was said and done, yet the latter forthwith kill the
former and then disappear for ever.[4]

We can find similar examples in the sagas. In the saga
of Gunnlaug Snake-tongue, Gunnlaug and another fight
a lonely duel in which both are killed, yet the incidents of

[1] *Supra*, p. 136.
[2] *Supra*, p. 12.
[3] J. Dunn: *The Tain*, pp. 1–4.
[4] Lady Gregory, op. cit., p. 203.

the duel and the conversation between the combatants are reported at length. In the saga of the Faroe Islanders the hero Sigmund Brestison is found by his enemy Thorgrim lying exhausted on the beach, where he has been thrown up by the sea. Thorgrim proceeds to murder him, but before being murdered Sigmund is supposed to relate his last adventures, including his conversations with his drowned companions, and all this is reported verbatim by the murderer.

"We can easily," says Koht,[5] "cut out from true history all the conversations reported from secret meetings of two particular persons. . . . Strangely enough, many modern historians have accepted such conversations as strictly historical, and still more strangely, some of them have relied upon the historicity of the account when Snorri pretends to record even the unspoken thoughts of his hero, St. Olaf." That the saga-writers were familiar with the ritual drama is improbable, but they were undoubtedly soaked in traditions derived from it.

We find similar incidents in many fairy-tales and ballads. The fairy with the goose foot, who marries a mortal, but forbids him to see her at her toilet, is spied upon and her secret discovered. She recites a rhyme, whereupon her husband's castle, with all its occupants, immediately sinks into the ground, and the site is covered with water.[6] In the ballad of the Demon Lover, the ship bearing him and his lass disappears into the depths of the sea, but nevertheless we have a verbatim report of their last conversation. Similarly, in a legend of Luxembourg, the Devil, having persuaded the Count's daughter to kill her father and elope with him, takes her into the middle of a river and drowns her; yet we are told what he said to her before doing so.[7]

The last three examples seem to me to be clearly of dramatic origin. It is only in the drama that supernatural beings appear, and it is very rare, except in drama, for

[5] Op. cit., p. 134.
[6] P. Saintyves: *Contes de Perrault*, p. 423.
[7] W. Edwards: *A. Medieval Scrap-Heap*, p. 131.

anyone to disappear suddenly and completely. The last incident would be very easy to act, and might well arise as part of a ritual drama or its derivative a morality play, but it would be impossible for anyone to imagine it to whom it had not in some such way been suggested.

As our next feature we shall take the various devices by means of which those listening to the recital of a traditional narrative are made to understand clearly what is happening and what is going to happen. These devices include the introduction, the prophecy, and the boast, and in my view all these devices have their origin in the ritual drama.

, We all, I think, when we go to the theatre, fail to realize the limitations of the drama. We start by knowing that the play is a comedy, or a detective drama, or whatever it may be, and that it will be over at eleven p.m.; we have a program on which are printed the names of the characters in the order in which they appear, and from which we learn that the final scene takes place in the hero's library. We may delude ourselves into the belief that anything might happen, but if we think it over we must realize that, apart from the law and the Lord Chamberlain, the conventions of the drama confine within very narrow limits the extent to which the dramatist may surprise us. It may be objected that these conventions arise necessarily from the conditions under which drama is performed, but this, though no doubt true in part, is by no means the whole truth, since we find similar conventions in the Attic drama, in which the conditions of performance were very different. We find, for example, the very clearly marked division between tragedy and comedy, which did not allow that a man should come on the stage, make some jokes, and then be killed. Such an incident would also offend against the conventions of the modern stage, yet it might be highly dramatic.

The element of surprise, in both ancient and modern drama, is confined within very narrow limits because it originally formed no part of the drama at all. The drama was originally not an entertainment but a religious cere-

mony, in which the whole community, or at any rate all
the initiated, took part. Since the successful performance
of any ceremony depends upon its being performed as it
has always been performed, and since any hitch or dis-
turbance is believed to impair, if not to destroy, its
efficacy, it is essential that all the participants should understand exactly what is going to be done. And there is a
further factor: the ceremony is intended to produce certain
results, and the method generally adopted is for the
performers to assert that they are themselves achieving
or about to achieve the desired result. I have already discussed this aspect of ritual;[8] the point here to be noted is
that these factors in the ritual drama lead to features of
which the modern theatre program is a degenerate survival,
and which appear prominently in the traditional narrative.

We need not dwell at length on the introduction, as it
is a feature of genuine history as well as of tradition. In
its simplest form it is seen when a character comes on
saying: "Here comes I, old Beelzebub," or when the entrance of a new character is announced by those already
on the stage: "Who comes here? The worthy thane of
Ross." In the sagas the characters are not merely introduced when they first appear, but are also, if they manage
to avoid being killed, dismissed when they leave the stage:
"And now Thorarin is out of the story."

In ballads we find a form of introduction which is
clearly dramatic:

"Now whether are ye the queen hersell (for so ye well
   might be)
Or are ye the lass of Lochroyan, seeking Lord Gregory?"
"Oh, I am neither the queen," she said, "nor sic I seem to
   be;
But I am the lass of Lochroyan, seeking Lord Gregory."

Professor Chadwick,[9] notes how boastfully the heroes
of the *Iliad* introduce themselves. When Idomeneus meets
Deiphobus in battle, he challenges him, recites his own

[8] *Supra*, p. 154.
[9] *The Heroic Age*, p. 327.

pedigree, and continues: "But now have ships brought me hither with consequences evil to thee, and to thy father and to the rest of the Trojans," [1] He tells the audience who he is and what part he is going to play in the drama; that is to say, he combines the introduction with the prophecy.

The prophecy is, of course, a conspicuous feature of the Homeric literature—the prophecies of Kassandra, for example, are proverbial—and it is also a conspicuous feature of all forms of the traditional narrative. But it forms no part of history. Historical characters have seldom attempted to forecast the time, place, and manner of their own or other persons' deaths, and, we may safely say, have never succeeded except where matters were entirely within their own control. Even the most expert of politicians, financiers, or racing men seldom succeed in foretelling the future course of events, even events in their own particular line.

Prophecy, again, forms no part of the art of the novelist or story-teller. Many types of story depend for their success on a denouement unsuspected by the reader or listener, and even if the latter knows what is going to happen, he cannot without loss of interest suppose his knowledge to be shared by all the characters in the story.

Prophecy, then, in any narrative which pretends to be historical, is evidence that it is not really so, and in any narrative which is told for amusement indicates that it had originally some other purpose. In both cases the ritual drama is indicated as the original form of the narrative.

The prophecy occupies a very prominent place in the traditional literature of Ireland, and affords one of many reasons for believing that in pre-Christian times the ritual drama played a very important part in Irish life. Let us take some examples.

The fate of Cuchulainn is announced by Morann the seer as follows: "His praise will be in the mouths of all men; charioteers and warriors, kings and sages will recount his deeds; he will win the love of many. This child will avenge all your wrongs; he will give combat at your fords;

[1] *Iliad,* xiii, p. 448.

he will decide all your quarrels." [2] In Cuchulainn's last battle he throws his spear, which kills twenty-eight men. Lugaid takes up the spear and asks: "What shall fall by this spear, O sons of Calatin?" "A king will fall thereby," say the sons of Calatin. So Lugaid flings the spear, and deals Cuchulainn his death-wound.[3]

King Dermot questions his magicians as to the manner of his death. "Slaughter," says the first, "and 'tis a shirt grown from a single flax-seed, with a mantle of one sheep's wool, that on the night of thy death shall be about thee." "Drowning," says the second, "and it is ale brewed of one grain of corn that thou shall despatch that night." "Burning," says the third, "and bacon of swine that never was farrowed—that is what shall be thy dish." All of which comes to pass in a manner clearly suggesting a sacrificial drama.[4]

Glas fights a duel with Madan, son of the King of the Marshes, "but as it was not in the prophecy that Glas should find his death there, it was the son of the King of the Marshes that got his death by him." [5]

The prophecies of Merlin are a prominent feature of the *Morte Darthur*. To Balin he says: "Thou shalt strike a stroke the most dolourous that ever man struck . . . and through that stroke three kingdoms shall be in poverty, misery and wretchedness, twelve year." He tells King Arthur that so long as he has the scabbard of Excalibur he shall lose no blood, "though ye have as many wounds upon you as ye may have," and also "the prophecy that there should be a great battle beside Salisbury, and that Modred his sister's son should be against him." His prophecies include that of his own fate: "I shall die a shameful death, to be put in the earth quick." [6] It is to be noted that these prophecies, however authoritatively made, never have the slightest effect upon the action. Even Merlin

[2] E. Hull: *The Cuchillin Saga*, p. 20.
[3] Ibid., p. 259.
[4] S. H. O'Grady: *Silva Gadelica*, p. 86.
[5] Lady Gregory: *Gods and Fighting Men*, p. 214.
[6] *Morte Darthur*, pp. 54, 57, 44.

himself goes to his fate as if unaware of his own prophecy.[7]
This is a universal feature, and one inconsistent with the
view that the prophecy is a warning; at least it is not a
warning to the actors, though it may be to the audience.

In the sagas the death of every prominent man is foretold
by prophecies, dreams, and omens; his friends urge him
to put off his journey or to guard himself, but he pays no
attention to what they say, and goes to meet his death
exactly as has been foretold.

It need hardly be said that prophecy is a familiar feature
of the fairy-tale. The fairy godmother, or other supernatural being, tells the hero or heroine what will happen
to them on a particular date or at a particular spot. In this,
as in all other cases, the prophet is a ritual personage, and
the prophecy is, or is part of, the myth—that is to say,
the form of words associated with the ritual.

Not only is prophecy a prominent feature of the traditional narrative, but prophecies are often in verse. Now,
it will hardly be maintained that historical persons were
in the habit of speaking in verse, or that it occurs naturally
to a story-teller to represent his characters as doing so.
All the evidence suggests that verse was originally ritual
in character, and to a great extent it still is so; among
many peoples the only kind of verse is ritual verse—that
is, verse sung or recited upon religious or ceremonial occasions—and even in modern Europe hymns, psalms, and
devotional poems are better known and more widely used
than any other form of verse. When these poems contain
any narrative, it is a narrative connected with the ritual.
The Greeks and Romans had no secular narrative poetry,
and in northern Europe all the narrative poems before
the twelfth century are myths or romances based upon
myths. It is in this century, so far as I can learn, that we
find rhymed chronicles with a definitely historical basis.
Of these the best-known is probably Wace's *Roman de
Rou*, composed about 1170–5, which contains an account
of the Battle of Hastings. Dr. Round has shown that this
account, far from being derived from reliable traditions,

[7] Ibid., p. 76.

is in part a "somewhat confused paraphrase of the words of William of Malmesbury," and that the rest contains numerous blunders and anachronisms.[8] In this, as in every other case, the "traditional" is the historically worthless, and the fact that it is in verse form by no means adds to its credibility, since our knowledge of such poetry as deals with historical facts teaches us that a poem can never be regarded as the primary source for a historical fact; the poem is historical only in so far as the poet derives his facts from written records. A reliable account of a battle can be made only by collating the evidence of those who witnessed its various incidents and phases, and there is no reason to suppose that any illiterate poet has ever attempted such a feat. The poems of illiterates, and often of literates too, contain narratives of combat because their ritual is dramatic, and in dramatic ritual the combat takes a prominent place. The traditional accounts of combats, from the Tale of Troy to that of Robin Hood, are either in verse or give us reason to believe that they once were. They were once, that is to say, connected with dramatic ritual.

The Irish myths, like the sagas, are in prose, but some of the most important parts, including the prophecies, are in verse. Before setting out to invade Ulster, Queen Medb consults a prophetess:

"*Tell, O Fedelm, prophet-maid, How beholdest thou our host?*"

To which the answer is:

"*Crimson red from blood they are; I behold them bathed in blood.*"

This is repeated five times.[9] Needless to say, the Queen is not in the least affected. The prophecy is part of the ritual, and the fact that it is in verse while the rest of the myth is in prose makes this fact all the clearer.

[8] J. H. Round: *Feudal England*, p. 416.
[9] J. Dunn, op. cit., p. 15.

Even when there is no prophecy, the conversation in verse, whether it occurs in ballads and fairy-tales or in pseudo-history, indicates a dramatic origin. In the story of Alfred and the cakes, which was interpolated into Asser's *Life of Alfred*, the cowherd's wife is represented as breaking into a Latin verse, which may be rendered:

"*Can't you mind the cakes, man, and don't you see them burn?*
I'm bound you'll eat them fast enough as soon as it's your turn!"

The genuine incidents of Alfred's career have, of course, not been transmitted in verse.

The rhyme also plays an important part in the fairy-tale. In the widespread tale of the little man who serves the farmer until the latter gives him a hempen shirt instead of the linen one for which he had bargained, the little man is heard to sing:

"*Harden, harden, harden hemp! I will neither grind nor stamp.*
Had you given me linen gear, I would have served you many a year." [1]

On the other hand, when the Cornish farmer gave the helpful elf a new suit of green, the latter put it on and went off, singing:

"*Piskie fine and piskie gay Piskie now will fly away.*" [2]

But whatever the elf sings, the point is that somebody is always just in time to see and hear him; his departure is dramatized. Similarly, in the Rumpelstiltskin type of story, the lady who has to find out the elf's name always happens to overhear him singing it in a rhymed verse, such as:

[1] J. A. Giles: *Six Old English Chronicles,* p. 60.
[2] J. Rhys: *Celtic Folklore,* vol. i, p. 324.

"Little does my lady wot That my name is Trit-a-Trot." [3]

The overhearing is represented as accidental, but it is really, like the rhyme, an essential feature. They are features not of a written or spoken story, but of an acted drama.

[3] R. Hunt: *Popular Romances of the West of England,* p. 130.

CHAPTER XXII

AGE AND TIME

In every drama the unity of time must to some extent be preserved. The imagined interval between the acts or scenes must not be so long that the characters in the first act could not survive until the last, and the characters themselves must not be supposed to have changed between the acts to such an extent that they cease to be readily recognizable by the audience. The observance of these two rules is almost universal on the stage to this day; on the rare occasions when they are departed from, in a play such as *Milestones*, for example, where successive generations are shown in successive acts, unity is achieved by a partial repetition of the plot with the same actors taking similar parts. Such devices are highly sophisticated and scarcely bear repetition.

These unities are far more fundamental than the arbitrary conventions that have been established at various times limiting the intervals between acts or scenes to so many hours or days. They are really essential to the drama. Let us set them out more simply:

Rule 1: All the characters in a drama must be contemporaries.

Rule 2: All the characters must remain the same age throughout.

The simpler and more primitive the drama, the more difficult it would be to depart from these rules, and in the ritual drama, which deals with the fate of a particular hero or heroine, it would be impossible.

Now, when we examine the traditional narrative, whatever form it may take, we find that these rules are always observed, and it seems to me that this fact supplies a strong

link to the chain of reasoning that connects the traditional
narrative with the ritual drama.

Let us start with rule 1 and the Greek heroes. Hesiod
tells us of the "divine generation of the Heroes, which are
called half-gods of early times over the boundless world.
Bad war and awful battle slew them all; some at Seven-
Gated Thebes, the land of the Cadmeans, died battling about
the flocks of the sons of Œdipus; and some War took in
ships over the great gulf of the sea to Troyland for the
sake of fair-haired Helen. Where verily the end of death
clouded them round. And Father Zeus, son of Cronos,
gave them life and familiar places far away from men,
settling them at the ends of the world, far from the im-
mortals, and Cronos is king among them. And there they
live with hearts untormented, in the Islands of the Blessed,
beside deep eddying ocean, happy Heroes, and the mother
of corn bears to them thrice in the year her honey-sweet
harvests." So the heroes of Greece were all contemporaries,
and they all died fighting. What happened after the sieges
of Thebes and Troy, Hesiod neither knows nor cares, but
he knows that the heroes came to life again and had a
good time. Does not the account suggest a stage-manager
saying to the prostrate heroes: "It's all over. You can get
up now, and supper is waiting for you behind the stage"?

Professor Gilbert Murray quotes Hesiod with another
purpose, but he has not failed to note that the heroes are
all contemporaries. He says: "There is an extraordinary
wealth of tradition about what we may call the Heroic
Age. Agamemnon King of Mycenæ and Argos, Priam
King of Troy, and the kings surrounding them, Achilles,
Aias, Odysseus, Hector, Paris, these are all familiar household words throughout later history. They are among the
best-known names of the world. But how suddenly that
full tradition lapses into silence! The Epic Saga can tell
us about the deaths of Hector, of Paris, of Priam; in its
later forms it can give us all the details of the last destruction of Troy. Then no more; except a few dim hints, for
instance, about the descendants of Æneas.

"It is more strange in the case of Mycenæ and Sparta.
Agamemnon goes home in the full blaze of legend: he is

murdered by Ægisthus and Clytemnestra, and avenged by
his son Orestes: so far we have witnesses by the score. But
then? What happened to Mycenæ after the death of
Ægisthus? No one seems to know. There seems to be no
Mycenæ any more. What happened in Sparta after
Menelaus and Helen had taken their departure to the islands of the blest? There is no record, no memory.

". . . It is the same wherever we turn our eyes in the
vast field of Greek legend. The 'heroes' who fought at
Thebes and Troy are known; their sons are just known by
name or perhaps a little more: Diomedes, Aias, Odysseus,
Calchas, Nestor, how fully the tradition describes their
doings, and how silent it becomes after their deaths!" [1]
We find the same phenomena elsewhere, and the explanation is, in my view, a simple one: when the drama is
ended, the curtain goes down.

Peake and Fleure admit that "though tradition and the
works of the chronologists hang well together, these dates
do not agree with the results of archaeological research." [2]
Ridgeway says that "we must not lightly discard the traditional chronology of Early Greece." [3] But what does he
mean by "traditional chronology"? There is no chronology
in Homer or the other poets. It is easy to take a myth or
a fairy-tale and estimate the age of the characters and the
intervals between the incidents; this is all that the Greek
chronologists did, and this is why their works hang well
with tradition. But this, though it may be called a chronology of tradition, is not a traditional chronology.

In spite of this pseudo-chronology, we find that rule 2
was observed just as well as rule 1. Helen has a grown-up
daughter before she elopes with Paris; indeed, at the taking of Troy she must have been, according to Jacob
Bryant's calculations,[4] nearly a hundred years old. Hermione was betrothed to Orestes, who had just reached
manhood, but the wedding was postponed, and it was not
till thirty years later that he avenged his father, and then

[1] *The Rise of the Greek Epic*, pp. 29–32.
[2] *The Horse and the Sword*, p. 73.
[3] *Early Age of Greece*, vol. i, p. 109.
[4] W. L. Collins: *The Odyssey*, p. 10.

married her. They were both, however, still in the first
bloom of youth.

Professor Halliday remarks how "the wicked Poly-
dectes is enamoured of the surely maturing charms of
Danaë," whose son was grown up, and notes that similar
improbabilities are habitually ignored in fairy-tales.[5]

In the *Odyssey,* Odysseus, returning to Ithaca after
twenty years' absence, finds Penelope still in the bloom of
youth and charm. His son, Telemachus, has just reached
man's estate; that is, he is about sixteen, yet he has been
the leading man in Ithaca for about eight years.

Nestor, at the beginning of the siege of Troy, is a wise
and very old man. At the end of the siege he is still a
wise and very old man, and he returns home and keeps
on being a wise and very old man.

In Ireland, as in Greece, attempts have been made to
fit the traditions to a chronology, yet who can say what
happened after the death of the great heroes? Here again
the characters never get any older. In Maelduin's voyage
"the mother of seventeen grown-up daughters is still
young and desirable." [6] The hero Finn mac Cumall performs feats of valour at a fight known as "the Little
Brawl"; so do his great-grandsons, Echtach and Illann.[7]

We find the same phenomena in the Arthurian legends.
All the heroes are contemporaries, and the Britain of the
legends has no past and no future. The characters, again,
never grow old. Guinevere has apparently been married for
some time before Launcelot's birth; he carries her off after
the death of his son Galahad—when, that is, she could
hardly be less than sixty.

"It is an essential character of heroic poetry," says
Professor R. W. Chambers,[8] "that, while it preserves
many historic names, it gives the story modified almost
past recognition by centuries of poetic tradition. Accurate

    [5] W. R. Halliday: *Indo-European Folk-tales and Greek Leg-
end,* p. 130.
    [6] A. Nutt: *The Voyage of Bran,* vol. i, p. 166.
    [7] S. H. O'Grady, op. cit., p. 382.
    [8] *Widsith,* p. 5.

chronology too is, in the absence of written records, impossible; all the great chieftains become contemporaries." But whatever modifies stories cannot be tradition, since the essence of tradition is that it passes on what it receives. The great chieftains are contemporaries because they are mythical—that is to say, timeless. In Bosnian poetry, as recited by the minstrels, "the characters mentioned by name are few in number and recur again and again in different stories, each district having apparently a favourite hero who is introduced as its representative on many different occasions." [9] It would seem that the chieftains are not merely contemporaries, but form a regular stock company.

As an example of rule 2 in the north, I shall take the saga of *Burnt Njal,* since it is one of the latest and most highly rationalized of the sagas, and its chronology has been worked out painstakingly by Dasent and sounds very convincing until we investigate it critically. We then see that it has no real foundation, but that the characters remain the same age throughout.

When we first meet Njal he is, according to Dasent, between thirty-five and forty, yet he is an old man, well skilled in the law, who takes no active part in life, but whom people come to consult. He remains exactly the same age till his death forty years later. His sons, when we first meet them, are, again according to Dasent, between ten and fifteen years old, but all are described as strong men well skilled in arms, and all marry within the year. Forty years later they are killed, still displaying the maximum of youthful vigour and rashness, and their wives are still childless brides, without dwellings of their own. Njal and his sons are avenged by Asgrim, who is the father-in-law of one of them and who, though he is at least seventy-five, is foremost in the fight. Gunnar reaches the age of twenty-nine without a love-affair, and then falls desperately in love at first sight with the youthful charms of Hallgerd, whose second husband has been murdered fifteen years before.

[9] H. M. Chadwick, op. cit., p. 103.

Another feature of the traditional narratives is that the characters are all adults. To this there are two exceptions: the hero or heroine may be introduced as a new-born babe in order that somebody may try to kill it or may utter prophecies about it, and may come back into the story as a youth or maiden of about the age of puberty, in order that they may embark on the series of adventures which will bring them to the throne. I have suggested the reason for this in Chapter XVII: namely, that between the rites at birth and the rites at puberty children take no part in ritual and have therefore no part to play in the ritual drama. It would not be true to say that children never appear in traditional narratives, but their rarity can well be realized by contrasting the best-known fairy-tales, such as Bluebeard, Cinderella, and Sleeping Beauty, or Sindbad and Ali Baba, even as they are edited for children, with modern children's stories, such as those of Alice or Christopher Robin. In the former class the heroes and heroines are nearly always adults, whereas in the latter they are always children.

Even when the hero or heroine appears as a child, as happens to a limited extent, as I mentioned just now, he or she is the only child in the story. It may be said that the same applies to history; but while this may be true of chronicle history, which never deals, as tradition professes to deal, with private life at all, it is certainly not true of modern historical literature, which often contains references to and anecdotes of childhood.

But whether the hero and heroine were ever children or not, they never cease to be young. Either they meet with an untimely death, or we are told that they lived happily ever afterwards, or, like Helen, they remain permanently young. If a character is to be old, like Nestor, he must never have been young, and even if he is to be middle-aged, like Odysseus, he must be middle-aged from the start and remain so indefinitely. The reason is that they are all characters in drama; an old Helen or Hallgerd and a young Nestor or Njal are as unthinkable as an old Columbine or a young Pantaloon.

To the rule that young children never appear in the traditional narrative there is one exception, and that is the case of Heracles, and some Celtic heroes such as Cuchul-ainn and Llew, who either grow up at a miraculous rate, or perform feats of strength at a miraculously early age. Light is probably thrown on these by an incident in a modern Thracian folk-play. The play begins with "the entry of the old woman called 'Babo' (i.e. unmarried mother) with the *liknon* containing a swaddled puppet representing a seven-month-old illegitimate baby, which she declares is 'getting too big for the "basket." ' " It has developed an enormous appetite and demands a wife. One of the girls . . . is brought to the child "now grown to maturity." He is married, killed, and restored to life.[1]

There is one other phenomenon in tradition connected with time, and that is the miraculous lapse of time in the Otherworld. In the usual form of the story the hero spends what he supposes to be one or more days in the Other-world, usually in the company of a lovely lady, and finds to his astonishment, when he returns to the real world, that he has been away a corresponding number of years. This suggests the interval which is often supposed to elapse between the acts of a drama, but while the idea of a lapse of time between the acts might arise from the miraculous lapse of time in the Otherworld stories, it could hardly give rise to them, since in them the change takes place, not in the hero, but in the audience. It is more likely to have arisen in connection with a drama performed annually. In such a drama Robin Hood, or whoever the hero was, might well come on and explain that while the audience were a year older than when he last saw them, he himself was older merely by the length of a night spent with his May Queen. I know of no evidence for such an incident, but can think of no more plausible explanation. The attribution of widespread beliefs to casual dreams or fancies must in this as in every other case be unhesitatingly rejected. The idea that a lobster supper may lead to a new religion, though it seems to have a considerable vogue, is

[1] Quoted by E. O. James: *Christian Myth and Ritual,* p. 274.

quite unwarranted.

Apart from this, however, it seems clear that every aspect of age and time, as they appear in the traditional narrative, while suggesting more or less clearly a dramatic origin, affords further strong evidence to prove that these narratives have no historical basis.

CHAPTER XXIII

DRESS AND SETTING

✳

It is a feature of all ritual that great importance is attached to the clothes and ornaments worn by the principal actors. We see this clearly in the ritual of the Church, which, in this respect as in so many others, merely follows the example set by its predecessors. The essence of ritual is that its performance should in every way accord exactly with precedent, and the clothes of the actors therefore share the importance which attaches to all that they say and do. It is hardly an exaggeration to say that nowhere in the world is anyone allowed to take a prominent part in any ritual unless he is dressed for it.

Now, whereas in history there is very seldom any mention of what anyone wore, in the traditional narrative detailed descriptions of costume often occur, and this gives us another reason to believe that traditional narratives are accounts of dramatic ritual and have no connection with history.

We saw that all those who took part in the May-day festivities, even the King, wore Lincoln green, and this ritual costume appears in the ballads. In one of them[1] Robin Hood not only wears green cloth himself, but provides the King with a suit of it. In another ballad Robin's bride wears a gown of green velvet.[2]

In the sagas there are many descriptions of dress. Odin, in the *Volsunga Saga*, appears as an old, one-eyed man, barefooted, with tight linen breeches, a cloak, and a slouch hat.[3] It seems impossible to explain this description except as being that of the costume worn by the

[1] J. Ritson, op. cit., p. 55.
[2] Ibid., p. 111.
[3] Magnusson and Morris, op. cit., p. 6.

person who took the part of Odin in a ritual drama. The same applies to the goddess Hel, who, we are told, is "half blue-black and half flesh-colour (by which she is easily recognized." [4] She could hardly require recognition except on the stage.

There is a curious incident in the saga of *Burnt Njal* when Njal's sons ask for help at the Thing. According to the story, Skarphedinn is one of the best-known men in Iceland, and has been attending the Thing regularly for forty years, yet four of the chief men in the island use almost exactly the same odd formula in asking who he is. We are told that he "had on a blue kirtle and grey breeks, and black shoes on his feet, coming high up his leg; he had a silver belt about him, and that same axe in his hand which he called 'the ogress of war,' a round buckler, and a silken band round his brow, and his hair was brushed back behind his ears." [5]

In the *Laxdœla Saga* we are told of Geirmund that "he was ever so clad that he wore a kirtle of scarlet cloth and a gray cloak over all, a bearskin cap on his head, a sword in his hand; that was a mickle weapon and good; ivory-hilted, no silver was borne thereon; but the brand was sharp, and rust never abode on it. This sword he called Footbiter, and never did he let it go out of his hand." [6] From the last remark we may conclude that the tradition of the ritual drama has survived into the saga.

In the saga of Eirek the Red there is a still more detailed description. We are told that there was a famine in Greenland, and that Thorbjorg, a prophetess, was summoned to ascertain when it would cease. She came wearing "a blue mantle, which was set with stones down to the hem; she had a rosary of glass on her neck and a black hood of lamb-skin lined with white cat-skin on her head, and she had a staff in her hand with a knob on it: it was ornamented with brass, and set with stones down from the knob; round her waist she had a belt of amadou on which

---

[4] A. G. Brodeur, op. cit., p. 42.
[5] G. W. Dasent, op. cit., p. 219.
[6] R. Proctor, op. cit., p. 85.

was a great skin bag, in which she kept those charms which she needed for her art. On her feet she wore hairy calfskin shoes, the thongs of which were long and strong-looking, and had great buttons of lateen on the ends. On her hands she had cat-skin gloves, which were white inside and furry." The saga goes on to tell how she was seated on a throne, furnished with a cushion of hen's feathers, and how "there was made for her a porridge of goat's beestings, and for her food were provided hearts of all living creatures which were obtainable; she had a brass spoon, and a knife with an ivory handle bound with copper, and the point was broken off." [7] By those who believe in the historicity of the sagas we are invited to consider all these details as part of a true story of discovery and adventure, transmitted orally for about a century and a half before it was written down. It may be said that these details are "embellishments," but why should anyone embellish a true story in this way? We have here, it seems to me, a case in which the ritual framework of the sagas, elsewhere more or less thinly veiled, is clearly apparent.

This fondness for the description of ritual costumes may have been derived, like much else in the sagas, from the Irish myths, in which they are numerous. We are told, for example, that the god Manannan, son of Ler, "wore a green cloak of one colour, and a brooch of white silver in the cloak over his breast, and a satin shirt next his white skin. A circlet of gold around his hair, and two sandals of gold under his feet." [8]

Fiachna mac Retach of the men of the *Sid* or fairies wears "a five-fold crimson mantle, in his hand two five-barbed darts, a gold-rimmed shield slung on him, at his belt a gold-hilted sword, golden-yellow hair streaming behind him." [9] Another fairy who has golden hair is Midir, but Sir John Rhys tries to explain this away,[1] since it does

[7] Quoted by Gathorne-Hardy, op. cit., p. 34.
[8] A. Nutt, op. cit., vol. i, p. 131.
[9] Ibid., p. 180.
[1] *Celtic Folklore*, vol. ii, p. 680.

not fit in with his theory that the fairies were real people of a small, dark race.

Of Conchobar we are told that his face was like the moon, and that he had a forked beard and reddish-yellow hair. The description goes on: "A purple-bordering garment encircled him, a pin of wrought gold fastening the garment over his shoulder. Next to the surface of his skin was a shirt of kingly satin. A purple-brown shield, with rims of yellow gold, was beside him. He had a gold-hilted, embossed sword; in his white, firm right hand he held a purple-bright, well-shaped spear, accompanied by its forked dart." [2] We have already seen how the description of Cuchulainn's appearance occupies a page and a half.

The Homeric poems, though derived from the ritual drama, have got a good way from it, but even in them we find descriptions of dress and equipment more detailed than occur in historical records. The shield of Achilles was probably attached to the statue of a god, and borne by the person who took the god's part at his festival; the transformation of the appearance and garments of Odysseus to those of a beggar takes place instantaneously, after the manner of the drama but not of real life.

I said at the beginning of this chapter that in history there is very seldom any mention of what anybody wore. It is difficult to prove a negative, or to be sure that one has not missed descriptions of clothing in books which one did not read with this idea in mind, but I have been unable to find any mention of what anybody wore in the works of any classical historian or of any old English chronicler—in fact, of any writer before the sixteenth century—and I believe that our knowledge of what was worn in earlier times is derived from pictures, statues, and brasses, and not from written descriptions of what people wore. If the traditions were simply oral chronicles, we should expect that the practice of describing at length the dress and equipment of the leading figures would be carried further in the written chronicles, since it is obviously

[2] E. Hull, op. cit., p. 10.

easier to record what was worn by a contemporary than by a person who lived some centuries before. If I am not mistaken in my facts, we have here further evidence of the gulf which divides history from tradition.

Not only does the dress of the characters of tradition suggest a dramatic origin, but so also does the setting in which we see them. The usual setting for a ritual drama is a doorway or gateway. The reason for this is probably that the ritual was originally performed at the king's palace or tomb, which was often the same place. With the centralization of kingdoms and cults, and the gradual secularization of kings, came the development of shrines— that is, buildings in which there was just sufficient imitation of the royal palace and tomb for ritual purposes. A shrine with an auditorium—that is, an area in front of it fenced to keep out unauthorized persons—becomes a temple, theatre, or church. The place where the ritual can most appropriately be performed—that is to say, where sacredness can be combined with visibility—is the entrance to the shrine, and it is there that the ritual drama is performed. The scene of the Attic tragedy is usually laid at the entrance of a palace or temple, and the medieval mystery play was usually performed at the entrance of the chancel. This explains why characters in fairy-tales and other traditional narratives are in the habit of blurting out their secrets in some gateway or doorway, where other incidents often occur that in real life would be unlikely to occur in such a situation.

Lugh has a ritual dialogue with Nuada's doorkeeper, and plays chess in the doorway,[3] and the Black Book of Carmarthen contains a poetical dialogue between King Arthur and a porter.[4]

"We may note especially," says Professor Chadwick,[5] "the long and detailed account of Beowulf's arrival at the Danish king's hall, and the conversation which the chamberlain holds with the king on the one hand and the visitor

[3] A. Nutt, op. cit., vol. ii, p. 175.
[4] E. K. Chambers: *Arthur of Britain*, p. 63.
[5] Op. cit., p. 82.

on the other, before the latter is invited to enter." "The
second poem," says Professor W. P. Ker,[6] alluding to the
Fiolvinnsmál, "also in dialogue, and in the dialogue measure, gives the coming of Svipdag to the mysterious castle,
and his debate with the giant who keeps the gate."

The tragedy of Absalom's death, which strongly suggests
the ritual drama, is staged in the gateway of Mahanaim,
the speaking characters being David, Joab, a watchman,
and two messengers.[7] Another tragedy staged in a gateway is the slaying of Jehoram and Jezebel by Jehu.[8] In
both of these tragedies we have the well-known stage
device by which a watchman reports to those on the stage
what is happening off.

Another common feature of ritual and drama is the
procession, in which, of course, the principal characters
come last. Dr. Krappe[9] notes that in ballads and fairy-
tales such devices are common as "a procession will come
of ladies fair in the extreme; it is thought that the queen
is among them, but we are told that she is not; these are
only her handmaids. Next comes a procession of women
fairer still, but again the queen is not one of them. At last
she comes herself and is a thousand times fairer still."

When Janet is to retransform her lover, the Young
Tamlane, from a fairy to a man, he tells her that she is
to let the first two companies of fairy horsemen go by, and
seize the third rider in the third company, which will be
himself.

Cormac comes to join Queen Medb with three splendidly arrayed companies. When the first appeared, "Is that
Cormac yonder?" all and everyone asked. "Not he, indeed," Medb made answer. The same happened with the
second company, but the third time Medb replies: "Aye,
it is he." [1]

Koht notes another type of this rule of three in the
sagas; "when somebody is hidden, and is to be found, it

[6] Op. cit., p. 114.
[7] 2 Samuel xviii.
[8] 2 Kings i.
[9] A. H. Krappe, op. cit., p. 182.
[1] J. Dunn, op. cit., p. 11.

is a rule that the search for him is to be made three times." [2] The connection of the number three and of the third time of asking with ritual is, of course, well known, but there is no reason why it should figure more prominently in the unfettered imagination than it does in historical fact.

[2] H. Koht, op. cit., p. 122.

CHAPTER XXIV

SHAPE-SHIFTING AND
TALKING ANIMALS

A prominent feature of every type of traditional narrative is the human being in animal form, or, what is in my view merely a variant, the animal that talks. That persons disguised or partly disguised as animals are an almost universal feature of ritual and ritual drama is so well known as hardly to need demonstration. Why ancient Egyptian ritual was performed largely by people wearing animal masks; why Greek gods and goddesses were often represented as animals or birds; why the Hindu god Ganesh has an elephant's head; why an African chief is invested with a lion-skin and given some such title as Great Lion; and why in modern churches we may see Christ represented as a lamb—these are questions the answer to which lies outside the scope of this work; my object here is to try to show that similar features appear in all types of traditional narrative, and afford further confirmation for the belief that these narratives are derived from the ritual drama.

It should be sufficiently obvious that human beings never really turn into animals or animals into human beings, and that animals, or at any rate quadrupeds, never talk, so that whatever else these incidents in the traditional narratives are based upon, they are not based upon fact.

The generally held view about such rites and such tales is that they arose from the inability of savage man to distinguish between animals and human beings. Thus Professor Gilbert Murray[1] speaks of "men who made their gods in the image of snakes and bulls and fawns, because they hardly felt any difference of kind between them-

[1] *Bacchæ*, p. 85.

selves and the animals," and Sir James Frazer assures us that "it is not merely between the mental and spiritual nature of man and the animals that the savage traces a close resemblance; even the distinction of their bodily form appears sometimes to elude his dull apprehension." [2] Such a view may be supported, as Sir James supports it, by the statements of early travellers and missionaries, but is quite untenable by anyone with any real knowledge of savage mentality. In questions that involve the weighing of evidence or the application of scientific principles the savage, like the less educated European, is often at sea, but his powers of direct observation are as good as those of the scientist. Failure to distinguish between a human being and a snake or a bull would be, among savages as among the civilized, an indication not of dull wits but of hopeless insanity. The savage may believe, as the Council of Trent believed, that people can take the form of animals, but that is very different from confusing men with animals. People in animal form are quite different from real animals; between a man and a wolf there is a great gulf fixed, and so there is between a real wolf and a werewolf. The latter always has traits that mark it out as a human being in disguise; it is, in fact, not a real animal but a magic animal, the product not of confused thought but of superstition.

It seems probable that such superstitions arose out of the ritual. Men disguised, or partly disguised, as animals have been, from the earliest times of which we have any knowledge, familiar figures in ritual. People seeing such figures in circumstances calculated to produce the maximum of emotion and awe might well come to believe that they existed independently of the ritual. Just as we have good reason to believe that a devil was originally a man ritually disguised as a goat, and an angel was originally a boy ritually disguised as a bird, so we may well believe that werewolves and wereleopards were originally men ritually disguised as wolves or leopards. And since men disguised as animals can speak, it may well come to be believed that

[2] J. G. Frazer: *Golden Bough,* vol. viii, p. 206.

magic animals can speak. If there is any person in the world who believes that real animals can speak, I have yet to hear of him.

In ancient Egypt it was not men but gods who changed themselves into animals. "The goddess Nut," we are told, "changed herself into a cow, and the majesty of Râ found himself seated upon her back. Then Isis transformed herself into a *djeri* bird, the form which she was in the habit of taking in times of stress, and flew up and alighted on the top of a tree."

"Horus then changed his form into that of a lion which had the face of a man, and he was wearing the triple crown with three solar discs, three pairs of plumes, two cabras, and a pair of ram's horns." [3] Can anyone seriously believe that the ancient Egyptians were unable to distinguish between a woman and a cow, or a man and a lion? We shall see later that these transformations undoubtedly took place in the ritual drama.

With the rationalization that begins once the traditional tale, or myth, becomes separated from the ritual, the miraculous incidents are gradually eliminated, but these animal transformations are among the last to go. Shapeshifting seems to have been expunged from the *Iliad*, but a good deal of it remains in the *Odyssey*. Athena flies off into the air like an eagle; Idothea disguises Menelaus and his companions as seals with the aid of fresh-flayed sealskins.[4] The latter was probably the method by which Circe originally changed the companions of Odysseus into swine.

The ass's ears of Midas, and of various Celtic kings, were probably part of a ritual costume. In the original rite which gave rise to the story of Balaam and the ass it is probable that, as in the thirteenth-century Laon Christmas play, it was "*puer sub asina*" who answered the prophet.[5]

The *Volsunga Saga*, which, as we saw in Chapter V, is the basis of most of the saga literature, contains a great

[3] E. A. Wallis Budge: *From Fetish to God in Ancient Egypt,* pp. 466, 449, 479.
[4] *Odyssey,* ii, 310; iv, 440.
[5] E. K. Chambers: *The Mediæval Stage,* vol. ii, p. 54.

deal of shape-shifting. "Now on a time as they Sigmund and Sinfjotli fare abroad in the woods for the getting of wealth, they find a certain house, and two men with great gold rings asleep therein: now these twain were spell-bound skin-changers, and wolf-skins were hanging up over them in the house; and every tenth day might they come out of those skins; and they were king's sons: so Sigmund and Sinfjotli do the wolf-skins on them, and then might they nowise come out of them, though forsooth the same nature went with them as heretofore; they howled as wolves howl, but both knew the meaning of that howling." [6] This passage suggests that the donning of wolf-skins, like nearly all rites, was periodical; that men who were disguised as wolves talked in a howling voice; and that werewolves were once royal personages.

Otter, son of the rich and mighty Hreidmar, is killed by Loki in the form of an otter. The gods obtain the wherewithal to pay the blood-money by catching a dwarf who was in the form of a salmon. Fafnir, Hreidmar's elder son, kills his father for the sake of the treasure, and takes the form of a dragon, in which form he is killed by Sigurd, who is himself apparently in the form of a wolf. There is much to suggest that the whole of this story is the account of a king-killing ritual which was eventually dramatized. There seems to be no doubt that Norse kings masqueraded as animals. In an early seventh-century grave found in Sweden was a helmet on the base of which was represented a procession of warriors. The leader wears a boar's-head helmet and a boar's mask, with the tusk protruding. "Here indeed," says Miss Phillpotts, "we have *Hilditonn*, the Boar-Tusk King." [7]

She also describes[8] a Swedish play, *Staffen Stalledreng*, which contains a mixture of heathen and Christian ideas. Staffen makes his speech mounted on his grey steed, which is composed of two youths fastened so that they are back to back. Each walks on his feet and on two sticks held in his hands, so that the horse has eight legs. We may thus

[6] Magnusson and Morris, op. cit., p. 20.
[7] B. S. Phillpotts, op. cit., p. 170.
[8] Ibid., p. 125.

understand how Odin's horse Sleipnir came to have eight legs.

Shape-shifting stories are also common in Celtic mythology. The children of Lir were changed into swans by a stroke of their wicked stepmother's wand; this is a widespread fairy-tale motive. Liban becomes a salmon and her handmaid an otter. Tuan mac Cairill was changed successively into a stag, wild boar, bird, and salmon. This brings us to the pursuit stories—Gwion, pursued by Ceridwen, becomes in turn a hare, fish, bird, and grain of wheat, while she becomes a greyhound, otter, hawk, and black hen.[9] Pursuit stories are found all over Europe, as well as in the *Arabian Nights,* and would seem to be allied to the stories of disenchantment by shape-shifting. In the ballad of Young Tamlane, the hero, before he can regain his proper shape after being enchanted, becomes in succession a snake, a bear, a red-hot bar of iron, and a burning coal. That this was a ritual procedure can hardly be doubted, and since it cannot have been carried out in reality, it must have been represented dramatically.

Of another type of story I will let Professor Saintyves[1] speak. "On Puss in Boots or his like," he tells us, "fox or gazelle, dog or jackal, depends not only the prosperity of the country, but even that of the king. By giving to the animal protector the role of ambassador, herald, and champion in the installation ritual of a king, one caused the latter to participate in the animal's powers and virtues. Besides this, the commentary which accompanied it, and which was nothing but a variant of our tale, showed clearly the debt which the king owed to the animal, and his obligation not to offend it, not only in the interest of the public, but in his own interest. *Puss in Boots* was most probably connected with the installation ritual of the ancient priest-kings of primitive societies, and doubtless served to recall to the sovereign the importance of the magico-religious duties of his office." An actual animal could obviously not have appeared, nor, since the part is an active one, would an image have been adequate, so

[9] J. Rhys: *Celtic Folklore,* vol. ii, pp. 611–13.
[1] Op. cit., p. 490.

here again we must conclude that, if Professor Saintyves is right, there was a dramatic impersonation.

An almost world-wide type of story is that in which an animal or monster is beheaded, and immediately there steps forth from its skin a handsome prince, who marries the princess and becomes king. Sometimes, on the other hand, it is a beautiful princess who steps forth. Many examples have been collected by Professor Kittredge.[2] In Gaelic stories a horse, a fox, a frog, and a raven become princes or handsome young men, and a horse becomes a girl. In Ireland an old man becomes a young man, and in England a cruel monster becomes a man. In Germany three dogs become princes; in France and Norway a cat becomes a princess, and in Norway, Sweden, and Russia a horse becomes a prince. In all these cases the animal or whatever it is is beheaded, but sometimes it must be cut open or skinned. Thus in Brittany the hero kills and skins a horse, and a prince emerges; the same thing happens when the belly of a black cat, born of a woman, is ripped up. Sometimes, as in Sweden and the Faroes, the skin of the animal, kid, or ass has to be turned inside out. A Zulu prince, born in the form of a snake, gets his wife to pull the skin off, after which he appears in his true form. In Armenia a spell causes the skin of a dragon to burst and a prince to emerge.

"The belief," says Professor Saintyves,[3] "in the cessation of an animal metamorphosis in consequence of a wound or a beheading, a belief which is found both in the stories of werewolves and in the tales which have just been cited, refers, in our opinion, not to real facts— this is quite certain—but to rituals in which animal disguises were the rule. The faith in werewolves and in the sabbath, as well as in many magical practices, is connected in part with ancient pagan or pagano-Christian secret societies, the members of which, during their initiation or in their sacred ceremonies, clothed themselves in the skins or masks of animals such as wolves, tigers, cattle, cats,

[2] G. L. Kittredge: *Gawaine and the Green Knight*, pp. 200, 217.

[3] Op. cit., p. 434.

bears or hares. The violent return to human form in certain variants of *Beauty and The Beast* impels us to suppose that narratives of this type arose when similar rituals were still customary. Neither must we ignore the frequency of the employment of animal disguises in the initiations of savages and of pagan religions. Did not nearly all the degrees of Mithraic initiation require animal masks?"

These disguises had no need to be complete. "In the nursery tales of the higher races," says Hartland,[4] "the dress (which transforms the heroine into a swan, etc.) when cast aside seems simply an article of human clothing, often nothing but a girdle, veil or apron; and it is only when donned by the enchanted lady, or elf, that it is found to be neither more nor less than a complete costume." Once the ritual and the belief have come into existence, the power of suggestion is almost unlimited, but to allege that the belief is instinctive is a very different thing. If belief in shape-shifting were natural it would be everywhere the same, instead of taking different forms in different parts of the world. It is found, however, in all forms of traditional narrative, myths, sagas, epics, ballads, and folk-tales, and this fact further demonstrates the absurdity of postulating a different basis for the different forms of traditional narrative. They are all, in more or less corrupt forms, descriptions of dramatic ritual.

The Science of Fairy Tales, p. 301.

CHAPTER XXV

THE ROYAL HERO

We have seen that in the ritual the chief part is played by the king, and in the ritual drama which arises from the ritual the chief part, if not played by the king himself, is played by a priest or actor who represents him. This explains why royalty plays such an important part in every form of traditional narrative. Royalty plays the chief part in the epic, the saga, the fairy-tale, and the folk-play because these are all derived from the ritual drama. On the commonly held view that folklore derives from the peasantry, there is no conceivable reason why all the features of village life, the festivals, the songs, the dances, and the stories, should revolve round kings and queens. The people who took part in these festivals and dances, and repeated these songs and stories, could as a rule have no acquaintance with royalty, any more than most villagers could at the present day. If they had originated their own festivals and composed their own songs and stories, they would have used material with which they were more familiar. The vast amount of traditional material dealing with the kingship must have been evolved among people to whom the kingship ritual was not merely highly important, but thoroughly familiar.

The development of kingship ritual without the king may be due to two causes: the first is the consolidation of kingdoms, as when the heptarchy became a single monarchy and the king's functions became increasingly secularized; this might cause the idea of kingship ritual without a king to become familiar. The second cause would be imitation; the tendency in all ages and all countries has been for the king and his courtiers to set fashions which all classes of the population strive to follow.

I cannot agree with Professor Karl Pearson when he says that in the *Märchen* "kings are as plentiful as blackberries, because every kin-alderman and clan-father has developed into one," [1] since we have no reason to believe that a kin-alderman ever developed into a king, nor does the king of the *Märchen* bear any resemblance to a kin-alderman. No more can we agree with him when he tells us[2] that "back in the far past we can build up the life of our ancestry . . . the little kingdom; the queen or her daughter as king-maker, the simple life of the royal household, and the humble candidate for the kingship." The king is always a sacred person, living a guarded and ceremonious life, and the candidature is always limited to those who can satisfy rigid ritual requirements. What we must rather suppose is that the king of the *Märchen* is the king of the village drama, performing his part amid rustic surroundings and with simple properties, just as the king of the folk-drama does to this day.

The importance of the part played by royalty in the folk-play and the fairy-tale requires no illustration; the heroes of the early sagas are all kings, and though in the Icelandic sagas the heroes are not actually royal, which since there were no royalties in Iceland they could not well be, yet they are always members of the leading families, and are represented as associating on familiar terms with the kings of Norway. In all epic poems the chief characters are royalties. "The characters brought before us in the *Iliad,*" says Professor Chadwick,[3] "are almost invariably princes, or persons attached to the retinue of princes, apparently of what we may call knightly rank." And the same writer tells us that "all the women mentioned in the Anglo-Saxon poems are of royal birth, while the men are either princes or persons, apparently of noble or knightly rank, attached to the retinue of princes." [4]

These poems, like the drama itself, are derived from the ritual drama, and the belief that drama—that is, seri-

---

[1] *The Chances of Death,* vol. ii, p. 56.
[2] Ibid., p. 90.
[3] Op. cit., p. 228.
[4] Ibid., p. 82.

ous or tragic drama—is concerned solely with the doings of kings persisted until recent times. Among the chief features in the ritual life of a king, and the life of an early king was simply a life of ritual, were his deposition and death, and it is these that were long regarded as forming the proper subject of tragedy. Chaucer's monk says that tragedy is a story:

> *Of him that stood in great prosperity,*
> *And is yfallen out of high degree*
> *Into misery and endeth wretchedly.*

This describes the fate of most of the heroes whom we discussed in Chapter XVI.

"The tragic hero," says Miss Bradbrook,[5] "was not thought of as a human being, on the same level as the other characters in the play. If he were a king, his royalty invested him with special powers; and the difference between comedy and tragedy was often defined in this way, that comedy dealt with common people and tragedy with kings and princes."

According to Daniello (1536), "the tragic poets treat of the death of high kings and the ruin of empires." Minturno (1559) thought that tragedy concerned "those of high rank"; Scaliger (1561) says that tragedy "introduces kings and princes"; and according to Castelvestro (1576), "the actions of kings are the subject of tragedy." [6]

This tradition is not confined to Europe. "According to Cambodian notions, as in Burma," says Ridgeway,[7] "the principal character [of a drama] must be a king, a prince, or a princess." He also tells us that "the themes of the Cambodian drama are drawn from the lives of the ancient kings, which present numerous tragic reversals." [8]

The same fact, and also the essentially dramatic character of epic poetry, have been noted by Professor Ker,[9]

---

[5] M. C. Bradbrook: *Themes and Conventions of Elizabethan Tragedy*, p. 55.
[6] A. Nicoll, op. cit., p. 85.
[7] W. Ridgeway: *Dramas and Dramatic Dances*, p. 265.
[8] Ibid., p. 264.
[9] *Epic and Romance*, p. 23.

who says that "in the main, the story of the Niblungs is independent of history . . . the relations of Achilles to his surroundings, of Attila and Ermanaric to theirs . . . are intelligible at once, without reference to anything outside the poems. To require of the poetry of an heroic age that it shall recognize the historical meaning and importance of the events in which it originates, and the persons whose names it uses, is entirely to mistake the nature of it. Its nature is to find or make some drama played by kings and heroes." We may go farther and say that to suppose that it originates in historical events is entirely to mistake the nature of it.

Not only must there always be a king or high-born hero in the traditional narrative, but he must always engage in a contest. In Chapter XVII I dealt with a particular type of hero, and the particular types of contest in which he engages. There are variant types of hero and of contest, but whenever the hero is represented as fighting, it is always evident that it is a staged combat and not a real battle. There is never any question of tactics or generalship; the hero never takes his adversary by surprise, nor turns the tables by bringing up reinforcements to a threatened point. All that he does is to hew his way through the ranks of the enemy until either he defeats them singlehanded, or else he meets in single combat the opposing hero whom he is to kill, or by whom he is to be killed. The combatants other than the heroes never perform any feats of valour; their sole function, if they appear on the scene at all, is to fall in heaps before the hero's all-conquering sword.

In the *Iliad*, minor heroes slaughter one another, and nameless warriors fall in scores, without affecting the issue; this is decided by a single combat between Achilles and Hector, at which the opposing armies look on.

The great Battle of Magh Tuireadh lasts for many days, but it is not till the last day that the superhuman leaders take part in it. They then slaughter each other in single combat.[1] Cuchulainn repeatedly defeats the armies of

[1] Lady Gregory, op. cit., pp. 55–9.

Queen Medb single-handed; at last his death is decreed,
but he can be killed only by a king, Lugaid of Munster.[2]

We saw that according to Nennius the 960 foemen who
fell at Mount Badon were all slain by Arthur's own hand.
It would seem that in his final battle with Modred all the
combatants on both sides are killed or incapacitated before
he and Modred engage; they can get their death-wounds
only from each other.

In the saga battle of Dunheidi, which is supposed to be
between the Goths and the Huns, the leaders are Angantyr
and his nephew Hlodver. The battle goes on for nine days
and thousands are killed; on the tenth day the leaders meet
in a long-drawn-out duel in the midst of the battle, and
when at length Angantyr kills Hlodver, the battle promptly
ceases.[3]

"In *Roland*," says Professor Ker,[4] "the fighting, the
separate combats, are rendered in a Homeric way." That
is the way of the ritual drama, and not the way of historical fact. Professor Chadwick[5] tries to explain these
single combats by supposing that the possession of armour
constituted an overwhelming advantage, and that the object of the battle was to kill the leaders, who were expected to distinguish themselves by personal bravery. The
same conditions would apply to feudal times, yet feudal
monarchs never performed such feats. Many of them are
reported to have performed acts of personal bravery, and
King Edward III is said to have challenged the King of
France to single combat, but I have been unable to find
any occasion on which rival kings or leaders actually met.
Shakespeare, indeed, represents King Henry IV as fighting
a single combat with Douglas, but this is quite unhistorical.

An interesting example of the traditional battle as a
ritual drama is afforded by the description of *Ragnarok*,
the destruction of the gods, in the *Prose Edda*.[6] We are

---

[2] E. Hull, op. cit., p. 259.

[3] *Hervarer Saga,* quoted by P. B. du Chaillu: *The Viking Age,*
vol. ii, p. 447.

[4] Op. cit., p. 294.

[5] Op. cit., p. 339.

[6] Tr. A. G. Brodeur, p. 79.

told that "Odin rides first with the gold helmet and a fair birnie," and later that "Thor shall put to death the Midgard Serpent, and shall stride away nine paces from that spot; then shall he fall dead to the earth." The adversaries of the gods included, besides the Midgard serpent, the Fenris wolf and the dog of Hel; it would seem that there was a procession of men dressed as the gods, and then a battle between them and men in animal masks. The mention of nine paces shows how meticulously the parts were laid down, and the fact that the future tense is used shows how little difference there is between a prophecy and a stage direction. In this, as in all other traditional battles, there is no concerted fighting; each god fights a duel with a monster.

The single combat that the hero fights is not an isolated phenomenon, but follows from the general rule which prescribes that he shall perform all his feats and all his journeys alone. Of course no real potentate ever acts in this way; no king or prince, feudal lord, Arab sheikh, or savage chief has ever left his palace, castle, camp, or village for any purpose whatever without at least two or three retainers. What chiefly distinguishes kings and rulers from ordinary men, both civilized and savage, is that the former are always closely attended. This applies not merely to royalty, but to such substitutes for royalty as governors, judges, and mayors. A royalty as a solitary figure is even more difficult to conceive; anyone attempting to describe the activities of such a person, whether real or imaginary, could hardly fail to represent him as surrounded or followed by guards and attendants.

Yet the hero of tradition is usually alone. We find him miles from the nearest habitation, often with a sword, sometimes with a horse, but never with any spare clothing or any provisions for the journey. His lack of provision never causes comment, though his loneliness is explained in various ways. A solitary journey through desolate country, connected with and usually leading up to a single combat, is, however, a normal feature of a hero's career.

Let us take some examples. Robin Hood, though he has

a large band of adherents, spends much of his time wan-
dering alone through the forest, seeking out the single
combats in which he is usually worsted. Sigurd, having
killed Fafnir and Regin, performs a long journey alone,
with a vast treasure loaded on his horse. Cuchulainn travels in a chariot, and must therefore have a charioteer;
accompanied by him alone, he makes many journeys
through desolate country, and fights a number of single
combats.

Malory wrote at a time when no archer went to war
unaccompanied by a servant, and he often mentions
squires, yet we repeatedly find the leading heroes, and even
King Arthur himself, riding alone through the forest to
their single combats.

Going back to ancient Greece, we find various heroes
who travel alone because they ride supernatural steeds.
Leaving them aside, we may note that Heracles travels all
over the Western World, and fights monsters of all kinds,
accompanied by nothing but a club and a lion-skin. Odysseus, having lost all his companions at sea, travels through
the wilds of Ithaca to attack single-handed his wife's suitors. Œdipus is travelling alone when he meets and kills
his father, King Laius, who is accompanied only by a
charioteer. Theseus had an easy voyage from Trœzen to
Athens by sea, yet he chooses to walk a hundred miles
alone, and apparently without even a wallet, through what
appears as desolate country, though it was really the most
populous part of Greece. He has several single combats
en route.

Jacob carries things even farther. The son of a wealthy
sheikh, who has many herdsmen and slaves, he sets forth
on a journey of five hundred miles to obtain a bride,
alone and on foot, and with no provision for the journey.
The first day, apparently, he covered sixty miles before
sunset, going via Hebron and Jerusalem, but he did not
stay at any town or village, but lay down supperless upon
a stone. His single combat with "God" took place on the
return journey.

We are told nothing of Moses' journey after he killed

the Egyptian, but he must have crossed two hundred miles of desert, apparently alone and on foot, till he, like Jacob, found a bride beside a well.

None of these incidents is altogether impossible, and a plausible case for any one of them can be made by a euhemerist, especially if he is "allowed to tell the story as it more probably happened." [7] It is not until we compare these stories with each other, and with recorded facts on the one hand and folk-tales on the other, that their real nature becomes apparent. In almost every folk-tale there is a future king (or queen) who performs a solitary journey, and it is with these, and not with the princes of history, that the affinity of our traditional heroes rests. The only king on record who roams alone in the woods is the "king of the woods" at Nemi, and he is not a real monarch, but a ritual survival. The impossibility of fitting our heroes into any historical setting has been tacitly recognized by the creation of a "Heroic age" and a "Patriarchal age" in which to place them.

There can be little doubt that the scene of the solitary journey and single combat is the stage. They are the features numbered 10 and 11 in the career of our typical hero, and we saw in Chapters XVI to XVIII that these features are all features of ritual. Now, ritual, especially royal ritual, is an essentially public affair; even if the whole community is not allowed to be present, there are always many officials, initiates, or other privileged persons who may or must attend. The hero must perform his feats alone, since it is by them that he demonstrates his fitness for the throne; he must perform them in public, since the public, or the required portion of it, must be satisfied as to his fitness. This result is attained by placing the hero on a stage or within an enclosure where he is separated from the spectators, but in full view and hearing of them. If we wish to see how a hero can fight a single combat with a monster, in the heart of a desolate forest, but within full view of hundreds of spectators, we need only witness a

[7] A. Weigall, discussing Abraham in *A History of the Pharaohs,* vol. i, p. 319.

performance of Wagner's *Siegfried*. The scenic accessories
of the ancient ritual drama, on which the hero stories were
founded, were, however, less realistic in all probability
than the pasteboard trees against which one sees the con-
ductor's silhouette.

CHAPTER XXVI

THE SPIELMAN

In Reinhardt's wonderful production *The Miracle,* the incidents of which are traditional and clearly derived from the ritual drama, there is a character called the "Spielman." He appears in a different guise in each act, but it is he who initiates each dramatic development and who goads the other characters into action. The action into which he goads them always leads to their own ruin, but without his stimulation it does not appear that there would be any action at all. His role, though ostensibly that of a minor character, is really that of prompter and stage-manager.

In *Faust* we find a similar phenomenon. Here Mephistopheles, though he himself plays no part in the drama, is the motive-power behind the other characters. Mephistopheles is the Devil, and the reason why he is the Devil seems clear. The ritual was very ancient and very popular; the Church was unable to suppress it, though the actions that the hero had to perform, such as killing a man and carrying off his daughter, were regarded as highly immoral. The result was a compromise, by which the hero was permitted to perform the requisite actions, but they were to be regarded as having been inspired by the Devil, and were to incur the appropriate penalty.

This attitude seems to have been foreshadowed in late pagan Scandinavia. "Among the gods," says Professor Gronbech,[1] "Loki occupies a place of his own. His part in the sacred drama is that of the plotter who sets the conflict in motion and leads the giants on to the assault that entails their defeat. His origin and *raison d'être* are purely dramatic; like his confrères in other rituals and mytholo-

[1] *The Culture of the Teutons,* p. 255.

gies he is a child of the 'games,' and herein lies the cause
of his double nature. As the wily father of artifice whose
office is to drag the demoniacal powers into the play and
effect their downfall, he comes very near representing evil
. . . but as the sacred actor who performs a necessary
part in the great redemptory work of the *blot* [sacrifice],
he, i.e., his human impersonation, is a god among gods,
beneficent and inviolable."

This equivocal character of Loki may be due in part
to Christian influence, since in some at least of the earlier
sagas it is Odin who appears as the Spielman, and he
incurs no odium whatever, though he urges the heroes on
to courses that bring them to misfortune and death. In the
Volsunga Saga his machinations lead to the death of the
heroes and all the principal characters, and not only does
he appear from time to time to spur on the characters, but
he is brought on, in his cloak and slouch hat, to speak the
prologue and epilogue. In the story of Harald Hilditonn he
takes the place of Harald's charioteer and sows discord
which leads to the Battle of Bravalla and the death of
Harald,[2] and he lends Dag the spear with which the latter
kills the hero Helgi, and thereby avenges his father.[3]

In the Arthurian legend the Spielman is Merlin, who
is always turning up in unexpected guises and urging the
other characters on to deeds, usually of violence.

The Homeric poems are of composite origin, and in the
Iliad there is no regular Spielman, though Zeus occasionally takes the part. In the *Odyssey*, on the other hand, the
part is taken regularly by Athena—that is, presumably by
the priestess who represents her. She makes the spears of
the suitors ineffective; she strikes the suitors with panic;
she causes Dawn to wake Odysseus; she infuses fresh
vigour into Laertes; she consults with Zeus (presumably
the presiding priest) as to the future course of events.[4] "It
is obvious," says Miss Stawell,[5] "that we cannot think of

[2] H. M. Chadwick, op. cit., p. 251.
[3] B. S. Phillpotts, op. cit., p. 54.
[4] *Odyssey* xxii, 265, 297; xxiv, 334, 513, 472.
[5] F. M. Stawell: *Homer and the Iliad*, p. 14.

her in this case as an all-wise prophetess, for . . . she is
urging her favourite on a course she knows will end in
bitterest grief." But it is no function of the ritual drama,
or of its director, to secure the happiness of the characters.
Is Shakespeare to be blamed for not giving *Romeo and
Juliet* a happy ending?

It seems probable that in the earliest ritual drama, in
Greece and elsewhere, the Spielman spoke but did not act,
and the other characters acted but did not speak. The
original speaker seems to have been the *"logios anêr,"* or
man of words, the words being, of course, the sacred
words. At Delos the part was played by the Homeros, who
took the character of Apollo, and led the hymns and
sacred dances in virtue of his victory in the contest of
minstrelsy.[6]

On the Roman stage there was a custom by which the
lyric portions of the text were entrusted to a singer who
stood with a flute-player at the side of the stage, while the
actor confined himself to dancing in silence with appropriate dumb-show. Sir E. K. Chambers, who cites this
custom, says that it was unknown in Greece,[7] but the
actors were apparently all Greeks, and the custom seems
to have been in the Greek tradition.

We find a similar custom in Java. "The subject of the
tópeng is invariably taken from the adventures of *Pànji,*
the favourite hero of Javan story. In the performances
before the sovereign, where masks are not used, the several
characters themselves rehearse their parts, but, in general,
the Dàlang, or manager of the entertainment, recites the
speeches, while the performers have only to 'suit the action
to the word.' " [8]

It is difficult to believe that this custom, whether at
Rome or in Java, could have arisen out of the ordinary
drama, and it seems more likely that in the original drama
—that is, the ritual drama—the words were so sacred that
they could be uttered only by the representative of the
god, and that the other characters began by acting in

[6] J. A. K. Thomson, op. cit., pp. 205, 207, 224.
[7] E. K. Chambers: *The Mediæval Stage,* vol. i, p. 6.
[8] T. S. Raffles, op. cit., vol. i, p. 374.

dumb-show only, and when they did begin to speak, still left the principal, or the most sacred, speeches to a Spielman, who was a sacred personage. In most of the traditional narratives the traces of this custom have been lost, but if I am right, they still survive in some of them, and in particular in the *Volsunga Saga* and the *Odyssey*.

CHAPTER XXVII

THE RITUAL DRAMA

The thesis of this book is that the traditional narrative, in all its forms, is based not upon historical facts on the one hand or imaginative fictions on the other, but upon dramatic ritual or ritual drama. I began by attempting to show that the belief that people have a natural interest in historical facts and a natural ability to transmit them is devoid of foundation. I then took a number of quasi-historical traditions and showed that there is no valid evidence for their historicity, and that many of them are demonstrably unhistorical. I next gave the evidence for connecting the myth and the folk-tale with ritual, and for believing that the hero-tale is derived from ritual and not from fact.

In the third part of the book I have taken a number of the features of the traditional narrative and shown that they suggest, if they do not prove, that these narratives are dramatic in origin.

If the views I have put forward are correct, it follows that the ritual drama, or at any rate dramatic ritual, must have played a far larger part in human affairs than is generally recognized, and it will be the object of this concluding chapter to show that this is the fact.

I have, perhaps, used the terms *ritual drama* and *dramatic ritual* somewhat loosely, and it is desirable to show where the difference lies. Ritual, in itself, is not necessarily dramatic. A rite may consist merely in muttering a spell over a weapon or pot of poison to make it more potent; it becomes dramatic when persons other than the principals are present, and they are to be impressed. A coronation is an example of a dramatic rite. If the archbishop were simply to crown the king in the privacy of his chamber, it would not be dramatic; it becomes dramatic when it is performed in Westminster Abbey in the presence of a large number of people, most of whom take little or no part in the proceedings. The difference between a dramatic rite and a ritual drama is that in the latter there is personification. In the coronation ceremony the king is the king, and the archbishop is the archbishop, but in the crowning of the May Queen, the latter is not really a queen, but merely pretends to be one. It is the same when the king pretends to be a god. The importance of the distinction is that the ritual, whether simple or dramatic, need have no story; its myth may be merely a formula, or set of formulas. Where it has a story, we may suspect that it once formed part of a ritual drama, to which a story is essential. The myth of a ritual drama must be in narrative form, since a person makes a dramatic pretence of being someone else only in order that he may pretend to do what that someone is supposed to have done. The chief actor in a ritual drama pretends to be a god or hero—as we have seen, there is no real difference between them—in order that he may be able to exercise the power which that God or hero is believed to have exercised. The myth then becomes an account of what the god or hero once did, and the ritual drama gradually takes on the character of a commemoration, enacted from motives of general piety rather than from a belief in its actual and immediate efficacy.

After this preliminary discussion, I shall proceed to examine at some length the Attic drama, since from it must come a large part of the evidence necessary to show that the secular drama is derived from the ritual drama, that the ritual drama was of the highest religious importance, and that the plots of the ritual drama are not derived from history, which has no religious importance, but are the myths that grew up with the drama, of which they formed an essential part.

The ritual origin of the Attic drama has been widely recognized. Thus Professor Allardyce Nicoll [1] says that "in Greece the choral song chanted round the altar of the

[1] Op. cit., p. 52.

god developed along the twin lines of tragic and of comic
or satirical expression," and Professor Stuart[2] that "tragedy and comedy both owed their origin to rituals of the
cult of Dionysus. . . . The ritual was not commemorative of past events. It dealt with the present and was performed in order to ensure fertility in the future."

Its religious character in historic times is quite evident.
Dramas were performed only at the festival of Dionysos.
During the days of performance the city was in a state of
taboo. Every citizen had to attend the performances as
an act of worship, but the principal seats in the theatre were
occupied by the priests, and by the image of the god.[3]
Yet even those who recognize these facts have failed to
realize their implications, and many scholars are still re-
luctant to recognize them. The well-considered attempts of
Professors Gilbert Murray and F. M. Cornford to reconstruct from the dramas the ritual upon which they were
based [4] have been met by the criticism that their theories
are valueless, since no such rituals are known to have been
performed. This criticism sounds plausible enough, but
when analysed it is found to be based on the belief that we
are in possession of full knowledge both of early Greek
ritual and of the development of the Attic drama. Such
evidence as we have, however, is traditional, and therefore
has no historical value.

The ritual of the dramas, if ritual it was, was certainly
royal ritual, but our knowledge of actual Greek ritual is
derived almost entirely from Pausanias (c. A.D. 170) and
other comparatively late writers. By the time of Pausanias
royalty had been extinct in Greece, except at Sparta, for
at least seven hundred years, and in spite of the conservatism of the priesthood, the rites described by those who
wrote after the beginning of the Christian era must have
been very different from those practised when the drama
first came into being.

The accepted view of the origin of the Attic tragedy

[2] D. C. Stuart: *The Development of Dramatic Art,* p. 103.
[3] J. E. Harrison: *Ancient Art and Ritual,* pp. 10 ff.
[4] G. Murray, in J. E. Harrison: *Themis,* pp. 341 ff.; F. M.
Cornford: *The Origin of the Attic Comedy.*

is that it was evolved among rustics, and in a more or less rudimentary form was brought to Athens by Thespis about the year 535 B.C. Thespis was the first to have an actor independent of the chorus, and a year or two later won the first prize in the tragic competition, which had been started in the meantime. Ten years later was born Æschylus, who raised tragedy to heights that were afterwards reached only by Sophocles and Euripides, and never surpassed.

It is only the belief in the historicity of tradition that prevents this story from being recognized as a tissue of absurdities. There is no historical evidence for Thespis at all. He is first mentioned by Aristotle about 330 B.C., and it is neither claimed by nor on behalf of Aristotle that he had any documentary evidence. He was, there seems to be no doubt, merely repeating a tradition which, like all traditions, is historically worthless. It is difficult to understand how any judicious person can believe that such a culture form as the drama, or indeed any culture form, could be invented by rustics; how, when introduced into a city such as Athens, it could immediately become the central feature of the most important religious festival; how a dramatic competition, previously quite unknown, could suddenly appear in full swing, and how a form of art which was entirely new to the world could in fifty years rise to a height that has been the admiration and model of Europe ever since.

Every feature of the Attic drama, both tragedy and comedy, as we meet it in the fifth century B.C., points to a long period of evolution. If we were told that the first beginning of Greek statuary was in 535 B.C., when a rustic came into Athens carrying a crudely carved wooden image, we should, of course, reject the idea with scorn, but it is in no way more absurd than the story of Thespis.

The development of the Athenian tragedy came to an end with Euripides because nothing more could be done within the limits of form and content set by the tradition arising from the ancient ritual. It must have taken many centuries for the ritual to develop, either at Athens or elsewhere, into so complex a dramatic form, and many more for the idea of the drama as ritual to decline to a point at which the idea of competition could be transferred to it from the games, which must have undergone a similarly long course of development and decline.

Having touched on the development of the Attic drama, we must now examine its content. It was, I must repeat, the central feature of a great religious festival; it was comparable to, and perhaps the prototype of, the mystery or miracle plays of medieval Europe, and as the plots of the Christian religious drama were drawn from the Christian Scriptures, we are entitled to suggest that the plots of the Greek religious drama were drawn from the Greek scriptures. A purely secular subject would be quite out of place in a religious drama. The characters in the miracle plays, Noah and Abraham, for example, are certainly not ordinary human beings, and were probably once gods. Similarly the characters in the Attic tragedy, such as Agamemnon and Odysseus, are not ordinary human beings, and were probably once gods. The evidence that the Greek heroes were once gods is stronger than the evidence that the Hebrew heroes were once gods, since, as we have seen, Greek heroes were worshipped as gods in historical times, and Greek gods were identified with heroes. The Spartans worshipped Zeus under the name of Agamemnon, and the fact that Agamemnon was Zeus explains his position among the heroes, which is exactly equivalent to the position of Zeus among the gods; explains why various kingdoms and various capitals were ascribed to him,[5] and above all explains why he was one of the most important characters in the Athenian religious drama. The only writer I have found who attempts to explain why the Attic tragedians should have set aside the stories of their own kings in favour of foreigners, which, on the assumption that they are historical, is as if Shakespeare had confined himself to writing about the Merovingians, is Dr. Pickard-Cambridge, who tells us "that it can easily be understood how enterprising and imaginative poets should have seized on the legends, experimenting freely, and ultimately rejecting stories which did not make good plays, and so settling down (as Aris-

[5] H. M. Chadwick: *The Heroic Age*, p. 240.

totle says) to the stories of a few houses." [6] That the
stories make good plays is quite untrue—some of the best
of the tragedies have no plot at all—and there is no evidence that the dramatists experimented; they certainly did
not settle down, since the range of Euripides, the last great
tragedian, is no less wide than that of Æschylus, the first.
Their themes were taken from the body of sacred legends,
but that does not necessarily mean that the stories were
sacred to them. The stories of Heracles, like those of Sam-
son, for example, formed part of the sacred legends, but
they could hardly be regarded as sacred in themselves.
The dramatists could treat the myths as they pleased, but
could not go outside them.

The one exception that has come down to us is *The
Persians* of Æschylus. It deals with a historic event, the
Battle of Salamis, and historical characters, Xerxes and his
mother, Atossa. Yet the play is purely fictitious. To cul-
tured Athenians the ghost of Darius and the masculine
part played by Atossa must have been highly unconvincing,
and they must have realized that Xerxes could not have
kept his throne if he had behaved as he is represented as
behaving, and that anyhow Æschylus could not have
known what passed in the palace at Susa. But all this did
not distress them, since what they were accustomed to was
not history but myth. Æschylus gave them myth with a
gratifying topical flavour and was awarded the first prize.

The subject of the Attic drama is inexhaustible; I hope
that enough has been said to show that it was religious in
its character and origin, and that its themes were derived
not from history but from myth.

There are indications that there was a similar drama in
northern Europe, the ancient religion of which has many
points of resemblance to that of Greece, from which it was
probably derived. Miss Phillpotts tells us[7] that "the Nor-
wegian Eddic poems bear the unmistakable stamp of
dramatic origin. . . . Yet these poems are not the remains
of folk-drama in the modern sense of that word. Modern
folk-drama is a degenerate descendant of the ancient re-

[6] A. W. Pickard-Cambridge, op. cit., p. 196.
[7] B. S. Phillpotts, op. cit., p. 114.

ligious drama, whereas these poems are the actual shattered remains of ancient religious drama."

"Four of the extant plays," she says later,[8] "make Thor
the hero of the encounter . . . and the representation of
his victories probably tended to ensure the safety of man-
kind against redoubtable foes. We may be allowed to note
a similarity between the Northern Thor and the Greek
Heracles of comedy and myth." They both visit the world
of the dead; they both fight Old Age; they both indulge
in ribaldry and tauntings, and both are gigantic eaters and
drinkers. "Thor never appears in heroic story; Heracles
barely appears in Homer. Both have comic associations
incompatible with heroic Saga. Their place is in drama."

Ritual drama is at the base of the sagas themselves. "So
the plain historical tale of how one Helgi Hjorvardsson
loved and died, of how Helgi Hundingsbane had the misfortune to kill his wife's brother, how one Hedinn fought
with his bride's father, was spared by him and seven years
later fought again, of how another Hedinn won his
brother's bride—these stories slip from our hands as we
try to grasp them. They are not history but literature, literature working on memories of a drama which was not
commemorative but magical."[9] Helgi and Hedinn, the
names of the heroes, are originally not names at all, but
descriptions of characters in the ritual drama; Helgi is "the
holy one," and Hedinn "the shaggy one"—that is, the
one clad in beast-skins.[1] We may remember that when
Gunnar disguises himself in "a great rough cloak" he is
called "Hedinn."[2]

"That the old heathen religion was an essentially dramatic one," says Professor Karl Pearson,[3] "can scarcely
be doubted; we have proof enough not only in written
statements, but in a vast number of dramatic folk-customs
of heathen origin. We find many cases in which heathen
customs were introduced into Christian churches . . . both

[8] Ibid., p. 135.
[9] Ibid., p. 174.
[1] Ibid., p. 163.
[2] G. W. Dasent, op. cit., p. 37.
[3] *The Chances of Death*, vol. ii, p. 281.

monks and nuns indulged in dances and masquerades
directly connected with heathen festivals. . . . Other records of a similar date [the ninth century] speak of the
monks mumming as wolves, foxes or bears and of other
'diabolical' masquerades. . . . Even in the fifteenth century the Church had not freed itself from these strange
performances. The 'feast of fools' had become an established institution. A fool-bishop having been chosen with
many absurd ceremonies, monks and priests conducted him
to the cathedral. With faces smeared with ochre or hidden
by hideous masks, clad as women, as beasts, or as jugglers,
these clerical mummers proceeded singing and dancing
to the very altar-steps. The fool-bishop read the service
and gave his benediction, while his bacchanalian following
threw dice and ate sausages on the altar itself. The burning
of dung and old bits of shoe-leather took the place of
incense, and the utmost license and disorder prevailed both
inside and outside the sacred building."

But this was not the only type of dramatic performance
which took place in the churches. There was the passion-
play, discussing which the same writer tells us[4] that "gallery, choir and crypt thus obtain a new significance, they
are the heaven, earth, and hell of the scenic ritual; and
their relative elevations are in accordance with folk belief.

"This was the basis of the elevated passion-play stage.
We have three floors, one above the other, connected by
stairs. The top floor represented heaven with the Trinity,
the angels, and sometimes the virtues; the bottom floor,
hell, with Lucifer, Satan, Death, the smaller devils, the
damned, and the patriarchs; the middle floor, earth, and
there the main portion of the play took place. By means
of the upper flight of stairs God and the angels visited
earth, and the souls of the blessed were carried heaven-
wards. In like manner the lower flight gave Satan and his
coadjutors access to earth, and enabled them to carry off
the damned; at the same time, it afforded facilities for the
rescue of the patriarchs."

This recalls the many Greek reliefs and vase paintings
in which the scene is laid on several floors, the human

[4] Ibid., vol. ii, p. 316.

beings or minor deities being at the bottom, the higher
deities at the top, while Zeus sometimes has a throne of his
own above all.[5] The boast of Zeus in the *Iliad* [6] that if he
let a golden rope down from heaven, and all the other
gods and goddesses hung on to it, they could not pull him
down but he could pull them up, suggests such a scenic
arrangement as Professor Pearson describes, as does Jacob's
dream,[7] in which angels ascend and descend a flight of
steps connecting earth with heaven.

Another type of stage used in the ritual drama was the
movable stage. "The English movable pageant associated
with the Corpus Christi procession," says Professor E. O.
James,[8] "introduced the wagon-stages in which the three-
storied plan of the stationary platforms became modified
to meet the requirements of transit. But the ancient plan,
nevertheless, survived though heaven was reduced to a
raised scaffold at the back of the stage.

"This arrangement recalls the Egyptian drama as recorded in the Ramesseum Papyus, in which the *dramatis
personae* were all divine beings each playing his part in the
forty-six scenes, introduced by a brief narrative recited
in all probability by a reader. Then followed dialogues
between the actors having a magical efficacy, with carefully preserved stage directions to ensure the correct re-
enactment of the royal installation at different 'stations' on
the banks of the Nile during the king's cruise through the
chief centres of his realm after his coronation. As the procession of the Host halted from time to time for the
performance of a miracle play, so the royal barge was
moored at the spot where the drama was to be held, the
Pharaoh himself acting the part of Horus. The other
divinities had their rôles in the representation and ascent
of Osiris (the dead king), symbolized by the setting up of
a ladder to the sky, and the threshing and carrying away of
the reaped barley. Other scenes were concerned with the
restoration of the eye to Horus in various symbolic forms,

[5] A. B. Cook, op. cit., vol. i, pp. xi, xii, xiii.
[6] viii, 18.
[7] Genesis xxviii, 12.
[8] E. O. James: *Christian Myth and Ritual,* p. 265.

the investiture of the king with his regalia, and the passion
of Osiris, which included the singing of a dirge-like lamen-
tation by two women impersonating Isis and Nephthys, the
production of a winding-sheet for the corpse of the dead
hero-god, and other articles required for its reanimation."

Discussing the Egyptian myths of Apepi and of Horus
of Edfu, Mr. Sidney Smith[9] says that "the incoherence of
the text as a story depends upon its dramatic use; to those
present at the performance not everything needed to be
said. . . . The text is rather a series of explanatory comments on things done than an ordered account of beliefs
about the origin of things. Direct speech, mostly in dialogue
form, again points to impersonation of the gods. When
narrative intervenes, that is generally because it deals with
matters that cannot be dramatically represented." This
incoherence, and this alternation of dialogue and narrative,
are characteristic of tradition, both the quasi-historical and
the quasi-imaginative.

"We shall probably not err in assuming," says Sir James
Frazer,[1] "with some eminent authorities, that the ceremonies of the nativity of the Pharaohs, thus emblazoned
on the walls of Egyptian temples, were copied from the
life; in other words, that the carved and painted scenes
represent a real drama, which was acted by masked men
and women whenever a queen of Egypt was brought to
bed. 'Here, as everywhere else in Egypt,' says Professor
Maspero, 'sculptor and painter did nothing but faithfully
imitate reality. . . . Theory required that the assimilation
of the kings to the gods should be complete, so that every
act of the royal life was, as it were, a tracing of the corresponding act of the divine life. From the moment that
the king was Ammon, he wore the costume and badges of
Ammon—the tall hat with the long plumes, the cross of
life, the greyhound-headed sceptre—and thus arrayed he
presented himself in the queen's bedchamber to consum-
mate the marriage. The assistants also assumed the costume
of the divinities whom they incarnated; the men put on

[9] In E. A. W. Budge: *From Fetish to God in Ancient Egypt*,
p. 430.
[1] *Golden Bough*, vol. ii, p. 133.

masks of jackals, hawks, and crocodiles, while the women donned masks of cows or frogs. . . . In general we are bound to hold that all the pictures traced on the walls of the temples, in which the person of the king is concerned, correspond to a real action in which disguised personages played the part of gods.' "

If this is correct, as there is no reason to doubt, then the Egyptian artists were acting similarly to the artists of fifteenth-century Italy, who painted endless pictures of the Holy Family and the Apostles dressed in the costumes of that century. This was not because they imagined that such costume was worn in Palestine in the first century of the Christian era, but because they were not trying to imagine anything, but merely to paint what they saw in the miracle plays and religious processions of their own day. And why should we suppose that the Greek artists acted differently? We saw reason to believe that the pictures of the Minotaur and of Ixion were drawn from real sacrificial rites;[2] it is equally probable that the pictures of the gods and Homeric heroes were drawn from scenes in the religious drama. The same applies to the Scandinavian carvings of scenes from the *Volsunga Saga*. There is no reason to believe that these artists or their patrons had any interest in or knowledge of history; that they were intensely interested in the religious drama is in many cases certain.

If the view here put forward is correct, then we should expect to find the ritual drama and the traditional narrative going, so to speak, hand in hand; where there is a large variety of one there should be, or have been, a large variety of the other; where there is a particular type of one, there should be a particular type of the other; and where there is none of one there should be none of the other. And this is what we do find. Professor Hooke and his collaborators[3] have brought forward a vast amount of evidence to show that an intimate connection existed between myths and other traditions and the ritual drama in Mesopotamia, Syria, and Egypt. In Greece we have seen that the deeds of the gods and heroes were enacted

[2] *Supra*, p. 158.
[3] In *Myth and Ritual* and *The Labyrinth*.

in the ritual drama, and that there is no good reason to
believe that in their human forms they had any existence
outside it. At Rome, on the other hand, there seems to
have been no ritual drama and very little dramatic ritual;
and there was correspondingly little in the way of traditional narrative—so little that when Virgil wished to write
a patriotic poem, he had to fall back upon the Tale of Troy.

A great deal has been written on the dramas of India,
China, Siam, and other countries[4] showing the close connection of the stage in those countries with religion and
with tradition.

In America the connection between the myths of the
Indians and their ritual dramas is well recognized, and
the same may be said for the Australian blacks. These
peoples have almost nothing in their traditions that even
suggests history.

In Africa it would seem that many tribes have a very
limited range of traditional narratives and of dramatic
rites, but we have a few examples of the ritual drama, in
which its connection with myth is clearly apparent. A cult-
hero of central Africa is called Ryang'ombe. During ceremonies to exorcize disease, "and also in the mysteries
celebrated from time to time," certain personages not only
are recognized as mediums of Ryang'ombe and other
superior spirits, but actually assume their characters and
for the time being are addressed by their names.

Having been mortally wounded by a girl who turned
into a buffalo, and helped by a maidservant called Nkonzo,
Ryang'ombe gave directions for the honours to be paid to
him after his death; these are, so to speak, the charter of
the society that practises the cult of the spirits. He specially
insisted that Nkonzo, as a reward for her services, should
have a place in these rites, and accordingly she is represented by one of the performers at the initiation ceremony.[5]
This is a good example of the way in which rites are referred to a mythical founder.

Dr. Meek gives us an interesting example. "Among the
Mambila, of the British Cameroons, there is a moon cult

[4] *Vide* W. Ridgeway: *Dramas and Dramatic Dances.*
[5] A. Werner: *Myths and Legends of the Bantu*, pp. 112–17.

in which the moon is personated by a man wearing a string costume and animal-headed mask. At the rising of the moon the masker appears and is ceremonially fed with beer, the priest asking that, by his graciousness, they may all have prosperity that month. A feast is held, and there is general rejoicing. When the moon is about to disappear the masker again appears and acts the part of a dying god. He bids farewell to the people, and forbids them to grieve, for in three days he will rise again and come unto them." [6] Here we see that the moon-god is not the result of speculation, neither is he a deified hero; he is simply a performer in a ritual drama.

For Polynesian traditions I shall rely on Mr. Percy Smith, and he, though he believes firmly in the historicity of these traditions, nevertheless gives us a number of indications that they are really accounts of ritual drama. Thus he tells us that "much of the old history of the Polynesians was regarded as sacred, and its communication to those who would make an improper use of it would inevitably— in the belief of the old priests—bring down disaster on the heads of the reciters. . . . This teaching [of the tribal lore] was accompanied by many ceremonies, incantations, invocations, etc. . . . There was a special sanctity attached to many things taught; deviation from the accepted doctrine, or history, was supposed to bring down on the offender the wrath of the gods." [7]

He later says that "there was a class of roving actors and players, who were also the custodians of much of the historic traditions," and that "the history of Onokura is a very remarkable one . . . the narrative is interspersed with recitative, which would take many hours in delivery. It is, in fact, a regular 'South Sea Opera.' " [8]

If these traditional narratives were really history, and if the teaching of history followed the same course in this country as it is alleged to in Polynesia, we should find professors imploring their pupils not to make an improper use of the Constitutions of Clarendon; boys learning the

[6] C. K. Meek, op. cit., p. 124.
[7] S. Percy Smith: *Hawaiki*, p. 14.
[8] Ibid., pp. 38, 222.

names of Henry VIII's wives with incantations and invocations; people convicted of blasphemy for mixing up
Thomas Cromwell with Oliver; and the history of the
Corn Laws related with vocal and instrumental accompani-
ment. These traditions are sacred, not because they contain
historical facts, which are never sacred, but because they
are accounts of ritual, which, whether dramatized or not,
is always sacred.

This survey of the ritual drama is anything but complete, but it may suffice to show that the ritual drama has
played a highly important part in the religious and social
life of many peoples, a part compared with which that
played by history has been inconsiderable, and that the
connection between the ritual drama and the traditional
narrative is often demonstrable. While there is not, or at
any rate I cannot claim to have found, evidence that the
traditional narrative is *always* connected with the ritual
drama, yet I hope that I have shown that this connection
is everywhere at least probable, whereas there is nowhere
any valid evidence to connect the traditional narrative with
historical fact.

BIBLIOGRAPHY

✳

(L. = London; O. = Oxford; C. = Cambridge)

Allen, T. W.: *Homer—The Origin and Transmissions.* O. 1924.

Ammianus Marcellinus, tr. C. D. Yonge. L. 1911.

Ancestor, The. L. 1902–5.

Arnold, T.: *Beowulf.* L. 1876.

Bain, F. W.: *A Digit of the Moon.* L. 1899.

Baker, Sir S. W.: *Journey to the Albert Nyanza.* L. 1867.

Baring-Gould, S.: *Curious Myths of the Middle Ages.* L. 1892.

Boswell, J.: *Journal of a Tour in the Hebrides.* L. 1928.

Bradbrook, M. C.: *Themes and Conventions of Elizabethan Tragedy.* C. 1935.

Briffault, R.: *The Mothers.* L. 1927.

Brodeur, A. G.: *The Prose Edda.* New York, 1929.

Budge, E. A. W.: *From Fetish to God in Ancient Egypt.* O. 1934.

Burn, A. R.: *Minoans, Philistines, and Greeks.* L. 1930.

Cambridge Ancient History. C. 1923.

Caton-Thompson, G.: *The Zimbabwe Culture.* O. 1931.

Chadwick, H. M.: *The Heroic Age.* C. 1912.

——: *The Origins of the English Nation.* C. 1907.

Chamberlain, B. H.: *The Kojiki.* Yokohama, 1883.

Chambers, E. K.: *Arthur of Britain.* L. 1927.

——: *The English Folk-play.* L. 1933.

——: *The Mediæval Stage.* O. 1903.

Chambers, R. W.: *England before the Norman Conquest.* L. 1928.

——: *Widsith.* C. 1912.

Childe, V. G.: *The Most Ancient East.* L. 1928.

Churchill, Winston S.: *Marlborough.* L. 1933.

Cobb, Wheatley: *The Story of Caldicot Castle.* Private, 1931.

Collins, W.: *The Odyssey.* Edinburgh, 1870.

Congrès Internationales de Sciences Anthropologiques, etc. L. 1934.

Cook, A. B.: *Zeus.* C. 1925.

Cornford, F. M.: *The Origin of the Attic Comedy.* C. 1934.

Dasent, G. W.: *Burnt Njal.* L. n.d.

——: *The Orkneyingas' Saga.* L. 1894.

Dictionary of National Biography. (*D.N.B.*).

du Chaillu, P. B.: *The Viking Age.* L. 1889.

Dunn, J.: *Tain Bo Cualnge.* L. 1914.

Durham, M. E.: *Some Tribal Origins, Laws and Customs of the Balkans.* L. 1928.

Edwards, W.: *A Medieval Scrap-heap.* L. 1930.
Elton, C.: *Origins of English History.* L. 1882.
Farnell, L. R.: *Greek Hero Cults.* O. 1921.
Fortune, R. F.: *The Sorcerers of Dobu.* L. 1932.
Frazer, Sir J. G.: *Folklore in the Old Testament.* L. 1918.
——: *The Golden Bough.* L. 1918.
Frazer Lectures, The, ed. W. R. Dawson. L. 1932.
Froissart's Chronicles, tr. Y. Johnes. L. 1844.
Gathorne-Hardy, G. M.: *The Norse Discoveries of America.*
     O. 1921.
Giles, J. A.: *Six Old English Chronicles.* L. 1875.
Gomme, E. E. C.: *The Anglo-Saxon Chronicle.* L. 1909.
Gomme, G. L.: *Folklore as an Historical Science.* L. 1908.
Gregory, Lady: *Gods and Fighting Men.* L. 1926.
Gronbech, W.: *The Culture of the Teutons.* L. and Copen-
     hagen, 1931.
Gruffydd, W. J.: *Math vab Mathonwy.* Cardiff, 1928.
Halliday, W. R.: *Folklore Studies.* L. 1924.
——: *Indo-European Folktales and Greek Legend.* C. 1933.
Harrison, J. E.: *Ancient Art and Ritual.* L. 1913.
——: *Themis.* C. 1912.
Hartland, E. S.: *The Science of Fairy Tales.* L. 1891.
Hastings' Encyclopædia of Religion and Ethics. Edinburgh,
     1908–21.
Hazlitt, W. C.: *Dictionary of Faiths and Folklore.* L. 1905.
Heath, C.: *Historical and Descriptive Accounts.* Monmouth,
     1805.
Herodotus, tr. H. Cary. L. 1872.
Hight, G. A.: *Grettir the Strong.* L. 1914.
Hocart, A. M.: *Kingship.* O. 1927.
——: *The Progress of Man.* L. 1933.
Hodgkin, R. H.: *A History of the Anglo-Saxons.* O. 1935.
Hooke, S. H., ed.: *Myth and Ritual.* O. 1933.
——: *The Labyrinth.* L. 1935.
Hull, E.: *The Cuchullin Saga.* L. 1898.
Hunt, R.: *Popular Romances of the West of England.* L. 1881.
Ingrams, W. H.: *Abu Nuwâs.* Mauritius, 1933.
Jacobs, J.: *Celtic Fairy Tales.* L. 1892.
James, E. O.: *Christian Myth and Ritual.* L. 1933.
Jolliffe, J. E. A.: *The Jutes.* O. 1933.
Journal of the Royal Anthropological Institute. (*J.R.A.I.*)
Joyce, P. W.: *Old Celtic Romances.* Dublin, 1920.
Keary, C. F.: *The Vikings in Western Christendom.* L. 1891.
Ker, W. P.: *Epic and Romance.* L. 1931.
Kermode, P. M. C.: *Manx Crosses.* L. 1907.
Kittredge, G. L.: *Gawaine and the Green Knight.* Harvard,
     1916.
Koht, H.: *The Old Norse Sagas.* L. 1931.
Krappe, A. H.: *The Science of Folklore.* L. 1930.

Lang, Andrew: *Custom and Myth.* L. 1910.
———: *Myth, Ritual and Religion.* L. 1899.
Leaf, W.: *Homer and History.* L. 1915.
———: *Troy.* L. 1912.
Leeds, E. T.: *The Archaeology of the Anglo-Saxon Settlements.* O. 1913.
Lewis, C. B.: *Classical Mythology and Arthurian Romance.* St. Andrews, 1932.
Lindblom, G.: *The Akamba.* Upsala, 1920.
Lowes, J. L.: *The Road to Xanadu.* Boston, Mass., 1927.
MacDulloch, J. A.: *The Childhood of Fiction.* L. 1905.
MacGibbon, D., and Ross, T.: *The Architecture of Scotland.* Edinburgh, 1887.
MacNabb, D.: *Report on the Chins.* Rangoon, 1891.
Magnusson, E., and Morris, W.: *The Volsunga Saga.* L. n.d.
Malone Society Collections. L.
Malory, Sir T.: *Morte Darthur,* ed. Sir E. Strachey. L. 1870.
Man, published monthly by the Royal Anthropological Institute.
Martinengo-Cesaresco, Countess: *The Study of Folk-songs.* L. n.d.
Meek, C. K.: *A Sudanese Kingdom.* L. 1931.
Müller, Max: *The Science of Language.* L. 1871.
Murray, G. G.: *The Bacchæ of Euripides.* L. 1931.
———: *The Rise of the Greek Epic.* O. 1924.
Murray, M. A.: *The God of the Witches.* L. n.d.
Myres, J. L.: *Who Were the Greeks?* Berkeley, Cal. 1930.
Nicoll, Allardyce: *The Theory of Drama.* L. 1931.
Nilsson, M. P.: *Homer and Mycenae.* L. 1933.
Nutt, A.: *The Voyage of Bran.* L. 1895.
Oesterley, W. O. E., and Robinson, T. H.: *An Introduction to the Books of the Old Testament.* L. 1934.
O'Grady, S. H.: *Silva Gadelica.* L. 1892.
Olrik, A.: *Viking Civilization.* L. 1930.
Oman, C. W.: *A History of England.* L. 1901.
———: *England before the Norman Conquest.* L. 1929.
Parry, J. H.: *The Cambrian Plutarch.* L. 1824.
Paston Letters, The, ed. J. Gairdner. Edinburgh, 1910.
Payne-Gallwey, Sir R.: *The Crossbow.* L. 1903.
Peake, H. A., and Fleure, H. J.: *The Horse and the Sword.* O. 1933.
Pearson, Karl: *The Chances of Death.* L. 1897.
Perry, W. J.: *The Children of the Sun.* L. 1927.
Phillpotts, B. S.: *The Elder Edda and Ancient Scandinavian Drama.* C. 1920.
Pickard-Cambridge, A. W.: *Dithyramb, Tragedy and Comedy.* O. 1927.
Pitt-Rivers Museum, Farnham, Handbook to. Farnham, 1929.
Prescott, W. H.: *The Conquest of Mexico.* L. 1843.

Proctor, R.: *The Story of the Laxdalers*. L. 1903.
Raffles, T. S.: *A History of Java*. L. 1830.
Raglan, Lord: *Jocasta's Crime*. L. 1933.
Rees, R.: *An Essay on the Welsh Saints*. L. 1836.
Rhys, J.: *Celtic Folklore*. O. 1901.
——: *Studies in the Arthurian Legend*. L. 1891.
Ridgeway, W.: *Dramas and Dramatic Dances*. C. 1915.
——: *The Early Age of Greece*. C. 1901 and 1931.
Ritson, J.: *Robin Hood*. L. 1823.
Rose, H. J.: *A Handbook of Greek Mythology*. L. 1933.
Round, J. H.: *Family Origins*. L. 1930.
——: *Feudal England*. L. 1909.
Saintyves, P.: *Les Saints Successeurs des Dieux*. Paris, 1907.
——: *Les Contes de Perrault and Les Récits Parallèles*. Paris, 1923.
Schweitzer, A.: *The Quest of the Historical Jesus*. L. 1931.
Seligman, C. G.: *Egypt and Negro Africa*. L. 1934.
Seligman, C. G., and B. Z.: *Pagan Tribes of the Nilotic Sudan*. L. 1932.
Skeat, W. W.: *An Etymological Dictionary of the English Language*. O. 1898.
Smith, S. Percy: *Hawaiki*. L. 1910.
Smith, Sir W.: *A Classical Dictionary*. L. 1899.
Spence, L.: *An Introduction to Mythology*. L. 1921.
Stanhope, Earl: *Conversations with the Duke of Wellington*. L. 1889.
Stawell, F. M.: *Homer and the Iliad*. L. 1909.
Stevenson, J. S.: *The Historical Works of the Venerable Bede*. L. 1853.
Strangways, A. H. F.: *Cecil Sharp*. O. 1933.
Stuart, D. C.: *The Development of Dramatic Art*. New York, 1928.
Sudan Notes and Records (*S.N.R.*), Khartum.
Tacitus: *Germania,* in *Minor Works,* tr. Church and Brodribb. L. 1885.
Theocritus: *Idylls,* tr. Calverley, ed. R. Y. Tyrrell. L. 1913.
Thompson, J. E.: *Mexico before Cortez*. New York, 1933.
Thomson, J. A. K.: *Studies in the Odyssey*. O. 1914.
Tiddy, R. J. E.: *The Mummers' Play*. O. 1923.
van Gennep, A.: *La Formation des Légendes*. Paris, 1910.
Waley, A.: *The Way and its Power*. L. 1934.
Weigall, A.: *A History of the Pharaohs*. L. 1925.
Welsford, E.: *The Fool*. L. 1935.
Werner, A.: *Myths and Legends of the Bantu*. L. 1933.
Weston, L. J.: *From Ritual to Romance*. C. 1920.
Wheeler, R. E. M.: *London and the Saxons*. L. 1935.
Williams, H.: *Gildas*. L. 1899.
Wood-Martin, W. G.: *Pagan Ireland*. L. 1895.

INDEX

FITZROY RICHARD SOMERSET, BARON RAGLAN, was born on June 10, 1885. He was educated at Eton and Sandhurst, and entered the Grenadier Guards in 1905. After serving as aide-de-camp to the governor of Hong Kong, as district commissioner in the southern Sudan, and as a political officer in Palestine and Transjordan, Lord Raglan retired as a major in 1922. In 1955 he was Her Majesty's Lieutenant for the County of Monmouth and President of the Royal Anthropological Institute. In addition to *The Hero*, he is the author of *Jocasta's Crime, The Science of Peace, How Came Civilization, Death and Rebirth*, and *The Origins of Religion*.